Café Shapiro Anthology

Café Shapiro Anthology

22nd Annual

2019

Original Artwork provided by:
Theresa A. Stanko
Learning and Teaching Project Coordinator
University of Michigan Library

Published by Michigan Publishing

22nd Annual Café Shapiro Anthology 2019

February 11, 2019
February 12, 2019
February 18, 2019
February 19, 2019
February 21, 2019

Selected Poems
& Short Stories

Contents

Anthology Introduction

LAURIE ALEXANDER

Welcome to the 22nd Annual Café Shapiro!

I am excited to introduce the 22nd Annual Café Shapiro anthology and invite you to read the following inspiring and thoughtful University of Michigan student authored poems and short stories. These works will draw you into the creative process, welcome you to think and rethink your assumptions, and connect you with the students through their individual expression. You will find a unique window into the Michigan learning experience.

When Café Shapiro first launched over twenty years ago, it was a bold experiment, a student coffee break designed as part of the University's Year of the Humanities and Arts (YoHA). Café Shapiro is an example of how past innovations become a part of current campus traditions. YoHA set out to explore the role of the arts and humanities in civic and community life through a variety of programs. Café Shapiro continues its tradition of featuring undergraduate student writers nominated by their Professors to perform their works and through during so continues to demonstrate the value of the arts and humanities.

The act of reading one's work out loud is a new experience for many of our students. Throughout several evenings in February, students will gather in the Shapiro lobby and share their works. They will be joined by friends, faculty, coaches, and family, as they demonstrate the power of speaking and performing. They will participate in an authentic act of creation, speaking possibility, expressing beliefs, and imagining the future.

Café Shapiro has become much more than a coffee break. It has become an annual event featuring undergraduate student writers as they think creatively and critically, reason, ask questions, and develop the skills that help them understand and participate in our world. We also publish this anthology of their work, making it available in print and through Deep Blue, the University's institutional repository. Through this process, students have the opportunity to learn about copyright and related steps to publishing their scholarship.

We thank the many librarians and library staff for making this event possible. Events such as Café Shapiro make visible the Library's commitment to learning. We provide a neutral and engaged space for students to practice, learn and grow their scholarship and advance their learning journey. We are enthusiastic partners with faculty and students, looking to enable the exploration of new ideas while capturing passions and self-expressions.

We hope you enjoy reading the work of these talented undergraduate writers.

Laurie Alexander
Associate University Librarian for Learning and Teaching
U-M Library

HODGES ADAMS

Senior
Major: Creative Writing & Literature and Art History
Reading: Poetry

Hodges Adams is a poet and playwright hailing from Northern Michigan. In their time at this University, they have been awarded four Hopwood Prizes for poetry. When not reading too much Shakespeare or shuffling a deck of tarot cards, they can be found working in the Graduate Library or climbing trees in the Arb. This is their second year reading at Café Shapiro.

Nominated by: Jose Casas

two can keep a secret

if i drop a letter in the ocean
        it won't reach its mark

but i'll feel better   someone

is receiving this love at least
        even swallowed

with mouthfuls of salt

i remove the heat
        from confession

and though i am a coward

i still enjoy the taste   even
        underwater there is breath

within me   the ability to speak

the name   if my love is unintelligible
        i am not   for once   to blame

unfinished portrait

the more i watch the painting the more it moves   like i am peeling
    paint and the artist left
instructions underneath   all the bitterness
    is encoded   the way an orange-rind sunset tastes like death

at the end of the day   how a mountain can be the shadow
    of the noontime sky   i am the careful reader

of thirty-six constellations   i have written into two
    oceans   perhaps there is one small thing

i understand within the hue
    and cry of a single day:

the world is an obsolete
    library filled with patrons who no longer know
how to read   or perhaps they know but have lost

    the desire   the work i do is futile   pulling down
a case of pages and attempting to decipher   i, who

    cannot hear   cannot speak   can hardly understand
the architecture of ink   perhaps there is one small thing

    i do understand   what i know is that i rewrite the draft
each time i see you   i hold a word suspended for a week

    until i lift it to your eyes to find a rhyme

i thought about you in a city
    to which neither of us were native   how you

and all your blood must have ambled across the marble
    floor   it had been the type of summer that could pull a planet

out of orbit—though i often wonder if i would have noticed
    the earth stop   since i didn't notice its spinning

they say one twin may feel the other die even
    across miles   i am sensitive, yes   and yet
not sensitive enough

but i have heard the depth
of your voice in the morning   not like the words

are rising a mile through well water
but rather like a body climbing a mineshaft

barehanded   i have seen the refraction of light
around your shoulders as you laugh with your hands
to your mouth   i hold those conversations for ransom

call me scholar   call me voyeur   i think i locked myself
in a library when it started to burn and have been reading
incautiously

the shelves were once full of students
who curled over to sleep and did not dream of classical

texts but rather of the sunshine and the taste
of apples   when we are awake   we show our devotion
and i have learned to never close my eyes

upon the next page is a painting   the foremost face
compels me to think of you

what is not forbidden is not a crime

some force has taken its thumb
    to the cloud and dragged it

down, smeared its paint into
    straight lines, made rain

which wanted to pour into bed
    with me so i let it. the regret

was immediate but the air was still sifting
    hot and colorless through

the window. how could i be angry?

    if it found the perfect foothold in the soft
hollow beneath my ribs and stepped
    up, reaching, and if i held it there, how

could i be angry? i gave my permission.

i wanted to be an ocean wave, striving,
    but i think i am the shore. blurry

and indiscriminate. wrapping my hands
    around the ankles of everyone who walks

into me. i even take poison into my veins.
    i even welcome blood

from the sand. i offer no warnings. only the appearance
    of a body forged from something once alive.

lean into me. let me wash
    over your shoulders and drag you back.

the afternoon was simmering. the sky
    was a threat. it asked where to
walk and i indicated my throat.

hindsight

he once told me absence is the catalyst
for appreciation. to be present is to disregard
the place.

but i remember watching a sunset
with my teacher and wishing there was more<
to be done. all things existing at once–

the horizon with its stitches torn open;
the startled red of her hair;
the conversation between water and shore–

i could not keep them. but i wanted to.

and i know i may not always recognize the sharpest moments
as they arrive. like a warrior who, only upon the moment of rest,
recognizes his own blood. aware of his wounds at last.

perhaps one day i'll weep to discover the damage
committed by stained glass.

perhaps beauty may be recognized in a moment,
but meaning requires distance.

nonetheless i believe he will be wrong. even if my affections
will multiply under the weight of missing<
i know i love this.
i know i miss it.

i know i am still here.

MAHMUDA AHMED

Junior
Major: English
Reading: Short Fiction

Mahmuda is a transfer junior at UMich, from Detroit, Michigan, majoring in English and hoping to one day work in publishing. She's been writing fiction and poetry for as long as she can remember, and absolutely loves it! Aside from this, she also likes to spend her free time drawing as well as reading!

Nominated by: John Buckley

Dead Leaves

Autumn is such a beautiful time of the year. Everything is coated in bright fallen leaves: the tops of cars, the roof of a house, the black shiny streets; my black boot as one lonely leaf settles perfectly on top, and *click*, the picture is taken, posted onto Instagram with a witty pun about leaves and autumn. These leaves are newly separated from their trees, so they are not yet crunchy as I step over them, but a faint *swish swish swish* as my boot sweeps them aside, like fingers as they sweep stray hairs out of my face. Soft. I clear the leaves from my windshield before taking off. The sunlight was beautiful.

Fifteen minutes into my drive, there is smoke, dark and billowing straight into my line of vision, covering the windshield just as the bright leaves did moments ago. I pull over into a side street and stare into the engine as if knowing where the problem lies. I try to call my brother—an expert in such situations—but I only get his voicemail. After taking another look at this oddity, this sudden burst of misfortune, I finally call roadside assistance. Within ten minutes, I am met by a tall man with cropped hair and black overalls getting ready to attach my car to his truck and drive it to the dealership.

"You can ride with me, if you want?" he asks, but I shake my head.

"I still have to get to work anyway," I say, turning my face into a frown and looking for an Uber. Although my manager would understand that sometimes cars break down, she wouldn't understand why I would have to miss my entire shift for it. *I'm sure you could ask a relative or a friend for a ride, or worst case, take an Uber! I've done it before!* Maybe this is what I get for deciding to work in retail. Or are all managers everywhere just like this? Completely insensitive to anything that'll cause a shift in their days?

The Uber is here in no time at all, before the tow truck guy has even departed, before he has even stepped into the truck. I approach the black Lincoln—an all too incredibly nice car—with tints so dark that I'm only able to see a silhouette of the driver. I check the license plate, just to be sure this is my Uber. And before I get in, I raise my hand in a goodbye to the tow truck guy and to my car.

"Giselle?" The man—John—asks. He turns slightly, his eye briefly meeting mine as I nod. "What an interesting name."

"Yeah, but I just go by Gigi," I say.

"Gigi." He says it slowly, swishing it around to see if he likes the taste. "I don't know, I wouldn't wanna take away from the beauty and uniqueness of a name like *Giselle*."

He lets out a laugh and turns around completely so that I'm able to see his whole face—handsome, older, maybe by a few years—but it's his eyes that hold my attention. Piercing blue, bright, clear, like the ocean pierced with sunlight. His laugh bounces around the small space of his car until it dies out and the light turns green and we're off again. The bright trees begin to blur and so do my thoughts because I can't be sure if this man—John—was flirting with me or if he's like this with everyone. And I can't be sure how I feel about it. He's attractive, sure, but I'd never openly flirt with someone I just met. Not to mention that he has to be *at least* five years older than me, probably more experienced too, while I've just started college with only one notch on my belt. I decide to let this go and focus my attention on my phone as I text my manager to let her know why I'm going to be late today.

"So, the mall, huh?" John asks. We're at another red light, so he turns around again to look at me.

"Yep," I say, my voice rising an octave. John smiles, probably suspecting my nervousness. His eyes slide down my body, pausing at my naked knees, where my skirt doesn't quite reach my boots. I try not to fidget under his gaze, but as soon as he turns away, I tug my skirt down and shift my legs closer to the door, away from his wandering eyes.

"What happened to your car?" he asks.

"Oh, I'm not sure. Something with the engine, I think?" I don't look up from my phone this time. I don't think I'd want to meet his intense gaze again. And what if he *is* flirting with me? I don't want to give him the wrong idea. Maybe I should say something? Make it clear somehow that I don't like him. Like, *hey John, sorry but I'm not really interested in you! But I'm flattered you like my knees and think I have a unique name!* Or maybe if I just look really busy and disinterested, he won't try to start another conversation with me. But, is that rude? Honestly, having any kind of conversation with an Uber driver that goes beyond "how are you" is uncomfortable to me. Do they really need to know why I'm going to the mall on a Tuesday afternoon? Or why do I need to know that you—John, my Uber driver, a complete stranger—prefers to call me *Giselle*?

I unlock my phone and scroll through Instagram to distract myself from my spiraling thoughts. A dog with a flower on his nose, a screenshot of a scene from a movie, that painting Hugo has been working on for days, my crush posing in front of an autumn tree in an orange dress and high heeled boots, all blurring by like the trees and cars and buildings outside, until finally they all stop and I'm staring at a back entrance to the mall that I've never seen before.

"What part of the mall is this?" I ask. I look closer at a faded sign posted on the door, indicating the shipping entrance. I've been on the other side of this door once to help my manager bring in some boxes for our holiday floorset, but I don't think I'm allowed to go *in* through here.

"Well the main entrance is always so busy, I thought this would be much more efficient so you're not too late to work," John says, and I finally look at him again. His eyes are less intense, but they seem earnest, and... I don't know? A little too crinkled around the edges? Like, maybe he's been smiling for too long?

"Oh, well this entrance requires a key, and I don't ha—" Wait. How does he know I work here? Did I mention that I worked here? Was I so busy with my spiraling thoughts that I might've missed an entire conversation we had? No, I doubt that.

"Huh, I didn't realize!" John laughs. "Why don't I drive you around to the main entrance then?"

I don't answer.

But maybe he just took a guess? I mean, I am dressed in all black, and even when I'm not working, someone always interrupts my shopping with an, "Excuse me, do you work here?" And why would I just leave my car and go to the mall unless it was for something important, like work? But even if he did guess this, something still feels a little off.

"You know what, that's okay! The Macy's entrance is not too far from here, I'll just walk. Thanks again!" I say quickly and get out of the car.

"Oh, no problem," John replies, but the end is clipped off by the car door slamming shut.

At least I'm out of there. I was starting to feel anxious, but I hope it didn't come off as rude. I decide to give John a little tip, just in case I did come off that way. But I'm only a few steps away from his car when I hear his door opening.

"Giselle, wait up! You forgot something," John says, but just as I'm turning around, the trees and cars and buildings all get blurry again.

Tree trunks are dark and slowly undressing, ready to embrace cold winds and long nights. The moon is overhead and the leaves are underfoot as they *crunch crunch crunch* from hurried steps through the woods, but I can't figure out whether they belong to me or to John, or to someone much worse. I almost hope it's a wild animal that finds me and kills me quickly. John would not offer such mercy.

For days—or weeks, or months, it felt like—I was hidden away in some dirty cabin basement, all a blur of screaming and fighting and *please, please let me go, I won't tell anyone it was you, please.* But he would just laugh and reply with a *don't be such a downer, we're having a good time!* A good time, like being stripped of nothing but my underwear and having the shit kicked out of me every time I made a run for the door. Having to swim just above consciousness with a concussion from when he struck me in the back of the head and shoved me into the trunk of his car. Of being cut up here and there to see how long I would last.

"You're my favorite so far," he'd whisper, with the smell of cologne and alcohol and blood flooding my nose.

But John got lazy, emotional. I began to notice small scratches at the base of his temple, a sign of frustration, but at what, I wasn't sure. Sometimes he would take that frustration out on me, calling me "Sandra"–an ex, maybe a woman he could never have?–and on it went, for days or weeks or who knows how long. I didn't get my chance to escape until tonight, when he stumbled down the stairs, dropping his glass in the process. He was too drunk to even hit me where he wanted to, so I pushed past him and ran. I didn't care that shards of glass punctured my feet as I dragged myself up the stairs, the stars that blurred my vision, or the aching in my head. But I had the sense to grab a phone on my way out; *there must be service somewhere*, I thought.

The crunch of leaves has quieted as I crouch down at the base of a large tree. I'm completely lost with no sure way out, but there are two bars of service and I'm hoping a call will go through. The phone I grabbed, it turns out, is mine. I unlock it with ease, and it opens up to my camera roll, where I find hundreds of new pictures. I cautiously swipe through them. Me, unconscious, with what I presume to be John's hand brushing the hair from my face. Me, unconscious, wearing a burgundy dress I had never seen before. Me, unconscious, completely naked. Me, unconscious, while John did this or that. Me, unconscious. All me, all unconscious, all one big blur.

The crunch of leaves, of hurried and desperate footsteps, starts up again.

KARI ANDERSON

Freshman
Major: Undeclared
Reading: Fiction

At the age of ten, Kari began writing her first novel, which by age 13 consisted of over 200 pages in 14-point Comic Sans. Although she never finished that first novel (considering that it most likely violated multiple copyright laws), she enjoys writing in her limited spare time in between a random hodgepodge of classes (due to the fact that she's woefully undeclared) and rehearsals for the Michigan Marching Band. Originally from the Seattle area, the 20 degree weather almost shocked her back to the Pacific Northwest, but she's glad she stayed. She has had a number of wonderful experiences so far this year and is looking forward to the opportunities to come.

Nominated by: David Ward

Holes

It had been three days since the start of school, and Ruby was already done. She was done with the letters and numbers and all the other nonsense they had to learn, and she was done with the kids who made weird faces at her, and she was definitely done with the teacher droning on in the front of the classroom. What was the point of all of this learning when it was so incredibly boring?

It wasn't like life at home was much better. Her mother spent all of her time sitting in the beat-up rocking chair in the corner of their living room, knitting a blanket or a scarf or a sweater that she never ended up finishing before moving on to the next project. Her older brother spent all of his time holed up in his room, occasionally emerging to yell about a recent conspiracy, including, but not limited to: the police chief that was secretly a member of the Russian mob, the serial killer in their neighborhood that had killed and buried sixteen people somewhere in the city, the chicken tenders at Mel's Diner that were *actually* made of 50% horse meat, etc. Worst of all was her father, who would return home from a day at work and would essentially ignore her existence. Not giving Ruby any attention? That would *never* do. Still, it was never her intention to run away. That said, when the opportunity fell in her lap, she couldn't find a reason not to take it.

It started as Ruby was coming home from her fourth-ever day of school, which had been just as wretched as the last three. She was taking the path that her mother had walked with her the first day, assuming that her daughter would be paying enough attention to take the route herself to and from school. She had been wrong, of course; Ruby had no trouble with the way there, but the way home always gave her some curveball she wasn't expecting. And so even by the fourth day, she found herself a half hour into her walk, facing a path she could have sworn she had never seen before. It was gravel, for one, and it went off in a completely opposite direction than she was aiming for. A quick 360 look determined the inevitable: Ruby was lost for the third time in four days. She must have taken a wrong turn somewhere, but where? She was completely surrounded by unknown streets in a neighborhood that was about $100,000 out of her family's pay grade: a hodgepodge of impeccably trimmed grass and decorative glass art and white picket fences. A prickling in the back of her neck made her feel like someone was watching her, judging her for her worn-out shoes and ratty jeans. Ruby shrugged it off and kept walking.

She rounded another corner, letting out a shriek as she nearly toppled into someone: a boy, dressed in a neatly starched white polo and carrying a knapsack.

"Shhhhh!" he whispered harshly.

"Jesus Christ, watch where you're going!" she scolded, a little embarrassed that she had scared so easily.

The boy's eyes were shifting, paranoid. "Be quiet!"

"Excuse you," said Ruby, on the defensive, "But I don't have to–"

"Please," he hissed. "They'll catch me."

"They?" she asked skeptically, raising a single eyebrow. It was a skill she was extremely proud of; usually people commented on it with amazement, but the boy didn't even seem to notice.

The boy shifted his eyes dramatically, then leaned in to Ruby. "Here's the thing: I'm running away."

Ruby's disappointment that the boy hadn't noticed her eyebrow raise was replaced with excitement and curiosity. "Running away?!?"

He shushed her again, then continued. "Yes. But you can't tell anyone. If they catch me, I'll have to go back."

"Back where?" Ruby asked. She was fascinated by this boy: she had never met anyone so unusual and mysterious, least of all someone so close to her own age.

The boy shuddered theatrically. "Private school."

"Private school?"

"It's horrible."

"How so?"

"Bullies," he said, bluntly. "Teachers. School uniforms. Communal bathrooms. Need I say more?"

Ruby shuddered. "No."

"So you understand that I can't go back," the boy said with a sweep of his arm.

"But where will you go?" asked Ruby, her curiosity brimming above the surface.

He leaned in again. "The forest," he whispered.

Ruby stopped, thinking for a moment. Life in the forest would mean no more numbers, no more conspiracy theories, no more adults. Ever. "All right," she said eventually, deciding that twenty whole seconds of thought was plenty of time to make a life-changing decision. "I've decided to go with you."

The boy looked at her, surprised, but she merely shrugged. "I'm quite lost right now," she explained, "and I don't have much of a chance making it home anyway, so I might as well run away with you. But before we continue, I've got to tell you that my mom told me to never go anywhere with strangers. What's your name?"

"Harry. Yours?"

She held out a hand. "I'm Ruby." They shook hands, and then she smiled. "See, now we're not strangers anymore. Lead the way, I'll follow you."

Harry lead Ruby through more winding streets lined with trimmed hedges and hired gardeners. Ruby was almost beginning to contemplate whether she'd made a poor decision when they arrived at the edge of a forest. Evergreens rose to great heights above her, consuming her within and making her feel small.

She loved it.

They walked silently through the forest, absorbing the soft sunlight filtering through the leaves. Ruby kicked dust up with her feet, letting glittering clouds of earth rise in the light of the afternoon sun. The air was tense with adventure.

"Look," Harry said, pointing ahead of them. "A clearing."

The two children sprinted towards the clearing with a sudden spurt of recklessness. They were just beginning to slow down when Ruby shrieked: her foot had caught on a root and she found herself face-planting in the dirt.

"Are you alright?" said Harry awkwardly, hesitating before walking over to his new acquaintance. He waited for her to stand, but Ruby's eyes were fixed on something in front of her face.

"Look at this," she said, shifting the underbrush slightly to reveal...

Harry's eyebrows raised. "A hole?"

Ruby stood shakily. "It's pretty deep too."

His eyes scanned the clearing. "There's another one. Right there."

Ruby squinted, and sure enough: another hole, half covered in branches and leaves, where Harry was pointing.

The two of them looked at each other, excitement twinkling in their eyes. "I bet I can find more holes than you," said Harry with a smirk.

Ruby matched him, smirk to smirk, overconfidence to overconfidence. "You're on."

After five minutes of vigorous searching and three territorial disputes regarding who had found what, they counted exactly 15 holes, all about six feet in width and five feet deep. No winner was declared due to the inability to reach a unanimous decision, but Ruby knew that she had won and celebrated her victory with a smug look that irritated Harry to no end.

"What do you think all of these holes are for?" asked Ruby, taking a brief break from gloating.

Harry's eyes gleamed greedily. "What if it's...treasure?"

They looked at one another, the fire reignited. "And if they've dug all of these holes it might mean they haven't found it yet!" Ruby said, jumping with excitement.

Harry yelped. "Look right there! There's a place that hasn't been dug up yet, but it's just the right size for another hole."

Ruby sprinted across to the flat spot, and nearly tripped again. Another root? No, something else...

"A shovel!" she cried, grabbing it with two hands, filthy from an afternoon of sifting through dirt and branches. She caught Harry's eye, and they mentally agreed on a plan.

They labored for half an hour or so, switching off every few minutes. Dust rose in the air, glowing in the light of the setting sun, and yet they dug, ignoring the blisters rising on their tender hands and the chill starting to settle in the air. The idea of treasure and adventure was enough motivation that they would've kept going for hours.

But it was only a few minutes after the half hour mark when Ruby (who was taking her turn, much to Harry's reluctance, who was hoping to be the one to make a big discovery) hit her shovel against something.

"Is it a box?" said Harry hopefully, leaning over Ruby's shoulder as she shifted the dirt around in hopes of revealing what had been buried.

"I don't think so," she replied, squinting her eyes at the vaguely round object that was starting to appear. "It almost looks like..."

Ruby shrieked, falling backwards onto her hands. Harry immediately ran to the partially uncovered hole. "What? What is it?"

Ruby was breathing hard, closing her eyes, trying to process what she had seen–no, *felt*.

"It's probably nothing," said Harry, perhaps for his own benefit more than anyone else's. "God, you're such a girl, I bet it's just a spider or something–"

His words broke off as he screamed–much louder than Ruby had, she noted with a small amount of amusement. But her fleeting moment of dominance disappeared as she and Harry shared a look: confusion, shock, disgust, horror.

"Was that...is that..." Harry gasped.

Ruby nodded solemnly. "It's a skull. A human skull."

SOPHIA ARBANI

Freshman
Major: Undeclared
Reading: Essay

Sophia is from the small town of Mars, Pennsylvania, right outside of Pittsburgh. She is a first-generation college student studying in the LSA Residential College. Although her major is undecided, she is currently exploring computer science and psychology. Sophia is a research assistant in the Department of Ecology and Evolutionary Biology and would describe herself as a generally curious person. Sophia loves travel, watching Food Network, and chatting with friends during her free time.

Nominated by: Sarah Messer

Tilting at Windmills

Hot air hits us like a brick wall as we step off the air-conditioned bus onto ash gray pavement in central Spain. We squint and place our hands on our foreheads as though we are saluting the gigantic windmills on the hill before us. The heatwave causes us to melt in the Spanish desert; the sun relentlessly beats down on us, making our heads full of dark hair feel like they're about to catch fire. The landscape around us is dry and yellowish-brown with patches of green here and there. The terrain is rocky but tall golden grass and low green shrubs grow on the side of the hill. We begin our walk uphill to the point where the pavement ends and sand, dirt, and beige-colored rock begins.

Twelve giants in the shape of windmills tower over us and try to intimidate us with their bulky stone bodies and long arms, which don't turn and spin like they used to when they were first built. Their bodies are cylindrical and stalky, the color of eggshells, and they wear triangular hats that are gray, blue, or black. The giants have square eyes just below their hats that surround their circumference, a rectangular nose, and a large rectangular mouth at their base. They loom over the town of Consuegra, a municipality located in the province of Toledo, Castile-La Mancha, which is home to about 11,000 inhabitants. The homes and shops and restaurants keep their distance from the hillside as if the sedentary giants will rise from the ground and stomp them in a sudden attack of mythic proportions. The air on the hill is stagnant and dry and it is mostly quiet with the exception of soft guitar music playing from the inside of the souvenir shop called *Cabellero del Verde Gabán*, the name of a gentleman who lodges the eponymous protagonist of the novel *Don Quixote*. We walk around and take pictures, posing like warriors with the brown landscape behind us as if we are Spanish conquistadors.

We stroll around and try to look at the new additions to our photo albums but the sun is too bright and our phone screens look black. Everyone starts to chat about what we're having for lunch, where we're going after that, and what we should do later that night. My thoughts wander and I think about the things I have to do once I get back home. Will my senior year test my limits? What is my college essay going to be about? Where am I applying? Will I get into the school of my choice? Am I in over my head? I feel myself tilting at windmills.

The windmills we are visiting rose to fame after being featured in the most influential piece of Spanish literature of all time, Miguel de Cervantes' *Don Quixote*. Originally published in full in 1615, the novel follows Don Quixote de la Mancha, a nobleman who has read so many epic novels and chivalrous romances that he loses his mind. Throughout the story, the delusional "knight" travels through Spain, slaying evil and defending good, determined to live in a time that no longer exists. His "squire" is a laborer named Sancho Panza, his "steed" is an old barn horse named Rocinante, and his beautiful "princess" is a peasant woman named Dulcinea. Although Cervantes originally wrote *Don Quixote* with comedic intentions, the theme of the novel has been analyzed many times and becomes darker over time.

In chapter eight of the novel, Don Quixote and Sancho come across *the* cluster of windmills which Don Quixote believes to be a group of giants. He goes to slay them and the arm of one of the windmills knocks him off of his horse and onto the hard ground. "Tilting at windmills" is an English expression derived from this moment in classic Spanish literature; it refers to fighting – "tilting" literally means jousting – imaginary demons. Don Quixote is determined to bring justice to Spain by fighting for chivalry, and in doing so, he fights things that don't actually exist. According to Merriam-Webster Dictionary, *Don Quixote* is linked to another term in the English language: *quixotic*, meaning "foolishly impractical, especially in the pursuit of ideals, marked by rash lofty romantic ideas or extravagantly chivalrous action." So, Don Quixote is fighting with all his might against things that don't matter, don't exist, don't harm, and don't effect anything.

Depending on how I look at it, the windmills could be windmills or they could be giants. They could hold their actual purpose, which is primarily grinding grain, or they could have their imaginary purpose, which is knocking people off their horses and terrorizing the town. I could choose to enjoy my time here or I could choose to tilt at windmills.

I come back to reality and look around. My friends are still chatting and laughing about the inside joke of the day. I join in. My Spanish teacher calls us over to the front of one of the windmills and insists that we have to take a group photo. He walks over to a Spanish woman wearing a blue and white flowy dress and asks her to take our photo; she takes his camera with a friendly grin and gets accustomed to the device before it's time to snap our group shot. He runs back to us and sits on a makeshift stool and we make a line around him, placing our hands on each other's backs. Our teacher is wearing a white shirt with PITTSBURGH 25 written across the chest in bold black letters outlined in a mustardy gold. We are very far from home.

I wonder if the people of Consuegra ever tilt at windmills. The town seems so sleepy and tranquil that I find it hard to believe that anyone would ever find the need to joust imaginary giants like Don Quixote. The people of Spain are known for their laidback lifestyle; they go to work in the morning and have a two to five hour break in the middle of the day for a *siesta* and then return to work in the late afternoon. They always make time for friends and family and going out and enjoying themselves. They eat dinner around midnight in the summer months and bask in the moonlight hours after eating, sitting and talking around the table, a time they refer to as *sobremesa*, which does not have a direct translation in English. Life seems so carefree and relaxed here that I can't relate to it, coming from the hustle and bustle and nonstop stress of the American lifestyle.

We soon get bored of standing in the brutal direct sunlight and venture to the souvenir shop, which is housed inside one of the windmills. Knick knacks line the circumference of the circular room and a woman with dark hair stands behind the counter, conversing with an American man practicing his Spanish. The air is cool and it is dimly lit inside the shop. Despite the cool shelter, it's uncomfortably crowded and we can't move without bumping into sweaty bodies with every step, so we quickly look at the shot glasses and tchotchkes and walk back into the arid desert.

After a while, our tour guide tells us we have five minutes until it's time to get back on the bus and go to lunch at a local restaurant. My friend whines about how hot it is. My Spanish teacher recounts his hellish experience of reading a thousand pages of *Don Quixote* as a Spanish student in college. Tourists take pictures with their kids. We descend down the hill while getting rocks and sand in our sandals. It's hotter once we hit the pavement. The bus creates even more heat and the putrid smell of fuel emissions fills the air after a while. The bus driver sits in the driver's seat but doesn't unlock the door, so we huddle and gossip about the boys in our tour group and discuss how we would spend our perfect afternoon. We fantasize about eating pomegranate gelato while we sweat in the summer heat. We fan ourselves with our museum maps from the day before until the bus driver finishes his crossword puzzle and opens the automatic door. We pile onto the bus and plop down onto the red 90's patterned seats and blast the air conditioning on our faces. The sound of conversation engulfs me and I zone out. I look out the window at the brown hillside and try to see the whole view, tilting my head to look at windmills.

Works Cited

"Don Quixote Summary." *Sparknotes*, 2018, https://www.sparknotes.com/lit/donquixote/section2/.

Photos from personal album. 16 June, 2017.

"The Windmills Route, The Toledo Area of La Mancha." *España*, 2018, https://www.spain.info/en/que-quieres/rutas/rutas-culturales/ruta_de_molinos_de_viento_mancha_toledana.html.

SRIKAR BAIREDDY

Junior
Major: BCN – Biopsychology, Cognition, Neuroscience
Reading: Fiction

Srikar Baireddy was born in California, moved to India at the age of nine, and then moved back to Pennsylvania at the age of eighteen. As a junior, he spends more time staring into blank space and dreaming than working. His stories usually tend to be unnecessarily tragic, a habit that has plagued him for years. His love for cats dwarfs his love for anything else.

Nominated by: Elinam Agbo

Horizon

"You've only seen Hirvin, haven't you?"

The old man had our attention already. Rashik was his name, he said. He had seen many things beyond our wildest imaginations, he said. He had explored the world, beyond Hirvin, beyond the seas that enveloped our land, to the giant, monstrous landmasses leagues away, he said.

Rashik is an old fool, the others said.

But if he was a fool, he was at least an entertaining one. Someone who seemed to elevate himself beyond the dirt and grime of everyday life with the light in his eyes when he recounted his tales. Real or imagined.

We were in a battered tent of some sort, where Rashik usually was. People could hear him call out and ask for them to listen to his story, but no one ever did.

Other than us, that is.

I heard the quiet sound of cloth rustling as Aleandra shifted her position, her eyes fixated on his lips, waiting for his next word. Her clothes were too fine for the floor, so she had delicately placed herself on the rug.

I nodded.

"Ah, there is so much more...so much more. Decades ago, when I was young and strong like you, I set out on an adventure. I wanted to see the world. I wanted to explore the secrets that no one else had. So I set out. I stole a boat from one of the fishermen, and during the dark of night, I sailed away. There were enough provisions on the ship to last me several months. It was weeks before I saw anything...at times I wondered if I had been driven mad. Day after day, sitting in isolation, watching the sea shift around me. Wondering if I was even moving at all, or if I had been sitting stationary, all this time, But finally! I saw land! Lush and green, tapering off to form the soft yellow of coastline. And the people! Dark-skinned and beautiful, sharp of mind and wit. Their food burst with taste, with senses I had never felt before. My days there were more potent than any other time of my life. But I knew I had to leave one day, to share my discovery with the rest of the world. I collected rations from my gracious hosts and headed back to my home town...but no one ever believed me. For years, I've been telling my story, but no one would listen."

His gaze fixed onto Aleandra. He had her complete attention.

"Until you two."

The spell broke, and Aleandra leaned back a little and blinked. I remained silent.

* * *

Walking in the street with Aleandra was always an unsettling affair. People would look at the two of us and whisper, wondering why an elf clearly born into royalty would be associating herself with a dirty commoner like myself. I had grown used to it, partially because I didn't quite understand it myself. The first time I'd met her, she had waltzed into our grocery store and taken possession of me, like an oddity she had mild curiosity in. Every time she was in the area, I would accompany her. An escort, a friend, a servant. Maybe a confidant. I was never sure. Did she have other people just like me? I didn't know. I didn't even know what I was.

Even now, it seemed like she was floating above the rest of us, untouched by the bustle and grime of our district. People parted before her, almost in reverence. I walked behind her, attempting to mask myself in her presence.

Aleandra claimed that she wasn't really that different from the rest of us. She was only a distant relative of the royal family, so she didn't really wield any power. She insisted that the only thing special about her was that she had to maintain appearances in public. That was the only difference between the two of us, really.

I watched her carefully lift the hem of her handwoven dress so it wouldn't be dirtied.

She ate bread and rice for dinner just like the rest of us, she said.

I couldn't remember the last time I had eaten dinner.

We made our way through the marketplace and were greeted by the fresh, salty smell of the Ocean. The scent of fish wafted in from a store, where a woman was enthusiastically alerting passerbys of their deals. Before us, a row of sailboats bobbed up and down with the waves. A group of fishermen had returned from their trip.

"There they are." There was a breathiness in Aleandra's voice. "The key to adventure."

I looked at the boats and resisted the urge to pinch my nose to block out the smell.

"That's what he used, right? Old man Rashik." She looked at me, her eyes sparkling in the sunset. "It's how he explored the world."

I nodded. She got like this sometimes. Swept up in her latest interest until it fizzled away and was replaced with something else.

She took note of my apathy. "You never seem interested in my ideas. Sometimes I wonder why I keep you around."

I wasn't sure either.

She took a seat on a low wall at the edge of the beach and motioned for me to sit down as well.

"This land...it's all I've known all my life. The capital city, the towns around it, I've seen it all, you know? There's nothing more for me to see here."

Her eyes shifted to the horizon.

"And...I want to see more. What's beyond what I can see, here? The Ocean is so vast. What's on the other side? I want to explore it. I want to see what Rashik saw. I know," she said, looking at me. "I know what you're going to say. That he's an old man who wants attention. But isn't the world a bit more magical if what he said was real? If there were people somewhere, far away, that we don't know about? It's like a grand adventure. And I'm the main character."

She did seem like the main character type.

"I want to see things that other people have never seen before. It feels like it would give life meaning."

My mother had always told me that life didn't need meaning besides living.

"Sure am lucky that they don't really protect these ships..." she chewed her lip thoughtfully. "Here, come along."

We walked up to the ships, and she touched a few of them thoughtfully while walking by them. "This one." She stopped at one and looked at me. "This one hasn't gone out on to the Ocean yet, has it?"

It hadn't. It was due to set sail soon.

"Good. Then they've probably loaded it up with provisions. Marley, huh? What a pretty name." The name, scrawled onto the side of the boat, had caught her eye. "I wonder why it was named that."

All boats were named after their owner's oldest daughter, but I held my tongue. I was sure her mind would come up with a more creative answer.

She leaned against the boat. "I'm sure I could get one of the servants to help me out...there are some fishing families that are indebted to us. I'm sure they'd agree to send someone along with me as recompense. Ma and Pa wouldn't like it, of course, but they wouldn't know. Just a written contract they find after I'm long gone."

Her fantasy was a bit more detailed this time. Almost worryingly so.

"In three days, I could get it all ready." She paused to study my face. "If I left, would you come with me?"

It was tacky, it was added on. A formality more than anything. And she knew what my answer was without me saying anything.

"Didn't think so. Well, go off now. Go back to your dull, mundane life, and remember that it could've been so much more."

I got home late that night, but my parents had heard about Aleandra's appearance, so they knew why.

"I still don't know what that girl wants with you," Mama said worriedly. "I don't trust the elves. They're emotionless and alien." Her tone was hushed, as though she feared that someone was eavesdropping.

Papa gave a grunt of approval, idly reading a newspaper while Mama cleaned the dishes.

"I don't think I'm going to have to be around her much longer," I said.

"That's good." I could hear the relief in her voice. The dishes had a calming rhythm to them, as they clinked and clanged and were placed to dry.

I had the urge to ask a question, something I hadn't done in a while. Curiosity was the Devil's work.

"Mama," I said. "What do you think is beyond the Ocean? Do you think someone could travel there?"

A missed beat. The tempo broken, and hastily resumed. A brief rustle as Papa flipped the page.

"Why do you ask? That is not for us. We live a simple life here. Our work is what we should think of. Not mindless fantasies." The relief was gone, replaced with an urgency. "Don't talk about such things in public. People will think you have gone mad."

It was about all I could hope for. "Yes Mama."

For once, Papa seemed to want to say something. He cleared his throat, like he always did before saying something important.

"Hirvin is the only land on this planet. God made it this way, because we are God's chosen ones. We are on God's chosen land. We are His favorites. We are surrounded by the Ocean so that we remember that this land is all we need, and all we ll ever need. So the scriptures say, and so it is."

I'd heard this all before.

"There is a bit more to this story. Should we forget the gifts He has given us, should our greed drive us to greater lengths, should we seek even more...those who attempt such a thing would be punished. We must live on our land, work our land, and die on our land. This is our life. We are not to venture any further."

It was what I'd heard all my life but worded differently. It felt more sinister, somehow. Just as suddenly as he spoke, he resumed his usual position and continued reading.

It had the customary vagueness that came with all of the scriptures that we were told, and I had to quash my curiosity about what exactly this punishment was. It wasn't my place to question the ancient teachings.

Aleandra was an elf, anyways. They were said to be nearly immortal, nearly impossible to kill. She would be fine, probably.

It dawned on me that I was assuming that she would even go through with her scheme in the first place. She wouldn't, that would be ridiculous.

* * *

I never heard from Aleandra ever again.

Later that week, there was a furor near the beach when people found out that a boat had been stolen. It was all anyone could talk about. I didn't ask which boat is was – I already knew. Marley's father was on the ground, sobbing, robbed of his livelihood.

There was a storm that night. I heard the wind whispering around me, sometimes shrieking in rage. The rain lashed against our town with a violence that seemed nearly sentient. That was all anyone could talk about for a while.

Soldiers came to town once. They asked me if I had any idea what had happened to her. I lied. I didn't know why I lied. It was wrong. But it felt right.

Soon, people forgot. Marley's father took up a different trade. The rain damage was repaired. Life went back to normal.

Sometimes I could feel people looking at me, wondering where my companion was.

Sometimes I would look out to the Ocean and wonder if she had found what she'd been looking for.

Sometimes I would sit by the beach and wonder if she had found a different land, with different people, different traditions, different food.

Sometimes I would feel jealous, jealous of the fact that she could just leave her life behind and follow her dreams.

Sometimes I would walk up to the Ocean, touch the water and wonder what it would've been like if I went along.

One time I found a piece of wood. Shattered, jagged, beaten by the water. I could make out the letters A and R on it. There was something that looked like the end of an M.

I threw it back into the sea. I wished I had never seen it.

EZRA BEEHLER

Freshman
Major: FTVM – Film, Television and Media
Reading: Fictional Short Story

Ezra is a freshman majoring in Film, Television, and Media. He comes from a small up-north town named Frankfort. He has written short stories since he was a small child. He has followed his passion for telling stories as it evolved into his current love of film and it's production. Other than that, Ezra also participates on the Club Wrestling Team. After graduating, Ezra hopes to pursue a career as a film producer.

Nominated by: Oluwapemi Aguda

A Light In The Dark

She held the oil lantern out in front of her with one hand, illuminating the way through the desolate wasteland. Her lantern only lit a few yards into the impenetrable darkness around her. The ash drifting down from above cast speckled shadows as it passed her lantern. Soft plumes of ash erupted from the ground with each step. A large object drifted into her globe of light, revealing a tree as she approached it. Reaching out, she brushed a gloved hand against the surface of the tree. The surface was bare and its branches barren of leaves. It had been many years since any light had breathed life into this tree. It was dead, like nearly everything else in the world. A lone rope swing hung from one of the branches, empty.

She no longer needed her compass, her memory now guiding her. It wasn't far now. She trudged back through the ashfall, the tree once again enveloped in the dark. The sound of a claw digging into the wood met her ear, as one of them reminded her of their presence. It was no use turning to try and see it though. They never enter the light, staying just beyond the amber glow, waiting for her light go out, just like everyone else.

Eventually, she found the entrance, just as she remembered. A lone wooden door set within the wall of the small white house that was shrouded by the dark. The dead remains of vines still clung to the wall, almost like veins through pale skin. The door stood slightly ajar. The woman climbed the three stone steps to the door. Slowly with one hand, she reached out to the door. Her fingers spread across the wooden surface pushing through the fine coating of ash...

I held my 4-year-old son with one arm, the other clutching the oil lantern I found in the basement. A heavy bag was strapped to my back, holding our supplies. I stood on the top platform staring out into the now unfamiliar world of night. We had to leave the house, I couldn't live there any longer. I closed the door behind me and started down the steps. As my light left the door, I heard it creak open, and the creature slither out onto the steps. Leave us alone, I screamed, before heading out into the void.

Her vision cleared, and she pushed the door inwards. It crashed into the wall, echoing throughout the empty house and knocking a fine layer of soot loose into the air. She entered the house for the first time in years, pulling down the scarf from over her mouth. Her breath agitated the ash lingering in the air.

With each step items from the past came into view, seeming like a distant memory. The entry room. Shoes of all sizes were scattered across the ground, coats still hung on the hooks. Her footsteps were muffled by the thin blanket of sediment that covered the floor. The kitchen. Plates and bowls still littered its counters. She breathed in, hoping for the once familiar smell of cooked food, but instead the everpresent acrid odor of smoke met her nose. The living room. A bookcase filled with unopened tomes. The couch. White, spattered in red and brown. Spattered in blood....

He laid across the couch, eyes closed. The perpetual sound of the generator running in the basement kept him up. I sat nearby, mending the knee in a pair of pants. A crash from the other room was followed closely by the cries of our son. He sighed, and began to sit up. No I got it, I said. I placed the needle and cloth on the floor, and rose from my seat. I crossed the house and entered the room where my son sat alongside his toy workbench, which was now on its side. Tears poured from his eyes. I picked him up and began wiping away his tears, whispering soft words into his ear. Another crash silenced the generator and erased away the lights. I stood there, my son in my arms, our shadows projected across the room by his battery powered night light. John, I called out, John what happened. No response came. I reached down and picked up the light. Cautiously, I made my way down the hallway, my breathing, the only sound, growing quicker and quicker. I entered the living room. I could see his arm, up and across the back of the couch. Maybe he had finally fallen asleep. I rounded the corner of the couch and saw his body. I began to scream. He laid there, his lifeless eyes staring into the ceiling. His mouth open, as if trying to gasp for his last breath. His throat, slashed open, blood still pouring from the wound. The red spreading across the white couch, a crimson flood. All illuminated in the blue light of my son's dinosaur lamp. Something scampered out of sight into the dark.

She wiped away a lone tear, a single line tracing its course through the grime on her face. She left the living room and made her way down the hall. The creature followed her, it's quiet movement audible in silence. The rug breathed out a puff of ash with each step she took. She passed the bathroom, expecting to see her reflection in the mirror, but only meeting an matte grey layer of ash. She walked into what was once her bedroom.

The bed sat in the middle just as before. The floral comforter was faded and partially eaten away by moths. Placing her lamp on the floor, she brushed off an area at the foot of the bed and sat upon it, resting her legs from the hours of walking. Directly ahead of her sat the tv. With the sleeve of her jacket, she cleared the powder from its screen, exposing her reflection

The news played on the tv. They said that Yellowstone was due to erupt any day now. They had been preparing the world for it for years. Scientists predicted that the ash would most likely fill the skies, creating a perpetual night. We had years worth of food and supplies in the basement. We should be okay. A hand placed itself on my shoulder and I looked up to see my husband. His soft brown eyes glowing beneath his short cut hair. We will be okay, he said. I know, I said. I love you Rachel. I love you too.

Rachel stared ahead in horror at the reflection of what she had become. Her face was gaunt and her once thick blonde hair was now sparse and broken. Her skin was pale and purple. And her eyes had changed. The bright spark that had once shown in her hazel eyes was gone, replaced with an eye that no longer showed emotion. It was not her. She could look no longer. She rose, grabbing the lantern and quickly exited the room.

She froze in the hallway, just before a closed door. A picture of a dinosaur hung on its surface, ever so slightly crooked. Moving slowly and painfully, as if she were being physically restrained, she reached towards the handle to the door. But she couldn't do it. She couldn't face her past, not yet. She instead turned and walked down the stairs into the basement.

There were plenty of supplies in the basement, left behind when she made the decision to leave. She could only carry so much in her bag. And now, years later, she has returned to her hoard of food. For the next few days, she lived in that basement, surviving off can after can of preserved food. She slept on a futon in the basement, refusing to go upstairs. And always present was the sound of the creature, circling its prey.

It was ironic, she thought, that the government was so focused on preparing everyone for the ash. Food was stockpiled, and society was prepared to work in this new world. Only that their new world was dismantled by what was also released in the eruption. The creatures of the dark. She had never seen more than the quick blur of motion on the edge of her vision of them, but that was more than enough. They left only a lone path through the ash, almost like that of a snake. They were born of the dark, and that is where they resided. And in it they were deadly. The light was her only salvation.

After nearly a week, or so she thought, she found herself sorting the remaining food, brushing off the dust so she could easily read the labels. Beans. Peaches. Soup. And applesauce; his favorite...

I chose to stop at an old restaurant, hoping to possibly find a few left behind cans. I sat him in a highchair and placed him at a table. His blue onesie was covered orange dots. I set down one of the lanterns next to him and lit my own. I drew a jar out of my bag. Applesauce. I opened it, slid a spoon into the thick mush, and gave it to him. Stay here while mommy goes and checks for food, I said. He was silent, the spoon already entering his mouth. I walked across the restaurant and through a doorway labeled employees only. A shelf on the far wall had multiple cans stacked on top of it. I reached up and pulled down a can, trying to read the label. Mommy, I heard him call. One sec honey, I yelled back. I grabbed as many cans as I could and turned back towards my son. I passed the doorway and he came into view. A loud crash reverberated through the building as I dropped the cans and began to run towards him. Mommy look what I have, he said, as he held the lantern far above the ground, his undersized hands gripping its handle. Put it down I called in mid stride. Okay, he said and dropped the lantern. It fell through the air, and that's when I saw it, something, waiting at the lights boundary. The lantern shattered against the floor, extinguishing its light. It was only a second before my light reached the chair, but it was already too late. He was gone, sucked into the void by some nameless evil. The jar of applesauce rolled to a rest on the table.

She needed to face it. She went back up the steps, and to the closed door, her hand once again hesitantly reaching forward. She found her resolve and twisted the handle, pushing the door inwards. Her lantern illuminated the room. Blue walls, covered with crayon drawings of what were supposed to be dinosaurs. Toys were scattered across the wooden floor, a small bed sitting in the corner. A glass object reflected her light back at her. She approached the object, revealing a picture frame. And in it was her son, Jack. Or a picture of her son at least. His blue eyes shining out beneath bangs of dirty blond hair. His cheeks red, dimples at the corner of his smile.

She grabbed the picture frame, bringing it to her breast, and collapsed upon the ground her back against the wall. She sat her lantern next to her and held the picture with both arms. One by one, sobs racked her body. It was her fault that her son died. She should have never left him. He was too young, he didn't realize the danger he was in.

She heard the creature slide into the room and glanced up enough to see it slide behind the door through tear soaked eyes. It wasn't her fault. It was the monster who killed him. Not her. Her anger grew. This creature had taken all that she had ever loved from her. She wanted to kill it, and looking down at her lantern, an idea formed.

She snatched her lantern, and exploded forward, slamming the door into the wall and trapping the creature behind it. The door barred it, and the light blocked its escape. The creature slammed against the door, trying to escape, but she held strong. Unhuman shrieks and cries emanated from behind the door. Holding the lamp in front of her, she threw the door open, exposing the creature to the light.

"Go to Hell you motherfu..."

There lied a child, in the fetal position. Dirty blond hair. Blue onesie with orange spots. It was him. Jack. She fell to her knees and scooped him up. It was her son. But what was wrong with him. Smoke rose from his skin, which was nearly perfectly white, blue veins blossoming out underneath. His hair was sparse and thin. Long bone nails extended from his fingers.

"Jack," she said. "What did they do to you baby?"

She slowly pulled his head back to look at his face. It was even worse. His once cherubic cheeks were now gaunt and bony. And where his eyes used to be were bottomless black pits. His cracked white lips moved in a whisper exposing sharpened teeth.

"Mommy."

She cried out and threw it back against the ground. That thing was not her son. She grabbed the lantern and ran out the door. She darted around the corner and ran into empty space where the stairs led to the void. Time slowed.

The lantern slipped from her grip, getting thrown up into the air above her. She twisted, landing on her back, her breath escaping through her lips. She slid down the stairs, each one sending lances of pain through her back, until she hit the wall. She laid there, helpless as she watch the lantern sail towards the ground in front of her. And as it neared the ground, she briefly saw at the top of the staircase, just within the light, the creature, standing there, staring at her with those dark holes.

The lantern shattered. Everything was dark. "Mommy."

Rachel started to scream.

NOA BERMAN

Sophomore
Major: Cognitive Science
Reading: Short Story

Noa is a sophomore Cognitive Science major from New York City. She loves writing plays and short stories, and is really excited to have her work read for an audience for the first time! She dedicates nearly all of her time to writing and theatre, but outside of that she loves good books, Broadway cast recordings, talking about how weird the brain is, and eating ice cream.

Nominated by: John Buckley

The Truth About Children

Characters:

Arnold: Hopeful, naive, adventurous. He was written as a dinosaur but could be anything.

Taffy: Assertive, cynical, motherly. She was written as a fairy but could be anything.

Ethan: 8. Arnold's kid friend. Cheerful, imaginative, fun.

Mom: Ethan's mom. Loving but very adult.

The end of the world, or so it seems. Lava flows around Ethan and Arnold as they prepare for the worst.

Ethan: This must be the last obstacle before we get back to the portal. Arnold, are we ready?

Arnold: We have to be. I believe in you, Ethan.

Ethan: Okay. All we have to do now is cross the lava bridge.

Arnold: Roger that. I'll go first, and then I'll catch you.

Arnold steps from one stone to the next.

Arnold: Ready?

Ethan: 3...2...1!

Ethan jumps, but can't quite make it. He lands just short of the stone.

Ethan: Help! Save me from the lava!

Arnold: You're not sinking! You must be immune!

Ethan: But for how long? Quick! Catch me!

In one swift motion, Arnold pulls Ethan up onto the stone.

Ethan: Phew! That was close.

Arnold: Wait...I hear someone coming.

Ethan: No. Please –

Mom: (*from offstage*) Ethan! Are you ready?

Ethan: No, not yet!

Mom enters. She does not register the peril at hand, nor anything or anyone except Ethan.

Mom: Ethan, you were supposed to be ready five minutes ago.

Ethan: I know, but then Arnold found the last clue to get into the time portal –

Mom: You can help Arnold with that later. Right now, I need you to put on your shoes and – (*as she's walking over to pick up Ethan's shoes, she accidentally steps on Arnold's foot*)

Arnold: Ow! Hey!

Ethan: Mom! That was Arnold's foot!

Mom: I'm sorry, Arnold.

Ethan: He's over here.

Mom: Ethan, I don't have time for this. Put on your shoes and go to the bathroom so we can go.

Ethan: Fine. See you later, Arnold.

Arnold: See ya.

Ethan follows Mom across the lava offstage. Unlike Ethan, Arnold is not willing to step in it. He sits down on his stone, careful to avoid letting his feet touch the floor, until he lets out a sneeze. He wobbles and begins to cling on for dear life.

Arnold: Help! Ethan? Anyone?

Taffy enters. With a wave of her wand, the hellscape disappears. Turns out it was just a blanket and a few books.

Arnold: I didn't need you.

Taffy: Oh, my bad. You're welcome for saving your life, by the way.

Arnold: But you got rid of everything! We liked it the way it was.

Taffy: Ethan won't notice.

Arnold: But I will!

Taffy: What's wrong with wanting the floor to not be lava?

Arnold: Now we're never gonna get to the time portal. We were about to save the dinosaurs.

Taffy: You can start again when Ethan gets back.

Arnold: It won't be the same. You ruined it.

Taffy: Oh, relax. You know, I remember when you used to be more mature than Ethan.

Arnold: Why do I have to be? It's not like I'm his mom.

Taffy: Hey, watch it.

Arnold: Eww, Taffy likes Ethan's mom! 'Cause they're both LAME!

Taffy: Shana is not lame!

Arnold: Please. Her idea of fun is sorting socks and stepping on my feet.

Taffy: All right, for the record Shana had way better adventures than you and Ethan ever did. We've been to space. We made a rocket. And the whole sky.

Arnold: You *made* it?

Taffy: Shana could make anything. Think of that next time Ethan thinks three books on the floor is turning it into lava.

Arnold: And a blanket.

Taffy: Whatever. Anyway, did you really want to be stuck sitting in lava until Ethan gets back?

Arnold: I don't mind. I want to be ready.

Taffy: Does he still not get bored?

Arnold: It's saving the world. Why would he get bored of that?

Taffy: I mean, what is he now, eight? That's when Shana started getting bored.

Arnold: That's different. Shana's not a kid.

Taffy: You think she was never a kid?

Arnold: Well, kids aren't tall. And kids don't spend all their time looking for shopping lists and making other kids go to the bathroom.

Taffy: That's the thing about kids, though. They grow up. There's nothing wrong with that.

Arnold: Maybe for her. But it won't happen with Ethan. We're best friends. Best friends don't let each other become lame.

Taffy: Oh boy.

Arnold: What?

Taffy: It's nothing. It's my fault. We should have had this Talk a long time ago.

Arnold: What Talk?

Taffy: It's okay. Everyone with a kid friend finds out about this at some point. (*She motions for Arnold to sit next to her.*) It's just...kid friends are not forever friends.

Arnold: Okay. What about forever and ever friends? That's what Ethan and I are.

Taffy: Nope. When kids grow up, friends like us become less important.

Arnold: But that takes a really long time, right? Like it must be at least fifty years or so.

Taffy: Maybe if your kid friend was a hobbit or something, sure. But human kids? I'd give him one or two more years, tops, with you.

Arnold considers this.

Arnold: Okay.

Taffy: Okay?

Arnold: Yeah.

Taffy: You're taking this surprisingly well.

Arnold: What's there to take well? It's nothing bad. It's no different than when the floor turns into lava.

Taffy: What?

Arnold: It's my next adventure. I have to stop Ethan from growing up.

Taffy: You can't do that.

Arnold: That's what you said about crossing the lava bridge, right? (*He begins pacing around the room.*)

Taffy: Well, you couldn't. I had to catch you –

Arnold finds a piece of paper and some crayons on the floor. He picks them up to begin sketching his plan.

Arnold: Do you think using the time portal might be a help?

Taffy: No, I don't.

Arnold: Stop ruining my dreams. You can help, if that will make you feel better. Maybe...you can stay like a million miles away and let me know if you hear it working from there. Yeah. And then when it works, me and Ethan will travel the whole million miles just to say "I told you so."

Taffy: Arnold, I don't want you getting your hopes up for something that won't happen.

Arnold: It will happen. He won't want to forget me.

Taffy: I didn't say he'd want to forget you.

Arnold: Then he won't. Ethan isn't Shana.

Taffy: (*beat*) Shana didn't want to forget either.

Arnold: Well, she had no reason to. You never go anywhere. She could turn around and look at you anytime she wants, right?

Taffy: She can't. It doesn't work like that.

Arnold: She never talks to you. She never even mentions you. I think that means she doesn't love you anymore.

Taffy: Would you stop?

Arnold: But luckily, Ethan has always wanted me around. Which means he will always want me around. Unlike Shana, who doesn't want you at all –

Taffy points her wand at Arnold, throwing him to the ground. This finally shuts him up.

Taffy: Arnold. Why do you think Ethan calls you his imaginary friend?

Arnold: Because...we go on every adventure that comes out of his imagination?

Taffy: It's because you live in his imagination. He's the only one that can see you.

Arnold: Then how come his mom knows who I am?

Taffy: Why do you think she's always tripping over your feet?

Arnold: I have big feet. It's not that big a deal.

Taffy: Yeah. Especially when you can't see the feet you're stepping on. Trust me, Shana used to see the world the same way Ethan did.

Taffy waves her wand, creating a space for a young Shana to enter. In a sort of dream sequence, she grabs Taffy by the hands and dances with her around the space. She mirrors Ethan's mannerisms from the beginning, looking at Taffy with complete adoration. When Arnold attempts to enter the image, she becomes indignant and pushes him out – how dare he interrupt her game.

Arnold: No way.

Taffy: Yep. And then one day she said, "I can't play today, I have homework to do." And by the time she was ten or eleven, she stopped giving excuses.

The Shana image begins pushing Taffy away, becoming more adult in posture and mannerisms each time she does. As Taffy reaches out for her one last time, she exits. Taffy waves her wand again, coming back to reality.

Arnold: You're saying Ethan will want to do homework instead of play with me? He hates homework.

Taffy: So it'll be something else. Maybe...soccer practice, or something. And then one day he'll start getting taller, maybe go on dates –

Arnold: He doesn't want to go on dates.

Taffy: And six years ago he didn't want to use the toilet. Anyway, eventually he'll go to college, and he won't ask you to come. He's stopped looking for you by then.

Arnold: But I'm gonna miss him.

Arnold starts to cry. It's a pitiful thing to watch. Taffy awkwardly tries to comfort him. She is not a hugger. It makes things so much worse.

Taffy: Um...there, there. It'll be okay.

Arnold: No it won't.

Taffy has no response for this. It hurts.

Taffy: You may have been right. I don't really know if Shana wants me around anymore. And I miss when she wanted to go flying with me. But...it's not like she's lost everything.

Arnold: She's boring now.

Taffy: She still loves flying, though. And she keeps a telescope in the backyard. She might not know it's because of me but it's something.

Arnold: It doesn't hurt that she doesn't play with you anymore?

Taffy: Of course it does. But she's reached a point where she can't. I hate to say it, but I'm glad we're not best friends anymore.

Arnold: How can you say that?

Taffy: She has a whole family for adventures now. But it's hard to lead those without some help. So sometimes when it seems like she needs it, I whisper to her: let's go look at the stars tonight. I don't know if she knows she's hearing me, but she does listen.

Arnold: But I don't want Ethan to not hear me.

Taffy: Listen: If Ethan is your best friend, you want what's best for him, right?

Arnold: Yeah.

Taffy: At the point Ethan's at right now, he doesn't need to be reminded to use his imagination. It's just what he does. But grownups aren't as good at that. At least, not on their own. You're made of imagination. You'll have to share some of that with him.

Arnold: He'll still be in my life?

Taffy: Yes. And you'll still matter to him. Just in a different way.

Arnold: I don't know if I'm ready for this yet.

Taffy: You don't have to be. It's hard whether or not you know it's coming.

Arnold: So if it's hard either way why did you bother telling me?

Taffy: No one told me. I don't want you to wonder what's going on the day he comes home from school and steps on your foot without apologizing.

A key turns in the lock. Ethan and his mom are home. They talk offstage.

Ethan: So can you help me with my habitat diorama? I want to make mine volcano themed.

Mom: Sure. Go wash your hands and let's get started, alright?

Ethan runs into his room to take off his shoes. As he's running, he trips over Arnold. He pauses as he gets up, dusts himself off, and then –

Ethan: Sorry, Arnold.

Arnold: That's okay! That's great!

Ethan: What?

Arnold: Nothing. Just happy to see you. Have fun with your project.

Ethan: Thanks!

He runs back out.

The End

KRISTEN BOLSTER

Freshman
Major: Public Policy
Reading: Slam Poetry

I grew up in Monroe, MI. I enjoy writing slam poetry, realistic fiction, and prose. I'm currently part of Michigan Research And Discovery Scholars (MRADS), Michigan Pole Dance Society, and Active Minds. My love of writing started my junior and senior year of high school when I wrote my first novella and I've been writing ever since. When I'm not writing I enjoy playing volleyball and drawing.

Nominated by: John Buckley

Mom

Slam Poetry

I don't believe in god anymore, but I believe in my mom.
I believe in my mom.
I believe my mom when she tells me she should have never had me.
I believe my mom when she's curled up on the side of her bed shrinking like a burned cigarette.
My mom doesn't smoke but
She whispers,
I don't think I'll make it through this year.

100,000 dollar tuition is a lot of money.
How much do you think a life's worth?
My professor is 15 minutes late to class, and I wonder how many sessions she could have had.
I get a C on my test, and I wonder if she could have been able to go to my graduation.
I drink warm wine at a party, and I wonder if she'll be at my wedding.
But I'm not that naive.

My dad says he can take out another mortgage on the house.
My mom says might as well, we won't be around to pay it off.
He's 53 and retirement is a foreign word when all he's ever known is that
He has six mouths to feed
Four to send to college
And only one job.

As if my future is more important than her life.
It's hard to be a daughter and a therapist,
But I know it's even harder to be a mother and a patient.
Insurance doesn't cover it,
Because if she ain't bleedin, she ain't broke right?

Some days she can't leave the house,
Some days she can't look at me.
Just because you're breathing,
Doesn't mean you're alive.

Everyday this voice in her head claws at her,
Rips up her insides,
Sets fire to her heart,
Strangles her confidence,
And beats the happy out of her.
Black shirt, Blue jeans
Is the only thing she'll wear
Because she doesn't want people to look at her.
I haven't seen her smile in smile three weeks,
But she's still breathing right?

I sit in class,
That's got a $3,000 cover,
My mom hides from the world,
Locks herself in a bathroom.
Jail can be kinda lonely when you're the only prisoner in the only cell,
And I haven't been writing like I said I would.

I'm late to class,
And I wonder if I'll get a phone call.
The same phone call I got about my grandma,
The same phone call I got about my nana,
They'll tell me that the bathroom swallowed her whole.
That the voice slit her throat.
They'll tell me it's not my fault.
Then they'll ask me how college is going,
About all the good I'm doing,
How bright my future looks,
How many lives I'll save with my degree,
They won't mention the woman I killed to get it.
They say knowledge is power,
I guess I should've realized power came at such a high price.

I fall asleep in class,
And I wonder if she would have been cured by now?

Because mental disorders ain't cheap but college ain't cheap neither,
And I'm still trying to live with the fact that I chose the latter.
That I chose my education over her life.
And I'm still *pissed off* that as a 17 year old girl in our healthcare system,

I had to make that choice in the first place.
Because everyday I'm here, I know she's ain't getting any better.

Some days I wake up,
And I find myself writing her eulogy,
And I give credit where credit is due,
So I sign my name at the bottom.

Players

Slam Poetry

Play nice,
Play hard to get,
Make foreplay last,
Don't hate the player hate the game.

But I don't remember signing up,
I don't remember trying out,
I never had any practice,
And I wasn't ready for this game.

Because he was a senior on varsity and
I was freshman team.
There was no whistle.
No time out.
No water break and
I like to tell myself I was too out of breath to talk
To say anything.

I had a bad coach.
I don't know why he picked me to be his starting player,
Maybe it's because I wasn't as fast or as strong as the other girls and
He thought he was giving me a chance?
He should've known I wasn't ready.
I should have known I stood no chance.

If an athlete loses their first game,
But no one chooses to report it
Does it go on their record?
Am I just one one win on his record?

I've played many games since,
And I don't hate the player anymore
I hate that I play this game too.

But it's funny how every loss for me is a win for you,
Like no matter what both of our records are going up,
And wouldn't you want to play someone with more experience anyway?

I mean you could've won the title,
But you were like three inches short for my goals.
You still playing like you're in high school,
And don't you know I'm a D1 college?
I should have known the game was going to be a quick one.

I heard you called me easy,
Even after I let you play me like that.

Most days I wish I stayed on the bench,
but that's not an option either when
They need me back there
Like the home team hasn't been the same without me,
And the only time I feel like I have a purpose is when I'm on the court.
Is when I'm underneath someone.
Is when I let you run all the bases.

Back then I was bad at defense,
And you were good at offense,
So it only made sense,
That you scored.
These days I'm still bad at defense.

You say you love playing games with me,
I say #metoo.
Because not only am I competing against you,
But I've been trained to compete against every other women.
And when they look at my score they think:
Whore.
Slut.
That's terrible form,
Keep your legs shut.
Stick to cheer.
They like us better on the sidelines anyway,
Our most natural state is being watched.

But don't worry,
Even then sometimes they'll act like they don't see,
Like, like if the Ref ain't catch it must not have been a foul,
Must not have been holding... me down.
I must not have been targeted–If anything I was asking for it.
It must not have happened at all.

So go ahead,
Shoot your shot.
Whether I want you to or not,
you'll score.

KALEB A. BROWN

Sophomore
Major: Creative Writing
Reading: Poetry

Kaleb A. Brown is Michigander pursuing a BA in Creative Writing. His goal is to become a successful journalist and a renowned novelist. He has published a journalism piece in the Ann Arbor Observer. His favorite genres of fiction include fantasy, science fiction, realistic fiction, and romance. In his free time he enjoys reading books, watching movies, writing, amateur photography and playing video games.

Nominated by: Sarah Messer

Scopophobia

I never liked having my photo taken. My mother's the same way. My hair fights the comb like a mad dog. My eyebrows are like brown, fuzzy caterpillars. The way the camera captures my skin makes me look like a corpse. Even when I'm smiling, the photographer always believes that I am frowning. But alas, I'd be remiss to not have my picture taken by this good, patient man. Mr. W.D. Wyver told me so. He said all the stars had their pictures taken – that way they could put them on the posters. I still didn't really consider myself a star that twinkled in the night. I didn't see people grouping me in a constellation. I didn't imagine people would be upset if the city lights blocked me. I couldn't see myself in a limo, nor going to some high-class party with drinks that are contraband. Mr. W.D. Wyver (after insisting I called him Will) agreed – he didn't equate me to Polaris or Sirius or Betelgeuse or Altair. He said I was like the most important star of all. So important and vital that fine people often took it for granted. He told me I was like the sun – so bright that I outshone all the other stars. So important that people oft forget my presence. That Mr. W.D. Wyver sure knows to make his lips sweet. How could he not? The film was apparently a smash hit, after all. People from Ohio to California are writing about it. It's because he knows how to spin a yarn. Nevertheless, because he says I'm the sun, because he's been so good to me and sister and mother dear, because we are now living comfortably, I am having my picture taken. I hope that all goes well. If Mr. Wyver is to be believed, my brightness will make it so the picture is pure white.

September 28, 1921

Kindle

This arrangement is only a temporary matter. The councilmen made a mistake. The councilman are beating themselves up over their foolish folly at this very moment. They'll find me innocent. After a night, this freezing floor and these barbaric bars in this cell will give way to my wooden home. I'll be back soon; I can tell.

Denial

O' goddammit it all! But I suppose *God* doesn't care much about I, seeing as *He* left me to rot! He wants me to burn! I shouldn't have saved that brat whose skin was pale as the freezing snow, whose coughs bellowed like the wind. His mum accused me of 'craft. I was always too kind. My slain mum cried that I must look out for number one.

Anger

If they set me free, I promise that every Sunday, I'll walk into Church, loving the Lord. I won't spend my money on herbs to make remedies or components to make spirits dance. I'll buy fresh Sunday clothes. I'll buy a hat, a pretty dress, and shoes, to match! I know I haven't done the things I should, but if they give me a chance, I'll be a good girl.

Bargaining

But I know my chance is up. My goose is good as cooked. My book has been shut, and I know that no one will put up a fuss. I was always the strange one, always the one that they gossipped about; always the one that mothers snatched their children away from. And sitting here, I wonder why was I born, I wonder why I was endowed with this "gift."

Depression

But no use crying over the rising of the sun. I was borrowing time since the day I was born. I knew that when they killed my mum. But what I have truly *is* a gift. Maybe one day, long after I'm gone, us with gifts won't cause rifts. Maybe one day we'll be accepted with wide arms. I pray, to a God that doesn't care for me, that their perceptions will shift.

Acceptance

So I walk tall, chin up as they jeer and let out screams high in pitch.
My smile is still as I am told my crimes; I give them not a twitch.
With resolve, I let them bind my arms and legs to the stake for being a witch.

Then I burn

1,000 Cranes

I was just two when the bombs came ten years ago. They tossed me through the window like a ragdoll. I was fine. My family called me a miracle child. My family said I could never die. So I know that I'll be fine. In a few days, I'll be home. In a few days, I'll be out of the hospital. I made a crane. It helps me forget the pain. I take a piece of paper and fold. When I ask Mom what's the matter, I'm dismissed with the gift of a yukata and a smile. I know her smile is a lie. I've made five cranes. I hope they come alive and take flight. I want out of this despair-filled head. I need out of this small bed. Today, I have 25 cranes. My best friend, Rumiko came. She told me the legend of the crane. She says if you make a thousand, you get a wish. I already know mine. I wish to live. It was hard, but I have 99 cranes. I keep having a bout of screaming. I keep thinking it's a dream, then I remember this is my reality. 154 cranes. I wake in the middle of the black night. At least I can fold in the dark. 230 cranes. I hear them through the wall; they're in the hallway. The doctor says I have something called leukemia. He says it's because of the radiation from the bombs. According to him, I have less than a year left. In tears, I realize I am the miracle child no longer. With 302 cranes, scattered in the room, they must think I'm insane. But the nurses just smile and put them neatly on a shelf. After all, who are they to judge a dying girl? 370 cranes done and much more to go. My friends are flocking to me from high and low. I dismiss them when their eyes get misty. I get pissy when I'm pitied. I have them give me construction paper. Notebook sheets. Wrappers. All is welcome in my quest to cheat death, to become the miracle child once more. Then, I won't need their pity. Everything will be back to normal. 541 cranes and I want to hurl. My leg is a disgusting shade of purple. I can no longer play soccer. They'll yell, "get back," because I'm a monster. I've been a monster since I was two. It just took awhile to show itself. 630 cranes and I can't complain. It's one of the better days. Rumiko came today. We talked about boys and toys. I dare say, for once, it was a normal day. 729 cranes. Why the hell did this happen to me? I was a baby, I didn't do anything wrong. I didn't kill anyone. I didn't fight in the war. I didn't ask for the emperor to have us fight to the last man. I didn't fucking ask to be born in this country. I didn't ask for blond-haired, blue-eyed assholes to blow up block after block of my city. I didn't ask for this disease. With 799 cranes done, I wonder what's the point as I bear aching joints. I've been in this hospital for nearly ten months, with no signs of leaving. After 844 cranes, I had an out of body experience. The nurses say I was delirious, but I swear I was floating further and further from the hospital. I was terrified. I want my wish. 999 cranes and I'm scared. Next crane will be it. What if it was just a myth? I can't do it. But I have to. 1,000 cranes. I'm still in this bed. 1,000 cranes. There's a ringing in my head. 1,000 cranes. I'll still be dead. 1,010. Why. 1,020. Won't. 1,030. My. 1,040. Wish. 1,050. Come. 1,060. True? 1,100 cranes and I wish I had failed. I wish I could live the rest of my days with "what-if." 1,300 cranes and all my friends and family are here. I'm eating delicious tea on rice. It's nice that I'm

SAM CANTIE

Sophomore
Major: English and Business
Reading: Fiction

Sam is a sophomore dual degree student, studying Business and English with a creative writing sub concentration. She is a Music Writer for The Michigan Daily, and has a strong passion for film, literature, and music. She loves hammocking, coffee shops, and concerts, and genuinely wants to share the experiences of humans through story-telling with humility and curiosity.

Nominated by: Oluwapemi Aguda

A Bracelet On My Wrist

I'm walking, and I think: *what if I just randomly threw myself in front of this car?* It's a weird confession to make, but in random situations I feel an impulse to do something unhinged like that. Not that I'd actually do it, nor do I want to, but sometimes I'm just walking, thinking those thoughts. My mind spins through different crazy scenarios. I see a tree and think: *What if that thing just crashed down on me, right over there?* I start to think about surviving said tree crash, and how my injuries would be a badge of toughness, or maybe an indication that I've "persevered" or "made it through something." I can't help but glorify that possibility of the sympathy that people would grant me if I was a tree crash survivor. I'm not trying to romanticize the idea of being physically hurt, it's just thoughts.

The closest I've gotten to a crazy experience actually coming to life was a bad case of the swine flu in 5th grade, when my fever soared to 103 degrees. Those 103 degrees displayed on the thermometer gave me the ability to slow life down, and focus on what hurt. Everyone knew I was hurt, everyone *believed* I was hurt, so they showed me grace. I was granted a week off of school and friends visiting my hospital bed with sympathy cards and teddy bears in hand. I hate that I glamourize tragedies. I hate that I think like this.

On this particularly humid, summer day, I didn't have time for these day dreams. I was much too happy. My swollen eyes adjusted to the morning sun in a kitchen on the far west side of Michigan's mitten, in the city of South Haven, which laid on the edge of the vast expanse of Lake Michigan. South Haven was known for its enduring lighthouse, which abided through the assault of sun rays, only to be encased in ice come winter. Although South Haven's beach gleaned the most attention from locals and tourists alike, the true beauty of this town was held at the end of Sunny Dale Lane, where I stood rubbing my eyes, reaching for a glass of water. If the beach was South Haven's heart, Sunny Dale was its most important vein. My real haven, laid at the end of this particular vein, in a quaint house owned by my best friend Cora, who I'd like to believe would always show me grace, whether I was actually in a car accident or not.

In my haven I stood awake, while my five best friends (a squad of two girls and three boys) slept into the early morning hours. Six best friends, who would spend their summer days in a quaint lake house, three hours from home, helplessly intertangled in each other.

It was the girls' turn to make breakfast. At the start of each summer trip we'd take a disorganized attempt at buying groceries, each chipping in the necessary funds to achieve our perfect week in paradise. "Normal" life had always been too busy for cooking, but in South Haven, we cook for each other. No exceptions. This was a rule I absolutely adored. One day in the future, when I decide to cook breakfast for my husband, in our newly owned sky rise apartment, I will know that he isn't the first person I've ever cooked for. I spent my summers cooking for my best friends. They held my heart first.

The clock showed 8am. Moments before I had silently removed myself from the front room we all slept in, my footsteps unheard over the rhythmic breathing of five other bodies. With two sets of bunk beds, there was more than enough room for slumber, but for some strange reason we all chose to sleep on the floor, cramped together in the middle of the room. The stringy, green carpet was just really comfy. Good for sleeping.

A short time later, I was no longer alone in the kitchen, joined by Noelle and Cora, whose sleepiness evoked a zombie-like state as they worked their way around the kitchen. Cora connected her phone to the speaker, and we were moving, unloading the bacon, eggs, and hash browns from the over-cramped refrigerator. It felt good to have just us girls for a moment, falling over each other while the sweet air filled with the soft harmonies of Vance Joy. We delegated responsibilities, habitually, and mine was bacon. I despised bacon (my friends would never let me forget how "wrong" my taste buds were for detesting it), but I knew I could kick-ass at making it. The stove remained occupied by Cora and Noelle, so I took on an alternate route for cooking bacon, one that wouldn't need the stove. Preheating the oven to 400 degrees, I layered each strip of bacon onto the baking sheet, each strip slightly overlapping one another in the same manner as our sleeping arrangements. As I waited for the bacon to sizzle, I made bets with Noelle and Cora over when the boys would finally awaken. Sitting in the small booth of that kitchen, with my sunburnt back pressed against the high-backed bench, I couldn't even realize how content I was.

I swear the boys woke up to the smell of bacon, the scent of my creation sweetly invading their dreams. Rory walked in from around the corner, shirt off, exposing his pale Irish skin. His hair perfectly rumpled in a bed-head manner, probably from the carpet we all shared. My stomach dropped and my heart fluttered. I was the lighthouse of South Haven, and he was those relentless waves crashing upon the pier. I kept my head down, focusing on his bare feet as they elicited small creaks from the tiled floor, happy to add another human to narrowness of this kitchen. He opened the oven to see my bacon.

One by one my friends scoffed, questioning why I chose to make the bacon like this. Remarks were made about the unusual use of the oven, but I had watched my mom make bacon in this manner multiple times before. When the time came for the bacon to come out, I grabbed an oven mitt, and removed the baking sheet slowly out of the oven, the sweltering air splitting at my face and running up the sides of my cheeks. Unknowingly, my weight placed itself in my heels, causing the baking sheet to tilt backwards at the slightest of angles. I heard my shriek before I felt any pain.

The hot grease rushed down to the focal point of my wrist, singing my pale skin so effortlessly. The pain came in a sudden and powerful flash, my nerves toasting in utter agony. In an effort to save the bacon from my shaking wrist, I rushed to the back door, pushing through the creaky screen and dropping the searing hot pan onto the pavement of the steps. My state of pumping adrenaline assured me the damage surely would only be minimal. I pressed my lips tightly together in a wrinkled manner, as if suffocating my pain away at the tips of my lips. Holding my forearm at a 90-degree angle, I analyzed the wound. The bacon in fact wouldn't be saved, as my blood dripped down the sides of my wrist and onto the baking sheet below, blending into the remaining grease and acting as ketchup for the bacon that remained. I turned my body back towards the screen door, catching Rory's worried eyes as Cora and Noelle ran upstairs to get the first aid kit. I force a toothless smile.

In the meantime Rory sprung to action, grabbing a worn wash cloth and stepping his bare feet across the pavement to reach me and my wrist. Applying pressure to the wound, he spoke soft remarks about the severity of my burn, each wave of his mellow voice soothing the harshness of my pain. With him holding my arm, just the way he did, I became his sick puppy, and I quite liked this feeling. He was a hug in the darkness, a feeling that I'd chase for a long time thereafter. I would always wonder if this was a catalyst for my later infatuation with wrists.

When the winter months came and I felt least like myself, I could look into the deep purple burn mark centered perfectly on the largest vein in my left wrist, and remind myself of the humid summer days spent with my best friends. It was like a tattoo, and it was insanely difficult to think of it as anything else. I'd long for it, the interconnectedness we held in those summer months at South Haven. The connection seemed to drift away when we drove back east for the winter, or when the deep purple scar would fade to a less noticeable color.

The second wound my left wrist endured would be self-inflicted, and it would be a performance with no audience. I remember my head took on the feeling of a balloon, expanding with extreme tension as I took in each breath. Endless tears puddled on the white tiles of my bathroom floor. It was after a basketball game, my body still lined with sweat, where I sat naked on my shower mat, the steam of a shower at its highest temperature filled the room. It was the steam that prohibited air from entering my lungs, making my knees shake. It was the steam, blurring my vision, and making that bacon burn mark on my left wrist look just like an artistically crafted tattoo. It was definitely the steam, entering my conscience, making me think a nail cutter could be extended outside of its normal functionality and used as a tool for my creation. That steam, it governed my behavior, fuzzed my ethics, convinced my mind that it was a broken machine that needed a sort of outwardly apparent nursing. The inner voice in my head that was supposed to be there, simply wasn't. It was just the steam, its haze and mist making me too cowardly to grab a kitchen knife and get the job done faster.

When the summer months came back, it was time to go to South Haven again, and while the relationships between us were ever shifting, the desire to go back was still was the same. Sitting in the same kitchen booth of the cramped kitchen, my knees tucked to my chest, we started the day with a list. On a small piece of lined notepad paper we wrote out a schedule for the day. The event I looked forward to the most came at the end of that list, which read in fading black ink:

Bike ride to the beach for sunset

I rode my bike at the back of the pack. The sun sparkled through the green of the trees, which seemed to wrap around the bike path, wide at the base and tight towards the sky. The trees took on a crescent moon shape, enveloping our bike pack yet allowing for our freedom. Sticky air was soothed only by the wind created from the speed of our bikes. Sweat trickled down my forehead as I watched my friends bike ahead, in complete awe of this moment. Their bikes weaved in and out, constantly changing position. Jack would brake as Cora slipped in front of him, Rory leaned over to the left of the path and pushed at the pedals in a ferocious manner to catch up with Alex. Over and over the bikes would weave in and out, changing position, crossing over each other, only to straighten back out again. There was one calm moment where each bike perfectly aligned; the two bikes in the front row fit perfectly into the windows between the three bikes in the back row. And at once I could see all five of my friends, biking ahead, perfectly aligned. The moment came and it went.

On the beach, we all tried to fit onto one blanket. We picked a spot a good distance away from where our bikes rested, locked up. The walk along the beach included inside jokes which made me laugh until my stomach hurt, lyrics to songs we all knew, and shouts into the void of Lake Michigan. Along the way Jack found a piece of wood shaped like a dick, and preceded to slap us all with it, which he found absolutely hilarious. I pursed my lips together in the same way I did while my wrist bled onto the bacon last summer, trying not to laugh out loud at the sight of Jack running around with this piece of wood. Noelle managed to steal the dick shaped stick from Jack, and comically, but perhaps more sweetly, she used it to write in the sand: *Be Happy*. The boys roared with laughter, but us girls sighed sweetly, satisfied with the notion of what was written.

On the blanket, we laid down while the sun was slowly setting. If a pilot were to look down on us from above, I imagine he would see a sunflower, our heads forming the pollen producing center, each of our bodies a petal. Although no steam in the air, my breath ran short, as Rory's forearm delicately touched mine, our petals of the flower positioned directly next to one another.

Later, when the sun had set, Jack and Alex ran off to set a firework they had brought with. Noelle and Cora walked slower behind them, less enamored with the drug-store purchased device that would explode when ignited, but we all knew deep down they were looking forward to seeing that firework explode. As I took a step forward into the sinking sand, I was pulled back unexpectedly, by the hand of Rory grabbing my arm. A rosy blush flooded to my face, and I walked behind him under the notion that he wanted to talk.

We made our way to a damper part of the sand, at a distance from the single firework Jack had spoken of all day. I sat next to Rory, hugging my knees to my chest, facing the lake that softly vibrated from the crash of subtle waves. Although the sun had set, hues of orange and yellow still raced through the sky, following closely behind the sun, almost out of reach beyond the horizon.

I squirmed in my position, anxious by what might happen next, feeling slightly unaligned. I begged for earlier, when I could see each of my friends on their bikes in perfect formation. We made small talk, laughing about Jack's dick stick and tracing shapes in the sand. We spoke of his dad, who would certainly make him work extra hours at the shop when this trip was over, avenging the time Rory took off to be here. At one point he hung his rumpled hair down towards the sand, slowly reaching into his khaki shorts to dig out something from his pocket. He unveiled a bracelet, weaved together with strings of orange and yellow.

He reached out for my wrist, which made the blood underneath my skin freeze, for I was worried that he'd see the work of the nail cutter on that past winter day, the work of the bacon from a summer before. Slowly, he wrapped the bracelet around my wrist, my heart pounding in coordination with the waves against the pier. I searched his freckled face for some sort of reaction, but I only saw the intent of him wanting the bracelet he made to be a part of me, to hang securely on my wrist. In the dim light, I guess he couldn't see the scars. Or maybe, in this moment, they weren't even there. They were only mine to know, and I held them with me, with no one to show.

CHRISTIAN CHARLEY

Freshman
Major: Performing Arts Technology
Reading: Poetry

Christian Charley, also known by his stage names Ozone and DFRNC, is an American poet, writer, musician, songwriter, and producer. Attending the University of Michigan as a Performing Arts Technology major, he doesn't take his skills for granted. He is often regarded for his unique ways of storytelling in both music and poetry. He loves to share whatever is on his mind, which is currently Hamilton. After college, he plans to tour the world making music with friends and family and spreading a positive message. HIs favorite thing in the world, however, is intimate conversations, so he asks that whoever is hearing this brief bio to not be afraid to come up and say hi to him later.

Nominated by: Annika Pattenaude

Mabawa & Upanga

DFRNC

Let the richness of the nile take it over. A figure as built as the motherland that calls; melanin with meaning, shaded light and dark and in between. The machine has a methodical process built inside of itself. Flowing for years (is it tonal?), with no basis starting point, it can still be easily defined, chopped like tenderloins and served with anxious desire and a long anchor. A red floor, not splattered but ironed, envelopes the landscape, predominantly in that of original natives, but also where wire stays its natural temperature, and where the sun is a deadly laser. Back to melanin, back to coils locked in grenades and claymores. No sacrifices were made; two people have been born. They were created in the machine, or rather the machine was a helping hand.
Figures that the figure would take action.

A Creator, a Rose, and an Architect come together to create a dance. It was originally supposed to be no more than 50 steps. In a few months, they made over 108 steps.
The Rose got caught in legal trouble after making 10 steps. The architect made 26. The Creator wrote the other 72.

It's time to spend summer vacation with friends. For you, that may not be the case at the moment. Your parents wait for you at the bottom of the stairs to drop you off.
With your piano books in your bag, you follow the narrow stairway to the practice rooms. The door is closed for the room you normally go into. With a knock, you teacher appears.

Brian? you say.
What do you think you're doing? he responds. Can't you see I'm with another student?
A loud bang when the door shuts in front of you.
You shrug with a smile on your face as you walk back to your parents (you were young). Your parents eyes were teaching you something, something you already knew but never understood. You were being told not to react and to react at the same time, the chivalry gestures in your mind were confused.
What's wrong? you asked them.
We're finding you a new teacher, your mother responded.

With another regular day of college over, you relax in the lounge with other members of your major, to which they pay you no mind. As you sit to try and do your work, you overhear a conversation. One of them says, finally we got to hear about a black hip-hop artist. We never talk about them.
What are you getting angry for? is what you ask yourself after hearing them. You felt categorized. It doesn't stop you from saying What do you mean?
Huh? he responded
You said we never talk about black artists.
Yeah...what do you mean?
We've talked about a lot, like Julius Eastman and DJ Rupture.
Oh Shit...
That's what their faces said.
Oh, sorry, I guess I wasn't paying attention.
You nod your head and suddenly things become awkward, but you continue studying as if nothing had changed. You shouldn't have said anything. It's good you said something. You shouldn't have said anything. You felt that you were being talked to even though the intention wasn't there. Could the outcome have been different had you said nothing, had you kept to yourself?

We pulled ourselves into the world. Note what I just said right there.
I'm not gonna repeat myself, because I'm caught in the
eye of God,
In the eye of a hurricane, it feels so clear,
Blinding, push over me,
What do I do what do I do.
That's right...the notes.

Stop writing like you have no where you need to go.
Stop writing like you have no where you need to go.
Stop writing like you have no where you need to go!
Why do you write like you're running out of time?
Aaron Burr running through your mind for inspiration.
The sensation that I get when my kind rules this world with no supplements.

I imagine the spotlight so much it almost feels like a dream.
Is there where it begins? My legacy, so it would seem.
The fluids that run through my drums, the most
important ones coming from strife.
From the time that I was young, I secretly know this
would be my life.
MY LIFE!

What is life?
It is the culmination of your dreams and your soul.
Your soul, burning in your body because it wants to see,
It wants to see it's destiny that you left with your legacy,
Legacy that wants to breathe across the trees and the seven seas,
The seas is how far my eyes can now see
America you are dead to me!
Because all I want to do is
GROW
And everytime my talents shed their shell I want to
SHOW
Up into the spotlight as every time the hairs on my walls
become grayer and grayer
It grows, it grows, it grows, it grows!
MY ROSE!
....
How beautiful you are...
As you grow from the cement with...dried tips in the ground...
Take your time dear, take your time.
Take your time dear, take your time.
Take your time (x8)

I become timid with the glock in my hand as I hold to my head
WAIT!
....
Your melanin has meaning.
Your black coils with frost tips was always gleaming.
Come. Can I show you what I've created?

NAVANAS CHETSANDTIKHUN

Junior
Major: School of Information
Reading: Poetry

Navanas grew up in Thailand thinking the weather was too hot and immediately overcorrected when he chose to attend the University of Michigan. He writes in his free time.

Nominated by: Greg Schutz

Wild

-- A *date over Scrabble*

I swiped a mug from the self-serve counter, and said to her
But have you ever made up words, on the fly, like 'amazetastic?'
She said that it was a hundred percent against official rules.
Just this once, Janine, wouldn't it feel so good to be bad?
    She didn't laugh, but cracked a wince.
Not even once had she tried
to tie together a tmesis,
or bend a spelling, and
She'd also never tell a white lie,
or run a red
light,
even when the lanes went empty.
    But I did, on West Liberty.
Strictly, she squared herself, and stared

Still, in some way, as if to say
No.
And trashed the board flying straight
to the café floor, cascade
in cream-colored tiles, we basked, and she asked
me about my coffee.

She knew I didn't pay for it.

Viena

–I guess I don't know what it's like to be young with Parkinson's disease.

Funny seeing you here,
you never liked when the sky was out-of-whack,
        said it made you want to stay in bed.
Funny sitting in the beach chairs, with scarves
putting mayonnaise on fries.

I call and you turn but skirt away with your eyes
and say there's traffic on the highway,
big game today, people stuck
going to see Madrid play Barcelona.

But neither of us like football.

You roll a smoke, barely holding the tobacco.
I don't know if it's the cold, or you're having trouble
trying to light the end of it, blocking the wind with your knees
Last time you said you'd quit, I believed you'd really do it.

"I don't think I'd want to live until I'm fifty.
Maybe fifty-three, but not any more."

I drown the lump in my throat with water, to say something but the wind
is adamant to wisp the substance away, when I thought of how you played
guitar to Summer Latin Hits on Nit Boja, with
open chords; you couldn't hold the bars down.

We used to sing off-key to Vance Joy,
and Carlos Vives the second time around.
If I had stuck around I would
have learned to play one or two in Catalan.

Pretty Things

Matthew was sitting in Espresso Royale, pacing through the nauseous, ringing remnants of his St. Patrick's Day weekend, looking for a story to tell Chris. It was the first time that the two of them didn't hit a big party together. He closed his eyes, but couldn't string anything together past the fact that some kid he knew had tried cocaine. That was his ace. He opened his eyes back up, and saw Chris approaching from the counter.

"How're you doing? You look like shit," said Matthew. Chris took a seat next to him.

"Dude, I was drunk since, like, nine AM," Chris began, "And then I went until like- I partied until like three thirty. Woke back up at eight. Got Jimmy John's. Right back out. Peter and I punched a hole in the wall of a frat house, I think it was Delta Sig" Chris made a punching motion. "I've never felt worse, man" he added, smiling, "My intestines are swollen. Can just feel it." He looked straight at Matthew. Something about the way he held eye-contact seemed to communicate the fact that Chris didn't need Matthew to have a good time. In fact, "Peter" was a name Matthew was becoming more and more familiar with. Lately, Chris had been bailing out of plans with him to hang out with Peter.

"Who's Peter?" said Matthew.

"He's this guy in, uh, my team for a group project," said Chris.

"Right," said Matthew, "Is he cool?"

"He's not that cool," said Chris, "He's an alright guy, though."

Matthew nodded.

"Funny thing about that," said Chris, "I low-key hooked up with Peter's girl after the party. I don't think he knows." A smile plastered across Chris' face, showing all of his teeth, and his tongue out. Chris was recklessly charming that way. He had a real James Dean kind of face, and was exuberantly fun to be around. He was the type to die young, if there ever was one, Matthew thought. The guy can talk his way into all kinds of places.

Matthew told Chris about how the one guy had tried cocaine. Chris laughed and said, "No way," with enthusiasm all the way through Matthew's account of his wild and disorienting St. Patrick's Day weekend.

"Wow, maybe I should have been out with you instead, huh, buddy?" said Chris.

"Yeah," said Matthew, "Maybe."

"Oh," Chris said, "remind me to Venmo you for the Molly two weeks ago."

Matthew waved his hand at the thought like it wasn't a big deal. He had sold drugs to Chris almost every time they went out.

"Friends discount," said Matthew.

Chris' phone chimed. He picked it up and squinted as he scrolled through the messages. "It's Peter," he said. He typed something, and set the phone down. "He's bringing his girl to get coffee."

"What?" said Matthew.

"I know," Chris laughed, "I don't even care. Don't tell Peter what I said."

Matthew spent the next half hour witnessing Peter's unrelenting cluelessness, and Chris' blatant absence of guilt, as the two joked and laughed like childhood friends, in between the back-and-forth exchanges of gaze from Peter's girlfriend to Chris, and vice versa. Chris' outwardly friendship with Peter bothered Matthew, in a certain indescribable way – like vertigo, or a bad trip.

As the Winter semester wore on, Matthew saw less of Chris, and got even fewer messages. When Chris received a job offer from a big West Coast tech company, he made a post on Facebook that said, "Moving to a beach where the water's salty!" Matthew messaged Chris to congratulate him, and suggested that they get trashed to celebrate.

"Can't do, buddy boy," Chris replied, "The offer's contingent on me maintaining my GPA. Even legends have to graduate some time." Despite that, Chris would post pictures of his bar crawls with Peter on Instagram.

Matthew became increasingly aware of how painfully dull his weekends were without Chris – to the extent that no amount of drugs could make up for. At an afterparty for a dance showcase, Matthew stood for fifteen minutes waiting to buy drinks for himself and a girl he was talking to. Her patience ran out, and she left him in line at the bar to find other people on the dance floor. After finishing out both drinks, he decided that it was time he told Peter about what Chris had done, in a form of an ill-worded, shitfaced phone call.

The next time Matthew saw Chris was in front of Walgreens, when a winding fist connected just below his left cheekbone. Passersby had to peel Chris off of Matthew's half-conscious body lying on the curb. Matthew could hear Chris shouting something about graduation as he was being removed.

He found out through some friends that after his phone call to Peter, Peter was so mad that he asked the professor to remove Chris' name from the final project they were working on together. He had grounds to do so, too, since apparently Chris didn't contribute much to the project. Chris' job offer was revoked, because he had to stay an extra semester and retake the practicum.

"You didn't have to take his name off the project, you petty fuck," Matthew remembered saying to Peter, one time, when they ran into each other at a party.

"Yeah," said Peter, "and Chris only hung out with you for drugs."

KELLY CHRISTENSEN

Sophomore
Major: English and Communications
Reading: Fiction

Kelly was born and raised in Flint, Michigan and transferred to the university this year. She spent the last year at Sarah Lawrence College in New York. In her (little) free time, she enjoys cooking, travelling, gardening, and spending quality time with her cats.

Nominated by: Laura Thomas

Wonderland

The first time Virginia Townsend had received such a thick letter from the U.S. government, printed onto woven cream cardstock, was October 29, 1922. This new envelope that Virginia held in her hands nearly seventy years later was tattered around the edges as a result of the laborious, eleven-mile trip from the post office below. Four days of the week, Virginia's mail man, Adam, would climb over a thousand feet of winding mountain roads to hand-deliver mail to the only cabin left inhabited in the town of Elkmont.

Every morning Virginia would rise from her bed at 8:25 am and pour herself a cup of tea from the same iron kettle that her parents had used before her. Wrapping a quilt around her shoulders, she would open the cabin's creaking front door and step slowly down the cobblestone sidewalk to the 70-foot American chestnut tree in her front yard. On each side it was flanked with three other trees of the same species, however these ones had succumbed to the nationwide chestnut tree blight decades ago. Between the six husks, the last living chestnut tree was dotted with the first buds of spring

Mornings in the Smoky Mountains were characteristically brisk, but nonetheless, by the time Adam arrived at 8:40 am, Virginia would be nestled in her yellow vinyl lawn chair beside the mailbox. The chair had been there longer than Adam had been delivering her mail, long enough for pastel wildflowers to spring up along the aluminum legs, pulling it into the ground with their roots.

"You know Ms. Townsend, you gotta be the only person I've ever seen smile after receivin' a letter like that one," Adam laughed, leaning on the muddied postal pick-up truck as Virginia leafed through her delivery.

"I've been expecting this one for a while now," she explained softly. Adam gestured towards Virginia's mint-colored cabin behind them,

"I'm hoping it has nothin' to do with your home here?"

"Hate to see 'em get rid of your favorite route, huh?" Virginia winked. "Come inside, I have some gifts for you to take home." Adam chuckled from deep in his round stomach and offered his arm to help Virginia rise from the chair.

"Hey, if you weren't up here, my only stop would be the ranger station, and they definitely don't give me gifts!" Four days a week, if Adam wasn't leaving with new macrame decorations, he was leaving with pies and cobblers and anything that could fit into a mason jar. Climbing the wooden stairs to her cabin, Virginia pushed the bulging envelope into her pocket.

Inside, Adam took a seat in one of the wicker chairs positioned squarely at the dining table as Virginia shuffled towards her back porch.

“You don’t really think the Park Service would go back on their word after all this time, do you?” Virginia took her time to return to the table and to Adam’s question, and cradled an ivory macrame basket in her arms when she returned.

“If they decide that they want this land too, I’m sure that they’ll find a way to get it.” She transferred the bundle to Adam, who rose to accept it. Turning towards the front door to leave, he paused in front of the paned glass window in Virginia’s front room, looking out over the rest of the ghost cabins that once composed Elkmont.

“They don’t do anything with all these other nice houses up here, I don’t see why they’d need yours too,” Adam frowned. “I mean, look at the Trentham’s house…just sittin’ there.” Across the street, the once-manicured lawn had been reclaimed by vines, hemlocks, and maples. Virginia’s yard, while not as overgrown as the others, showed its heavy influence.

“I was hoping if I let the yard look like the rest, they might forget I was even up here.”

“With that magic chestnut tree here?” Adam gave the massive tree a pat as he passed it, “Hell, that’s probably what they wanted most making this place a national park!” Virginia absentmindedly nodded in agreement and waved goodbye to Adam as he climbed into the delivery truck and pulled back down the lightly-used dirt path.

After her father died, Virginia had done her best to maintain the yard as carefully as he had all his life. However, as she grew older the imperial bushes and vines began to grow faster than Virginia could chop them down. She caved in to the jungle around her.

The chestnut tree in particular had been ample in the mountains when Virginia was born in 1906. Looking back, Virginia couldn’t help but associate the beginning of the chestnut tree blight with the beginning of the national park movement in the 1920s. At the age of sixteen, she would climb high into the dying chestnut trees with the paperwork from that first envelope, detailing how the park would be moving in. There, Virginia would spend hours intent on finding a loophole to save her mountain town. Her dad would follow her, leaning against the trunks.

“It’s not that serious,” he would say, reaching up into the branches to offer Virginia a hankerchief for her puffy red eyes. “Like living next door to a giant park.” He explained that the government promised to let anyone living in Elkmont stay as long as they wanted. Even until they died. Later, the government offered Virginia’s father compensation for their house if he would voluntarily leave, but his dedication to nursing his ailing chestnut trees drove away any notion of that.

It was 1992 now, and it was a miracle that a single one of those trees stood in Virginia’s front yard, while the rest of the town had fallen to make room for hiking trails and tent pads. Inevitable red sores had begun to appear on the bark two springs ago, and Virginia knew it wouldn't be long before her final tree followed suit with the barren skeletons surrounding it. Already, some of the early buds had started to shrivel and fall off the branches almost as soon as they had sprouted. At the tree's base, Virginia had planted bright red cardinal flowers and spring beauties, *Claytonia virginica*, which her father named her after. Today they were in bloom for the first time and trembled with raindrops. Virginia slowly lowered herself to her knees and pulled at some of the weeds that had sprung up in her patch of garden.

Seventy years ago, Elkmont and much of the surrounding area had been clear cut by the logging industry, and while some plants thrived under so much sun, most of the indigenous plants withered away. Now, small green buds clung to honeysuckle branches and the rhododendrons had exploded into masses of pink and white flowers silhouetted against the shiny dark green leaves. Virginia had to admit it was much more beautiful this way. The only noise was that of bird song and the occasional pitter-patter of raindrops falling from leaves high above Virginia's head. The river babbled and the cicadas buzzed in unison, forming a single, unending hum. The town itself was silent.

Even after the National Park Service had made it clear that they were purchasing the land that Elkmont was situated on, it was never quite this quiet, at least not at first. For years, the suburbs and the campsite co-existed with few problems, aside from the inconveniences brought on by the choice to build the campground directly on top of the center of town. The Wonderland Hotel even continued to accept vacationers who preferred to sleep in a bed instead of a sleeping bag, until the National Park Service closed that, too.

Virginia rolled back on her heels and sat in the wild grasses, pulling the letter out from her pocket. Inside was a thick packet, barely held together by a staple. "UNITED STATES DEPARTMENT OF THE INTERIOR" was printed at the top of the first page along with the National Park emblem. It continued:

> 23 April 1992
>
> Dear Ms. Virginia F. Townsend,
>
> PURSUANT TO SECTION 34.5(c) OF THE LEASING AGREEMENT, THIS LETTER IS NOTICE TO THE OCCUPANTS OF 9567 DAISY LANE OF THE TERMINATION OF THE LEASING AGREEMENT ENTERED UPON BY MS. VIRGINIA FRANCES TOWNSEND, EFFECTIVE MAY 7th, 1992.

Virginia shoved the letter back into its envelope. She had read quite enough. Looking up, the leaves that once sparkled with dew suddenly seemed muted. For a moment she stayed there, knees pressed into the moist dirt beneath her. A lump formed in the back of Virginia's throat and her stomach twisted around itself.

Who did they think they were? How could these people sleep at night, stealing her land and leaving an 86 year old woman homeless? The longer Virginia dwelled on their nerve, the hotter her blood grew despite the chill of the cool mountain morning. In the silence of her ghost town, she felt utterly alone. She had no one to run to. No one to listen to her fury.

As panic began to bubble in her stomach, Virginia pushed herself to her feet. Restless, she headed in the direction of the Wonderland. After seventy years, the trail that ran through each of the abandoned properties had become rugged, and Virginia made slow progress. As the last resident of Elkmont, if Virginia had an accident it could be days before anyone came to help. But after walking this path thousands of times during her life, she moved confidently.

The Wonderland had been owned and operated by Mrs. Elizabeth Trentham, who was one of Virginia's closest friends as a result of the fact that for years, the two women were the only people permanently living in Elkmont. When the Park Service came, Mr and Mrs. Trentham were unwilling to leave their hotel in the same way that her father couldn't bear to leave his trees. When Mr. Trentham passed away in 1944, the National Park Service refused to extend his lifelong lease to Mrs. Trentham. Instead, they begrudgingly replaced it with a 20-year lease that they renewed twice, but refused to renew in 1984. When she was evicted, Mrs. Trentham was 87 years old.

Soon enough Virginia could spot the massive two-story white structure behind a wall of trees that had not existed before the National Park. Coming closer, she winced at the fresh plywood that leaned against the place where walnut French doors once were. Pulling the plywood back, Virginia stepped into the hotel's foyer. Unlike the other Elkmont houses that had been saturated by rainwater and scrapped for valuables by scavengers, the Wonderland remained mostly untouched, partially hidden from the road by the fledgling forest and religiously manicured by Mrs. Trentham until her last day in Elkmont. Only recently had the delicate, hand painted wallpaper begun to peel away where it met the cool, glittering stones of what was once considered the most beautiful fireplace in all of Appalachia. Nostalgically, Virginia recalled spending her evenings wrapped in a blanket in front of this fireplace, playing cards and listening to the stories of visitors who came to the national park from all around the world.

More clearly, Virginia could remember holding Mrs. Trentham in front of this fireplace on the day she received her eviction notice. Only fifteen years her senior, Mrs. Trentham cradled her knees to her chest in Virginia's arms. Her bony knuckles were white from clutching that thick letter from the U.S. government, printed onto woven cream cardstock. Sobs wrenched the woman's small body, and if it weren't for the fact they were the last inhabitants of Elkmont, Virginia would have been weary that someone would hear Mrs. Trentham wail.

Before they would break their promise altogether, the National Park Service found a loophole. Once they had handed down their first 20-year lease to Mrs. Trentham, the Park Service seemed to take a liking to them, as 6 years later in 1952, Virginia too held one of these letters in her hand, as did most of the families in her neighborhood. The letter explained that *all* of their leases were to be shortened to 20-year leases that could be renewed *only* by the original lease holder.

But even while Virginia held Mrs. Trentham as her agony gave way to acceptance and screams turned to sniffles, Virginia had still felt safe. When her father heard that the government was offering lifelong leases, he made the decision to put Virginia's name on her family's lease at the age of 21, already fearing for the fate that would eventually befall Mrs. Trentham. If her name was on the original lease, Virginia could renew it as many times as she pleased. Or at least that's what she had thought.

The hotel still appeared as though the owners might return at any moment, right down to the unburned firewood in the 40-foot fireplace, and the folded newspaper on the coffee table, dated from 1984. Virginia crumbled the newspaper, and poked it between the pieces of wood. Pulling a lighter from her pocket, Virginia lit the paper, cupped her hand around the flame, and gently blew on it. Satisfied with the spreading flames, Virginia pulled a canvas sheet from off the dull green couch and returned to her favorite spot. Pulling the letter from her pocket once again, Virginia read over the lines and watched as the grand fireplace grew large enough to once again send golden rays through the glass windows, casting the Wonderland and the entire town of Elkmont in amber.

SOPHIA CHRISTOS

Senior
Major: English Language & Literature and Creative Writing
Minor: Entrepreneurship
Reading: Fiction

Sophia is passionate about writing, reading, and creativity. She's one of the founders of EMPOWER, an online young women's magazine that promotes positivity and inspiration. Sophia's also a development intern at the Alzheimer's Association, where she is working to find the first survivor of Alzheimer's. In her spare time, Sophia loves to scuba dive and travel the world.

Nominated by: David Gold

Whatever's in the Fridge

It wasn't the first time the cops came to our house. And we all knew it wouldn't be the last time, whether we admitted it to ourselves or not.

Fotini stands at the edge of her bedroom door, her eyes traveling back and forth from all of us.

Mom's downstairs in front of the open door with Dad, refusing to let him up the stairs after demanding we stay there. The cops will arrive any minute now, so Dad's already cooled down and resorted to pacing back and forth in front of the door.

Pavlos sits with me on the top stair as we look down upon our parents, waiting for the moment the cops enter. The time in between the call and the cop cars pulling outside had always been filled with a tense yet knowing energy of what was to come. It had only happened twice before, but it was enough now to have become a pattern. A part of us remained uncertain of the consequences, but we also held some sort of understanding of what lay ahead, which would certainly include some reprimanding from the officers and a dose of discomfort at finding ourselves in this situation once again.

A beaten and accustomed energy rests between Pavlos and me. With Fotini, though, she appears invigorated at the morning's unraveling. I doubt she remembers the first time, when she'd been four. And it'd been five years since the second instance at the age of seven. Today, though, she won't forget. She'll soak up every last detail as if though we're some series finale on one of her T.V. shows.

"What happened?" she asks us for the fourth time. Her dark brown hair still bears the tangles it'd developed overnight. Her eyes are wide open, making the brown in them seem extra dark than usual, especially atop her rosy pink cheeks that haven't lost their color yet in the minutes she'd awakened. Her cheeks have grown chubbier over the last two years as has the rest of her body. She no longer has the slender body of her younger self, and now finds her body mirroring that of her siblings, which had grown thicker at the same age.

"Dad attacked me," I say. I catch myself from laughing at the incredulity of the situation and that the rare time Dad and I had ever gotten into it with one another was also the time the cops had been called. It was often Dad and Pavlos fighting with each other, over anything and everything. It was common for Fotini and Mom to argue with him.

But, I, just kept to myself in my room, spending my days writing endlessly on my own, working on my fantasy series, only coming out when I needed to eat or do chores. Most of the time things would be fine if Dad wasn't stirred.

He bothered me just as much as the others, but I despised the fighting and the shouting more than they did. I avoided it if I could, but the others either didn't care or realize when they'd do something that was bound to rile him up. Sometimes I think they were too pissed off to care or that maybe some small part of them still needed what they'd only ever known.

I can't blame them when we've all lived under Dad's rule for so long. He never means wrong, but somehow his temper and lack of control always bubble up to the surface.

There was a time a year ago when he and Pavlos got into it. I don't remember why they were fighting, or if I ever knew, for that matter, but it must've sounded bad enough for Mom to hop off the toilet and run naked through house with nothing but her underwear between her ankles. She tried to separate Pavlos and Dad, but Dad just took her and shoved her to the ground, where she slid on her butt across the wooden floor. After that, Fotini became so angry that she hit Dad with a hanger that broke upon impact.

I only know this because afterwards Fotini and Pavlos pushed open my bedroom door and told me what I'd missed. I'd heard the fight as it was happening, but I didn't realize it'd gotten so out of hand, more so than normal. From upstairs it sounded usual, like every other fight. I didn't pay much attention to it. I was too busy writing to go down and see what I thought I had already seen before.

As Pavlos and Fotini relayed the story to me, their eyes were wide with incredulity, but they laughed when they told me about Mom sliding across the floor and Fotini hitting Dad with a hanger. I laughed too. I don't know why. It's sickening to imagine, but I still can't help but laugh when I think of what happened.

"What did he do?" Fotini asks again, pulling me from the past. She walks over to Pavlos and me.

"Stop it, Fotini," I snap. I wasn't in the mood to talk. Something drips onto my right sock.

I look down and realize there's a pool of blood over my right thumb's nail. "Shit."

I rise and head into the bathroom with Fotini following behind. The sink water rinses out the blood, but I have to wrap two tissues around my thumb to stop the bleeding.

"What did he do?" says Fotini.

"He hit me with a lemon squeezer, okay? You happy now?" "Geeze, I was just asking."

I didn't want to be so short with Fotini all the time, but I somehow can't change. It pains me every time I hear the voice that reaches her, but a part of me thinks I do this to myself on purpose, punishment for God knows what.

Papou's face comes to mind as I imagine him discovering our current situation. He'll shake his head, disappointed but not surprised. I don't think we ever surprise him anymore. I wonder when the surprise stopped happening. Yiayia always had hope for us. She was the one who forced Mom to stay with Dad when Mom realized what Dad really was after three months of marriage. Her frantic, sob-induced call to Yiayia had left her with the only option available for a second-generation Greek.

I remember Mom talking to Yiayia for hours every day. I can't decide if Papou will tell Yiayia about today, now that her Alzheimer's – or, the disease, as Papou calls it – has almost consumed her. He's always worried about upsetting her now that she's become so sensitive, but he also pretends that she's the same as before.

We'd never been good at hiding ourselves, but somehow it's only the family that knows just how off we really are. I doubt any of our friends would suspect, mostly I think by choice. A part of me wonders whether Mr. Waters ever gets angry like Dad. I have a hard time imagining Daniel's dad getting angry like ours, but I don't know. We rarely see them now that we've moved three times in the last two years. Even though we're just in another Chicago suburb only an hour away, somehow the distance has separated us now that we're no longer on the same street.

An unrecognizable man's voice echoes from downstairs. The cops have arrived.

Fotini and I rush back into the hallway at the top of the stairs. A uniformed officer around Dad's age stands in between my parents.

"My husband has just lost it. He attacked my daughter, and we just can't take it anymore," Mom exhales to the cop. "I don't want him here."

"She attacked me first!" Dad exclaims.

"I'm going to have you step outside and go talk to my partner," the cop tells Dad, pointing to another cop who stands in the middle of the pathway leading to the front house.

Dad walks out to the second cop, leaving the one inside staring at the three of us upstairs. Underneath his reddish-brown hair are pink, freckled cheeks that hold a plumpness reflecting the rest of his body. A bothered, disinterested look rests upon his face. I shouldn't have expected a warm Olivia Benson approach after the last two times, but somehow I'm still thrown off.

The first happened in our old home, before the move. I hadn't seen the fight between Mom and Dad, didn't know if he'd really pushed her. After the cops came, I remember riding my bike with Pavlos and Fotini amongst all the cop cars in our cul-de-sac, hearing the cops exclaim how happy the three of us looked, expressing disbelief of Mom's words. Because that's definitely normal, seeing three kids riding carefree along the cop cars that have been brought out over their parents' domestic violence dispute.

The second time had been more or less the same. Dad had hit Mom in the laundry room when trying to resolve some argument. Pavlos, Fotini, and I didn't see it, but we heard it behind the closed door. The cops just gave him a warning. I was relieved back then, not wanting anything bad to happen to Dad or the family.

"Which daughter was involved?" the cop asks from below. Mom points to me.

"How old are you?"

"Eighteen."

"Alright. Why don't you come down here? Who else saw what happened?"

"My son did, and I came only at the end," Mom says.

"I'm going to talk to each one of you, and then I'm going to have you write up your statements."

I come downstairs, and the cop brings me into the kitchen. I take a seat at our table, but he remains standing across from me.

"What happened?"

TERESA CLARK

Sophomore
Major: History and Philosophy
Reading: Fiction Short Story

I am a sophomore from New Jersey. I am passionate about my majors in History and Philosophy, and I hope to pursue a law degree after graduation. I like horror movies and true crime, and I also really like podcasts.

Nominated by: Oluwapemi Aguda

Anna

"I know you have something to tell me."

I examined my cold white fingers, nails chewed short and adorned with chipped black polish. My nail beds were starting to dry up and peel, cuticles cracked and beaten dry by the autumnal chill. She slid her pinky next to mine. Her hand was translucent and kaleidoscopic and warm, like a pool of sunlight passed through stained glass. Golden light pulsed every so often around her form, sometimes so bright that I had to look away after a while.

"I can always tell when you do, you know."

I let out a sigh and pushed myself off the cold stone slab, my boots hitting the frozen ground with a thud. I swung around to face her, ready to resist her inquiries.

She was perched on her grave, rocking her legs back and forth, the back of her ankles passing through the stone at the end of each swing. She was luminous, giving off light from every surface of her body. She was a beautiful girl passed through a post-mortem filter. Her form danced with technicolor light, dizzying to look at for too long. Through her legs, I could read the letters on her grave, though they warped slightly as if underwater.

Anna Angel Adler
1999-2017

The first time I heard that name, I was in still life art class. In a room where sad art students lurked, smelling of vintage shops and cigarettes, she practically glowed. When she introduced herself to me after traipsing in late, iced drink in hand, she used her full name, like a contestant in a beauty pageant.

"Anna Angel Adler," she declared, beaming blinding white teeth and extending her tanned hand. Silver charms dangled from her delicate wrist. The room was quiet enough that I swear I heard them chime together. I was stunned by her brilliance. She exuded light, white blonde hair in a blurry halo around her sandy freckled face. Her smoky lashes and glittery eyelids reminded me of all the make-up I didn't put on that morning, all of the mascara left opened and dried on my desk. Baby face aside from the intent blue eyes, she had a gentle sprinkling of freckles over a Barbie doll nose, and that dentist-white smile seemed to take up her entire face.

"Sofie," I said. "Sofie Cohen."

"No middle name?" she asked.

"Nope," I said, shrugging. "My parents said that there weren't two names in the world special enough for me. Really, I think they were just lazy."

She threw back her head and laughed, a sound as high and clear as a bell that made my heart clench. The professor shushed us, and we dutifully turned back to our empty canvases, sharing a smirk.

Something about having a naked stranger on display in the middle of the room set a precedent of quick intimacy, and we became fast friends. Giggling behind our canvas whenever we met eyes with the flaccid muse, we portrayed his most tender areas as comically huge and feigned ignorance with wide eyes when our matronly professor gently suggested that we work on our proportions.

"You know what, Sofie?" she said after our professor walked away. "I think we are going to be good friends."

Art class giggles turned to hushed murmurs over plastic cups of wine in her sweet-smelling apartment. It was much different from my own. I had no notion of a throw pillow until I spilled my wine all over one of Anna's. We always left a movie on in the background that neither of us preferred to our own conversation. It seemed unlikely at the time that she, a persistent optimist and (I could only assume) Homecoming queen, and I, alumni of middle school Gothicism, would get along. We did, though. We charmed each other. We were gentle, kinder with each other than we had any reason to be. I think we both felt we had was precious, to be handled with great delicacy.

"You know," she said as we sat cross-legged on the couch one night. "You would look really pretty if you pulled this back." Her words were soft and slow, dripping heavy with cheap booze. She set down her cup on the coffee table and reached forward, resting her forearms on my shoulders. Her nails gently scraped up the back of my scalp as she gathered my hair in one hand and smoothed the baby hairs back from my forehead in the other. Her face was inches from mine, mouth curved in a thoughtful smirk as her eyes trailed across my exposed cheekbones.

I could not breathe. My eyes were locked on hers, my mouth embarrassingly agape. I desperately tried to imagine what she could be seeing. Her eyes flicked up to mine, and she broke into a beaming smile, perfect white teeth on full display.

"Sofie, you are beautiful," she said, and kissed me.

~

"So, what is it?" she asked, bouncing her legs with whatever phantom energy sustained her beyond the grave. "What's got you all weird?"

I realized there was no way I was going to get away with this one.

"Fine," I sighed. I paused, and then said, "I met someone."

"Oh, wow!" she said. "What's she like?"

"*He*, actually. And he's... nice."

She scoffed, and put her hands on her hips in feign indignation.

"Well, you have to give me more than that!"

"I don't know, Anna."

I turned, kicking at some leaves on the ground. I didn't know how to tell her about someone that would take her place. I didn't want to lose her.

~

The last time I saw Anna was eerily like the first. She was wearing the same outfit: her favorite worn blue jeans that made her already long legs look miles longer, and a soft white cotton tee that made her tanned skin glow. The setting sun drenched her in golden light. I am sure that I could not look away. She saw me looking and smiled in a way that way soft and sweet, like she knew that this was the last time she would take my breath away. She squeezed me to her chest and gave me a flutter of butterfly wing kisses on my forehead.

"Love you, Sof!"

In the next second, she bounced into the front seat of her car and tucked herself behind the steering wheel that would, in the next hour, crush her ribs through her beating heart and into her spine, mangling her almost beyond recognition and, as the doctors told me in a way that was supposed to be comforting but wasn't, killing her instantly. I got the news an hour after it happened. I called her phone. She should've been home by then. I called, and someone picked up. I could hear the alarms in the background. For half a second, I thought it was music, and I began to smile. Anna loved to blast her music as loud as sirens. As soon as the deep male voice answered the phone, though, I knew.

In the winter after her death, I faded into the background. No one knows how to comfort the new fling of a dead girl. It can't be compared to the grief of a parent. I was too close to relate to friends, and not close enough to relate to the parents. I didn't want to relate to anyone. I didn't know how I could.

The funeral was big. She was beautiful, intimidating smart, and everyone loved her. Even the still life model from our art class came, and I wished that she could have been there to laugh with me once more about what her parents would think if they knew. Instead, I sat in the third row and tried not to think about how mangled and bruised her body must have been in that grand oak coffin.

Her dad came up to me after the service and drew me into a hug that shouldn't have felt unwelcome but did.

"Sofie," he said, and then cleared his throat, as if buying time to figure out what to say next. "Anna really... she really cared about you."

I just nodded, gave some awkward niceties, and left. I could not stay and watch my world continue to crumble.

My world shrunk to the size of my apartment in the cold winter months after she left, and my skin shrunk around my bones. Friends I had neglected in the throes of my new romance kindly reached out and I shut them down one by one. I was asleep more than I was awake, and when I was awake, I might as well have been sleep walking.

~

"So, what's his name?"

"It's Henry. Henry Keenan."

"No middle name?" she asked, giggling,

I blushed.

"Yes, actually. It's Nelson."

"Oh, Nelson! Well, it's no Angel, but it'll do!" She was cackling, her head thrown back and her heels swishing back and forth, comically fast.

My stomach clenched. I turned away, cheeks burning.

"Very funny," I said.

"What? I'm just kidding!"

"Don't you have... I don't know, any protest?"

"Oh, Sof," she smiled at me, sadly and softly, like she did the last time I saw her. "No! Of course not. I'm happy for you, Sof, and you should be too. I'm dead! And I'm happy. I know somewhere, actual me, like *really* me is out there. I'm more a part of you than I am a part of me. I'm a part of us... what we were. And we were awesome, weren't we? But you're more than just part of *us*, Sof. You're the same whole amazing you that you were before me."

Hot tears poured out of my eyes.

"But Anna," I sobbed. "Anna, Anna, Anna. I don't *want* to do it without you."

"I know Sof, but you're already without me. You used to come here twice a week. Now it's once a month. You're moving on. You don't need me, Sofie. You never did."

I stopped crying, but my chest still heaved up and down. I look at her, and she looks more far away than ever, her usual spectacle of color faded to a pearlescent cloud. She smiled at me, so gently and softly it made my chest ache. I felt her in every cell of my being.

Her eyes were soft and sad.

"This is the last time, Sof. You knew that when you came. I knew it as soon as you walked up."

I took a deep breath and closed my eyes.

"I know." The fall breeze was cool against my cheeks. My right side began to warm, and I knew that she was close.

"Anna?" I asked.

"Yes?"

Her voice floated into my ear like a warm breeze. It was barely louder than a whisper.

"Is everything going to be okay?"

"Of course."

When I finally opened my eyes, she was gone.

ALIX CURNOW

Sophomore
Major: Theatre Arts
Minor: Creative Writing and Playwriting
Reading: Non-Fiction

In addition to theatre, one of Alix's biggest passions is literature. She is beyond excited to share her works with you all tonight!

Nominated by: Jose Casas and Akil Kumarasamy

Cavities

Cavities
A short story by Cool-Dad-Magazine
Hopwood Underclassmen – Fiction

He wanted me to count the cavities in his teeth. A few of them were rotting, black char eating pearly bone. He laughed when I told him I found ten. Then he counted the freckles down my spine. Through the years some of them jumped off and landed on his chest. My freckles were splattered on his canvas of thin hair and skin. It made for a perfect pillow on the nights I didn't feel like taking the L home. A rocking ship, lulling me to an ocean far away from a wretched world that was only made good because he was there.

"Wanna go on a hike?" he asked in the morning. His breath would've been embarrassing if it wasn't his.

"It's 7am!"

"The woods are best in the morning. We can wake up with the animals and the flowers."

"I don't think the flowers want to be disturbed right now," I pulled the quilt his grandmother knitted him over my head.

"Well, I want to disturb them!" he nudged me with a heavy hand. His fingers drooping with the metal of at least ten rings. One ring for each cavity in his mouth. I think that was purposeful. "You're disturbing *me*!"

"Wake up! Wake up! Wake up!" His fuzzy beard tickled my skin. I wanted to rip it off and put it on my neck. Be him for a day so I could see myself from his eyes. My cheeks flushed from his persistence. Grandma's quilt was thrown to the side and hiking shoes were laced up as he danced around the bedroom to a tune of his own creation.

We started on the dirt path in silence. The rings on his fingers shielded my hands from the brisk air. His lips pursed in satisfaction. The peak of them a poppy flower, the soft pinks dipping perfectly beneath his petite nose like the folds of a petal. His arms were covered in faux tattoos. He'd write all his thoughts on them in ink like they were a journal. Wearing his mind on his sleeve instead of his heart. His heart was reserved for his crossword puzzles and, occasionally, me. As an English major he believed in words like they were God. He used them like he was God, too.

The rising sun's golden rays made a constellation of light in between the autumn leaves.

The branches of the trees sighed together in the breath of fall. The rustling of leaves caused constellations of light to twinkle onto our faces.

"What're you looking at?" "Look up."

Alexi tilted his head, the blonde hair that usually hung over his eyes a golden mountain slope as it fell backwards.

"Pretty cool, right?" I asked.

"I think if I could stay here for the rest of my life, I'd be happy," he grabbed my hand and rested it on his wrist. My fingers next to the word "happy" underlined three times on his skin.

"That's a bold thing to say." "It's not that bold," "Happiness isn't that easy."

"It's that easy with you." The funny word traveled from his wrist to my index finger and he circled it three times with the pen he kept tucked behind his ear.

I smiled and he kissed me. For the hundredth time. I could taste his cavities in my mouth. They were sweet. I wanted my mouth to be full of holes, too. His friends wanted to be him. Some of them wanted to fuck him. Everyone was always telling me how goddamn lucky I was.

A look of suppressed shock on their face when I introduced him as my boyfriend. Mr. Charmer with the cavities in his teeth that he didn't give a fuck about. Dating Miss. Goody with the straight A's and the pearly whites. They didn't know him like I did, though. He'd never opened his mouth wide for them to inspect with prying dental instruments. Never showed them the decay beneath the blackness. He was my first everything. He took a lot more from me than the freckles on my back.

People's shock didn't simmer even after three years of introducing him to new friends. On my roomates 21st birthday, the alcohol sloshing in my stomach far surpassed the need for cordial introductions. I stumbled up to my bedroom, losing track of time and of people. Opened the door to his mouth sucking on the side of her neck, her naked body pressed into my bed sheets. The word liar written over and over again on both of his arms. I wondered if he took the freckles from her spine and threw them on his chest, too. Wondered how long I'd been sleeping on a pillow of another girl's skin.

"I think if I could stay here at my desk, emailing you for the rest of my life, I'd be happy," his email to Julia read.

"Oh, really? I don't think happiness is that easy...." hers said, complete with a winking emoji. "It's that easy with you," he emailed back. I looked down at my index finger, the ink from his pen still there. "Happy" stained in gory lettering like a cut that wouldn't heal.

Yeah, I was real fucking lucky.

On my way to the coffee shop the snow storm seemed to threaten to scoop me up. I hadn't seen a blizzard like this since I moved to Chicago four years ago. Part of me wished that it would take me away to some desolate ice land where the people eat only fish and sing songs around a fire. Maybe then, I wouldn't be so lonely.

"Yo! Welcome to Early Bird Coffee Haus, what can I get started for–oh, Fallon..."Alexi looked up from the cash register and his voice faltered. The bitter sound behind my name coming from a year of being broken up tasted good as hell in my ears. Who said bitterness only pairs well with coffee?

"I didn't know you worked here," the skin on my index finger was starting to itch.

"I didn't know you came here," Alexi said. Anesthetics, cool rags, oatmeal baths-I'd tried it all. Nothing could get me to stop from scratching it.

"I don't. My apartment's out of electricity." My fingernail dug into the tattooed skin so hard I almost yelped in pain.

"Got some homework to finish?" he asked like it was all I'd been doing in the year we hadn't been together. He wouldn't be wrong...

"Yeah, I do."

"What do you want? Grande coffee: black, right?" I wished I could look at my hands instead of at him but I'm sure they were bleeding by now. I've never been one for gore.

"Glad you remembered."

"I'm not one to forget." he said and blood dripped from my finger and into the coffee he handed me. I've never been one for creamer.

A coolness that surprised me simmered beneath his attempted small talk. His rings were clanging against one another as he made cups of coffee for the slew of customers in line. His co-worker stood next to him while he made drinks. Close enough that I'm sure he could see the cavities inside of her mouth, if she had any. She seemed like the type of person that would. Alexi charmed every person he met. I wouldn't be surprised if she was flirting with him, or vice versa. I wanted the hot beverages they were making to spill down the cleavage peeking out of her barista uniform. Interesting how easily jealousy can surface. After obtaining my bloody drink, I tucked myself into the corner of the cafe, ensuring I was out of direct eye-line of Alexi. Senior thesis' and ex-boyfriends aren't a good mix.

Him being there made it difficult to concentrate. He still hadn't cut his hair. I could see the tangled locks tucked back into a low bun. I wondered if his barista friend had any idea how long he'd probably spent in the mirror that morning getting it to look so effortless. Wondered if she pulled his hair out and tied it into around her wrist over and over again, like I used to.

Admittedly, I was a bit surprised he'd taken up a job here. He'd always dreamed of moving to New York City when he graduated from UChicago. On the evenings him and I had spent alone together, my freckles on his chest would whisper to me the secret fantasies his heart had told them. The rhythmic thumping a type of morose code exposing to them his sacred hidden dreams. Dreams that would be embarrassing, if they weren't his.

Everyone thought he'd be publishing novels by now. Be on the cover of New York Times the second he got out of Chicago. He was so full of words that they had spilt out of him and onto his skin. Sometimes, if you were lucky enough, they'd spill onto your skin too. Only a fool would think his writing wasn't going to make him famous. Being stuck behind a counter for hours on end every day didn't really strike me as his forte. "Maybe he stayed for Julia," I thought. Maybe he stayed for me.

"**THE PSYCHOLOGY OF LOVE**" read the title of my thesis in bold Times New Roman across my computer screen. I'd written five hundred pages on this. Yet I still couldn't explain why I kept looking at my index finger to examine the word he'd circled three times on my skin over a year ago. Couldn't understand why my hands perspired in nervous excitement when he walked past my table to hand another cup of coffee to a busy customer.

This thesis had been keeping me company for the past year. I'd taken it out on dates to libraries all over my neighborhood. My only companion in a city that was as full of people as it was loneliness. I wondered if Alexi had a companion of his own over the course of this year. Wondered if that companion was Julia and her emails. If her freckles had covered up mine on his chest yet.

"Hey folks," a slender man with a uniform a little fancier than Alexi's, interrupted my jealous fantasies.

"Just letting y'all know, this snow storm is getting pretty heavy. They sent out a weather warning, so if you wanna get home safely, I'd recommend heading out now."

A slow groan brewed through the tiny venue as people began to pack their things. Alexi didn't seem to be going anywhere, though. I traced my tongue along the insides of my molars–sticky. If I stayed in the same place as Alexi for long enough, maybe the plaque on them would start to feel good. I tried to ignore the fact that the freckle deprived skin down my spine was aching in secret hope of being filled again.

A few hours had passed, and the only sounds in the cafe were the clicking of my computer keys and the wiping down of a coffee table.

"Fallon-" Alexi started, uniform off and sporting The Velvet Underground T-shirt he bought in high school. His arms weren't covered by the sleeves of his uniform anymore. I could see ink stained into words on his wrists and biceps. A pen tucked into the corner of his ear. I scanned his arm and looked twice when I thought I saw the words "forgive me" outlined in blue ink. I'd had too much coffee and not enough creamer.

His denim jeans were cuffed at the ankles over a pair of dirty white converse he was always refusing to clean. His septum piercing was out now. I had drunkenly pierced it in his dingy apartment at 3am the night he told me he loved me. He screamed in pain, a little from the piercing needle but mostly from the love.

"We're closing up shop right now," he said, a candy sucker tucked into the pocket of his cheek. "Wait, what?" I looked up from my laptop. It was already 10pm. I had lived the last few hours in the pixelations of my computer screen. The shop was a barren wasteland. Chairs were flipped on top of tables beneath the dimmed lights and above the newly mopped floor.

"Oh, I didn't realize." I said.

"Yeah, I mean, we technically closed an hour ago, but I know how you get when you're working on school. Figured it wouldn't matter too much if you stayed an extra hour while I put all this shit away," he pulled the sucker from the pocket of his cheek, sugary saliva coating the outside of his mouth.

"Um, thanks. That's, uh, that's nice of you," I felt like I was talking to a stranger. I used to tell him I loved him by tracing my tongue along the outside of his lips and now I'm stuttering when we speak. The last night I had spent with him, I accidentally left my toothbrush in a container next to his sink. "I should ask him to give that back to me," I thought as I licked the eroded sugar off of my teeth. I hated the part of me that hoped my toothbrush was still there. Emotions I'd buried for years were digging themselves up from their graves like zombies. I'd never been one for gore.

"Fifteen more minutes. Please?" I asked for more time instead of the toothbrush. Ignoring the secret hope within me that one would lead to the other.

"Alright, Fallon. You're lucky I've got a crossword puzzle I've been itching to finish." He said, glancing down at my index finger.

He was always doing crossword puzzles. The last one I remember him doing was on the train ride home last Thanksgiving. We'd asked the older man sitting next to Alexi if he'd switch seats with me so we could sit together.

"That your pretty lady?" the man asked, his face in a blush. The man had chewing tobacco nestled in front of his bottom row of teeth. I wondered how many cavities he had.

"I don't blame you for wanting to sit next to her!" the stranger chuckled over the sugary coca cola he'd surely coined from the vending machine in the back.

"Thanks a lot for switching," I smiled down at him.

"My wife and I used to be the same way. Couldn't separate us for a minute. I wouldn't want you two to spend three hours by your lonesome with your partner so close in proximity! You're lucky to be in love, that's for sure!" he rambled on as he scooted out of his seat. I wondered if his wife ever counted the cavities in his mouth or if he hid them from her in rotten silence.

I plopped down in the old man's space and Alexi laced his fingers in mine. Pressing his lips against the back of my hand.

"Ahhh!" he sighed in relief, "a much better seat partner. Smells like roses and lets me hold her hand. Don't think that geezer'd like me pecking the back of his hand all to well, do you?" "Probably not," I laughed. He grabbed his crossword puzzle.

"In what popular TV Show does the character 'Rachel' find out her boyfriend has slept with another girl?" he asked, his ballpoint pen scanning down the puzzle in his lap.

"Friends," I said, and wrote the answer on the back of his arm in blue ink, feeling lucky to have just finished the last episode of the tenth season the night before. The word **OBLIVIOUS**, written in bold Times New Roman across my forehead.

The crossword puzzle Alexi had on the train was a lot thicker than the one he was working on in his corner of the cafe. I wondered if he liked to do them as much anymore. I didn't have time to think about it for all too long as my fingertips hit the keyboard immediately after he returned to the counter. *Great philosopher Soren Kierkegaard,* I began to type, *once wrote that the eye has the power to foster the good in the unclean; this eye does not see the evil but the pure, which it loves and encourages it by loving it.*

"Uh, Fallon," Alexi called to me from across the room. "What?" I looked up.

"You probably shouldn't head out..." his crossword puzzle was closed on the counter beside him.

"Why?"

"We're snowed in..." the candied part of his sucker had disappeared into the cavities inside of his teeth. Now it was only a flimsy white pick drooping from his mouth.

"What do you mean, 'snowed in'?"

"Like, we can't leave this coffee shop." He flung the white pick into the trash. Carelessly following behind it were a few of his teeth- black and rotted.

"What?"

"Look," he motioned me over to his computer screen. Blaring in abrasive red letters beneath a deceivingly chipper weather man was,

"WEATHER WARNING. SEVERE BLIZZARD. STOP ALL ACTIVITIES AND STAY INSIDE. ROADS AND SIDEWALKS CLOSED."

"Oh, shit." I could see my freckles on Alexi's chest protruding out from beneath his shirt. I didn't see any of Julia's, though.

"I wouldn't go out there. It's pretty brutal." The zombies were getting closer. I could smell their oozing flesh.

"Okay." I didn't need much convincing. Loneliness was scarier than zombies.

"Do you, like, need to call anyone? Like a boyfriend or anything?" he asked, my freckles on his chest were impossible to ignore.

"Uh, no. There isn't a boyfriend to call." "Oh, okay, cool."

"What about you?" I asked.

"I certainly don't have a boyfriend to call!" "God, shut up," I laughed.

"No, no. No girlfriend waiting up for me." I could hear the zombies groaning down the street. "Do you wanna see something cool?" He grinned. God, my thesis had been keeping me pretty good company this past year but it certainly didn't have dimples I could spend the rest of the day swimming in like he did.

"There really isn't anything else to do, is there?" I asked.

"That's for you to decide," he scurried into the back room, allowing his comment to hang like dead weight in the air. Was he flirting with me?

He brought out two cups of coffee. Inside one of the cups was white foam, with a kitten delicately etched into the top. I laughed.

"And look at this one! I've been wanting to learn how to make latte art since I started working here in August," he pulled me to the second cup. A latte complete with a dog traced on top of the foam. It's brows furrowed and teeth flashing in an intimidating manor.

"Very cool," I felt like we were on our first date again. The strange dychomdamy that all good first dates have was stewing between us. As though I had known the person sitting beside me for my entire life and simultaneously, for not nearly long enough. The only difference between then and now is the amount of cavities in our teeth.

"That one's for you. You know, 'cause you're a dog person," he said, handing me the cup. He took some of my freckles from his chest and sprinkled them on top of the drink.

"A little extra sweetener," he added, with a wink. He picked up his artistic creation and toasted it into the air.

"Cheers!" he grinned.

"To what?" the red dye from his sucker outlined his teeth. He was standing so close to me, I could've licked the red stains off for him.

"To these sick fuckin' designs I learned how to do."

"Uh, I don't think that kitten should be described as a 'sick fuckin' design'" "I don't know... that dog looks pretty scary."

"He's growling in like, an adorable way." I tried to ignore the groan of the zombies looming behind us.

"Okay, cheers to these absolutely adorable animals!" I chuckled, "I'm a big fan of the alliteration."

"Don't you mean you're an astounding admirer of alliteration?"

"No, I don't."

I tapped my cup with his, and took a sip. "Holy shit, this is so good!" I exclaimed.

"The reason I have so many goddamn cavities." "You had ten the last time I counted,"

"Ahh, I've got at least five more by now." He moved in closer, expecting me to inspect his mouth. God, I wanted to.

"Any news on the snow?" I changed the topic. "It's only been a few minutes," he said.

"Oh, right."

"I'm happy you came to the cafe today. I've been thinking about you." I looked at his arms. The word liar wasn't written there anymore.

"Oh, really?" I asked like I hadn't been thinking of him too.

"It hasn't snowed this hard in years. The universe must be telling us something." "The universe?" I asked.

"I'd say God, but I don't really believe in that kind of stuff." "I know."

"We never really said goodbye properly," he said. "That's what happens when you-"

"Don't finish that sentence," he cut me off, "Are you still mad?"

"I don't think so," I replied and his hand reached toward mine. I moved away. "I'm sorry," he said.

"It's fine, my hands are just, they're clammy right-"

"No, I'm not sorry I touched your hand. I'm sorry about, you know, about Julia." "Oh?" The last few freckles I had down my spine shivered at the sound of her name. "I'm sorry things ended the way they did."

"I miss you," the words were projectile vomit leaving my mouth. He kissed me. And for the hundred and oneth time I felt so fucking lucky. His cavities, contagious. Rotting my teeth. I missed being infected.

He placed his hand at the bottom of my spine. A spine that had been rid of freckles for far too long. His arm, which was resting around my waist, started to slowly vibrate against me. With each passing vibration, his arm began to glow.

Getting brighter and brighter until it lit up the dark room. Illuminating the entire coffee shop. So bright even God could see. Julia with a sparkly heart emoji, had texted him. "Babe, when are you coming home!? I miss my boyfriend!" the words were engraved into his arms in digital ink.

The eye has the power to foster the good in the unclean, yet my eyes couldn't see the good through the dirt that started to cover his arms the moment I saw Julia's text. At first, the dirt hid only her her message but soon, it was covering all of his faux tattoos. He became so unclean that he was unrecognizable. Eventually, the dirt began to crumble away, taking his skin with him. The cavity ridden teeth in his grin started to fall, one by one by one into the cup of coffee he had made. There were so many cavities. I couldn't possibly count them all. Rotting into his latte art. The perfect creamer.

The only part of him he left were parts of me. My freckles. Sprinkled onto my index finger. Spelling out a peculiar word I never could figure out the meaning to. "Happy" they spelt, now in brown detail. My only tattoo. Attempting to count the cavities in my teeth, I licked my molars. But, they weren't sticky anymore.

The roof of the cafe was concaving from the weight of the winter. Soon enough I couldn't distinguish between his body parts and the flakes of snow piling in. Mounds of crashing ice crystals caused his body to disintegrate. The wind picked up as the snow carried him away. I hope he was taken to some desolate ice land where the people eat only fish and sing songs around a fire. I imagine it isn't very lonely there.

HIBA DAGHER

Freshman
Major: Undeclared
Reading: Poetry

Hiba is a current freshman who somehow scammed her way into being published in CityWidePoets 2018 anthology and the Hopwood Undergraduate Award for Poetry. Her hobbies include reading, napping, and lobbying the United States Department of Agriculture into including Double Stuffed Oreos as a sixth food group.

Nominated by: Lorenzo Diaz-Cruz

epigenetics

A study from the University of Barcelona has discovered that
we carry the memories
of up to 14 generations,
our ancestors embedded in our
genes. Nestled in
the back of the cedar wood
trunk, in my grandmother's old apartment
in Bint Jebail I find
a pair of my mother's old jeans.

Inky and blue like the nazar charms
my tata hangs in all the doorways,
with frayed hems and a hole
in the back of the left knee
and three rumpled liras in the back pocket
that I use
to split a chocolate umbrella with my sisters

I later find out that these are not, in fact, my mother's jeans.
They're my grandfather's
and I imagine them
stretching to fit him and shrinking to fit my mom's
under my grandmother's deft fingers.

I tried them on,
and let the fabric embrace my hips.
To think my whole life fits into the stretched out fabric,
the brass button,
that zipper that struggles to crawl up its track and
the cuffs that stop right before my ankles and I wonder if they
stopped before my mother's ankles
before she was my mother.

I want to ask her if she wore lots of bracelets
because she liked the way they sounded when she ran up the stairs
or if she likes to sit on the edge of her apartment's balcony
and look down at the world beneath her
instead of hanging up her brother's school uniforms on the clothesline to

dry
or if she pulls dark curls from her hijab
half because she thinks it looks pretty
and half because she knows it makes her mama angry
or if she likes to stick her head out the car window on the drive back up from Bint Jebail
and swallow mouthfuls of the night sky
and take a deep breath
and exhale the stars in her lungs

like I do.

excerpts from a mother tongue

after melissa lozada-oliva's "my spanish" and safia elhillo's "alien suite"

1.

If you ask me if I am fluent in Arabic, I will tell you my Arabic is a ghost of a limb, still reaching for words and forgetting the hand that once was is no longer there.

If you ask me if I am fluent in Arabic, I will tell you that my Arabic is all of the birthdays that I cannot remember, is all of the pictures pressed into the scrapbook with scotch tape and I Love You's, is what my family told me.

If you ask me if I am fluent in Arabic I will tell you that my Arabic sits in the back of the classroom, ducks its head on the flat desk and does not raise its hand.

My Arabic is red pen dancing across my final examination and I wonder why the slash marks look so much like paper cuts.

2.

My Arabic will never be like my mother's, clear as the breeze

that darts through the olive grove in her village.

Sometimes my mother will open her mouth and a song will pour out, sweet like the roses in my mother's mother's garden back home.

Sometimes my mother will open her mouth and a scream will pour out, mourning a family left behind, for a home that is no longer home, for a country that is more ghost than country, is more graveyard than country, is more bullet casings than country.

Because how can there be exile, if there is no homeland?

3.

My mother took us to her home in the summer of '09.

That was the summer I sat on the curb of the streets in Beirut eating Khasta Ice Cream with sticky hands and toothy grins.

My cousins introduce me as their American cousin,

the hard “R” rolling from their tongue like a punch to the gut.

I do not understand their jokes, with their fast Arabic and their faster laughter.

Their giggles fill the sticky summer air before Rasha can finish explaining it to me.

I do not understand the love songs my cousins sing

as they curl their hair and rouge their cheeks.

Songs that are as much about a country than they are about a woman.

Come home soon, my cousins say at the Airport.

But that home doesn’t feel like a home.

That home feels like a cluster of villages drawn inside

a border cut by force to draw blood.

Home is mango tree in my teta’s backyard,

is her hands, gnarled like tree bark,

pressing cherry tomatoes like rubies into my hands

to take to Amto’s house next door.

4.

They keep us in the Airport for three hours.

The TSA agent looks at me.

Her eyes are two chips of dirty glass on an unsmiling face, her arms folded.

She dumps out my Hello Kitty backpack,

looks at me confused when she finds coloring books instead of explosives.

She opens the stiff blue book stamped with

Place of Birth: Dearborn, Michigan, USA,

asks where I am from and smirks when I say here.

Somedays there is more American in me

then I can stand.

Somedays I cannot remember the words to the Fairuz song,

Somedays I cannot find all of my mother tongue,

Somedays I cannot find all of my mother's tongue.

And I am the nine year old girl locked in the windowless room in the airport again.

And I clamp my mouth shut.

Ashamed at how polluted my mouth has become.

5.

Forgive me, I cannot teach you how to say my name.

I am from somewhere halved by water.

From an ocean of salt and from the sand in my shoes.

Forgive me, I do not have enough language to name a child.

I only come with a handful of names to describe a body that feels foreign.

بيرغ

Alien.

يبنجأ

Stranger.

ناث

Other.

I am shifting through my silences,

half illiterate in a motherless mother tongue,

an Arabic brimming with words I cannot say,

with stories always out of my reach,

with letters that will always remain silent,

with words that will always escape me.

KELSI DAVIS

Sophomore
Major: Communication Studies
Reading: Poetry

Miss Kelsi Lynn Davis was born in Kentucky and raised in Mackinaw City, MI. She is total chaos covered in freckles, and can't believe that somebody liked this collection of words she threw together enough to let her read them out loud. She is joyously alive.

Nominated by: David Wade

Three Girls Harmonize for Their Lord

Karly sings low
She has thick eyebrows and works at a verdant farm up the road
And I deserve a shiny gold trophy for making her laugh
She's had it rough
And the thick green carpet on her stairs is worn down
She's a dichotomist
And she doesn't know what on God's good green Earth she's gonna do with the shit I gave her

Savannah sings high
She is a beauty if I have ever seen one! I love her!
Wide hips and a thin waist and a mouth that won't stop running
And she can't dance
Soft soft skin but her kiss is so clumsy
She's a people-pleaser
But she would never step foot in God's house for fear He would wash her mouth out with soap

I sing the middle
And Karly and Savannah and I all have dark dark hair
The light from the stage shines from behind it
And turns mine red
Tendrils of brimstone seeping into the girls at my sides
I'm asleep at God's feet
And, you know, there's just not really a goddamn thing else for me to say about all of that

The Poor Woman's Waltz

Razors. No, the good kind.
Shampoo that makes my hair shine
A hair mask, because my split ends are bad
The nail polish color that one actress had

Mascara, eyeshadow, lipstick and gloss
Kohl, primer, foundation, and floss
Hyaluronic acid and eyebrow gel
Contour and blush shaped into a shell

Underwear for looking sexy, underwear for looking cute
Panties for when your period is trying to murder you
A bra with no back, no straps, no middle, and no sides
(You need duct tape to keep it on, trust me, I have tried)

Brazilian wax, threading, depilatories, take your pick
Whatever gets it over with, I don't have time for this
A pumice stone, a herringbone, glass files, and cornstarch
For even in my three-inchers, the men I must outmarch

A horsehair brush, some acetone, and job loss through the roof
False mink eyelashes, the criss-cross kind, to make me look aloof
Nail glue, rubbing alcohol, chicken cutlets and eyeliner
I'll be damned if women with more money get to look finer

Tampons, *Spanx*, panty liners, and pads
And *Steel Magnolias*, 'cause I'm gonna get sad
All of this money, all this time and this pain
For a man gone unshowered for two or three days

Persistent Deciduous Teeth

Nadie está benevolente.	*Nobody is benevolent.*
Y cuando te conviertes demasiado agradecido	*And when you become too thankful*
Para el pelo que crece de tu cabeza	*For the hair that grows from your head*
Tiene miedo	*Be afraid*
Hay mal en corazones mayores, pero son	*There is evil in old hearts but it's*
Los dientes persistentes caducifolios	*The persistent deciduous teeth*
Que morde tu garganta con placer	*That bite your throat with pleasure*
Tiene miedo	*Be afraid*
Pero cuando la sangre, la sangre!	*But when the blood, the blood!*
Cuando gatea de tu cuerpo como	*When it crawls from your body like*
Grandes, ensangrentadas, vibrantes babosas	*Great, gory, vibrant slugs*
No tengas miedo	*Don't be afraid*

It Has Come to My Attention That You Don't Know Who I Am

Oh it hurts!
Three teeth smashed from his mouth to the floor!
Oh the anger
Oh the evil, vicious, justified anger
"It tastes like metal doesn't it, baby?"
Oh not the anger, the blood, the blood!

Oh she is a demon
The machiavellian spirit runs through her just as much as her blood in all it's wicked, malicious,
        deceitful glory
She is violent and bitter but oh,
She is right

He will live.
"Oh," but she coos. "Death is free, baby."
He may not.

"Skin is flammable," she tells him.
Oh, she would know!
His fillings sparkle at her!
Oh what is left of them do!

"I will kill you," she tells him, oh so calm, like the sunshine
He spits blood
"And I will eat you raw."

A Hymn (for Bob, Aged 18)

There is a place in my bloody black heart
For shy little creatures
Who meow and bark and laugh incessantly
And as I watch the dust
Float through the spotlights' beams leisurely
I consider how much of it
Sticks to the insides of my lungs as breath

I thought his shoulder had healed in a dislocated position

And even now as I honor him the best I can
I speak about myself
And about my lungs rather than his little ones
But what can I really say
About a man whose existence was to eat and shit
And make me feel better
When he slept in the notch of my neck and shoulder

My mother is a woman of 49 and my father a man of the grave

He is dying faster than I can get back to him
And that's a fear of mine
His lithe little body has fought off for a long time
Tiny blood cells energetic
Too old when I met him to protest my loving kiss
He knew my troubles
Sat calmly as I undid his claw from Josh's shorts

S t r o l l thump s t r o l l thump s t r o l l thump s t r o l l

Thump. And I giggle a little bit because it doesn't
Seem like he hurts
But my mother groans with her fracture when she sits
Bobkitty, Mr. Bob, ki ki ki
Come to me so I don't have to talk to her today
Put your fur in my face
Leisurely like the dust in my lungs tries to choke me

Cats don't actually have ball and socket joints, I didn't know

It is a gigantic, kitty-cancerous tumor growing on him
With his bald spots
And his limp and his yelling to be held in a lap and adored
And the menopause
And the gray hairs dyed just one time before she gave up
He's just getting old
And she doesn't remember a lot of the things I say anymore

Spackle

Love,
and lack thereof,
Makes the world go 'round

And women spill emotions
Unto the concrete ground.

Tearing out their eyes
Onto the short sharp walk

And even then
the men
About their sex lives talk.

It's hard to punch a wall
Without knowledge of the studs

But I would bet
still harder yet
To wash out congealed blood.

A bold claim,
you accuse
Oh and it is, I agree

But not so bad
If you had had
Experience like me.

Untitled

Young and hungry
For meat!

Hungry!

To feel tendinous flesh shred
Between my canines

My teeth are sharp!
Serrated!

My grip is supposed to be dangerous
And my eyes are supposed to be red

I am the giver of scars and not the receiver!
I am the giver of black eyes and not the receiver!
I am the giver of pain and not the receiver!

Your blood is supposed to drip from my chin

What I've Got

a hole in my gums no four holes in my gums dry socket a diamond ring a husband three toothbrushes a guilty soul hair a bad haircut knuckles stamps patience a fear of being pregnant chapped lips three months worth of Prozac and not a day more easter candy not enough socks lingerie unfettered control of my husband's membrum virile vivacity viciousness a book about vaccines four holes I punched in my ear when I was only fourteen a new found realization about how young fourteen is christmas decorations a WIC card twenty dollars wrapped in a sticky note seventy-seven posts on instagram a cat a case of soda a sister anger a magazine subscription a couple shoplifted hangers at least six bibles a grandmother who thinks I'm a godless heathen a hole in the armpit of my nightgown and another in the knee of my blue jeans most of my teeth fat arms a craving for bread a mom who doesn't love me anymore a hole in my head

NICOLE DE LA MONTANYA

Senior
Major: English
Reading: Creative Non-Fiction Essay

Nicole is a senior from Oakland, California. She is an English major and spent her junior year studying abroad in Dublin, Ireland. She has worked for a local criminal defense attorney since she started at Michigan, and is planning on moving to Las Vegas, Nevada after graduation to work before attending law school. She likes her major, but she can't wait to never write another literary analysis paper ever ever ever again.

Nominated by: David Ward

Cyber Sex, Chemo, & Rock 'n' Roll

I'm going to say what every boy at Edna Hill Middle School was thinking, but felt too creepy to ever say out loud: Lauren got hot after chemo. My cute Texan girl next door lost her chubby cheeks as the poison ate away at her fat cells, making its way through her system. Her acne cleared up leaving a red carpet glow in its midst, her belly melted away, and in the wake of an awkward child came a knockout beauty on the brink of womanhood and her own death.[1] At twelve, diagnosed and never been kissed; at thirteen getting fingered by sixteen-year-olds between radiation rounds. I couldn't blame her. She had less than a 10% chance of seeing her next birthday. She had no time to lose.

Lauren moved away to Nevada when we were thirteen, but our friend Alyssa and I visited in the first few months for one last good crop of memories before the inevitable bedside goodbye. The three of us had been close since we were in first grade. I remember being a six-year-old at daycare eating rice cakes with my new best friend, Lauren, when we decided to start having play dates outside school. We were shocked to discover we were neighbors. We spent the next several years of our childhoods, pre-diagnosis, riding our bikes up and down our court, Heather Place, playing Lightsabers, and pretending to go through Ninja Warrior obstacle courses in my front yard.[2] We even had a bench in my backyard called "The Puberty Bench" where we went to discuss all the crazy shit happening to our bodies. I had no idea what she was talking about when she told me about her new pubic hair.

When we went to visit, she was on an upswing, growing out rich Shirley Temple curls to frame her face during a temporary remission, a welcome improvement from her stringy, sorta straight, sorta wavy dirty blonde hair pre-poison. After an afternoon of walking the neighborhood, and taking too many selfies (back when you took them with the back of your phone), we went to see *Twilight: Breaking Dawn- Part One*, where we battled to the point of shouting about Edward and

1. Lauren's early puberty and sexual growth came accompanied by radiation ruining her reproductive system, causing her irreversible infertility. In her words, "They fried my eggs.
2. Our post-diagnosis activities were less fun. I'd help her pop her hip back in place, which had been damaged by radiation. At Relay for Life, I'd wheel her back and forth in her wheelchair as fast as I could underneath the misters to escape the California summer heat (this caught the attention of watery-eyed parents who were walking in honor of their deceased children, and always drew a crowd; we pretended not to notice them).

Jacob.[3] I watched them rap along to the lyrics of *Super Bass*, and I mouthed a hopeless version of the chorus until we found ourselves in Lauren's Reno home.

"Come see my room!" she said, and sprinted up the stairs before we could answer. Lauren never looked back to see if we were following her; she knew we were. She opened the door to a room as glamorous as one could have fresh out of junior high with a family drowning in medical bills. Multi-colored Christmas lights lined the ceiling, every Pinterest-conceivable version of a photo collage decorated her walls, and animal print patterned bed linens were strewn over her twin bed. I glanced at the photos. In nearly every one, she donned her signature ski cap; the ropes simulated hair between her fingers.[4]

This was not the first time Lauren was bullied in middle school for having cancer. A girl named Sylvia wrote "Lauren is a bald-ass bitch and a fucked up excuse for a cancer patient" on the bathroom wall. Lauren was warned against retaliation, but made a Facebook page, right in the peak of the cyber bullying discussion, called "Sylvia is a fucking bitch", which got upwards of a thousand fans. Lauren was nearly suspended. Lauren began documenting and living life hard after receiving her death sentence, with thousands of pictures taken in those final years, and plenty of tattoos, boys, and experiments tried. A faux for her, not-so-faux for me, lesbian kiss occurred in her bedroom just weeks after the diagnosis. I had wanted that kiss for years before I even knew what it was. I remembered us as children, playing pretend wedding with a quick dodge to the cheek at the kiss the bride moment, or immersing ourselves under the covers making fake moaning noises between giggles, recreating movie scenes.

"I wanna dye my hair," she said after the bedroom tour.

"Why? The color's already nice," I said.

"Just a little more chocolatey! I haven't had long hair in so long. So I want you guys to dye it," she pointed to a boxed dye *Medium Ash Brown*. It wasn't a question. We migrated over to the tiny hall bathroom and Lauren perched herself on the toilet seat like a throne. If Lauren's new home felt at all too-nice for her family, the familiar crunch of kitty litter beneath my feet brought me back to her old Brentwood duplex. Lauren's mom, Cherri, and I despised each other, and I believe she only grew to like me when she saw that I won the "most tears

3. Lauren, Team Jacob. Alyssa and I, Edward. I have since converted.
4. This hat was the subject of great controversy in middle school, as a bully ripped it off her once to reveal her stubbly head for the first time, long before she grew comfortable showing off her baldness. The next day I cornered him and pointed to his ear, which was missing a chunk from a skateboarding accident, and told him I'd rip the rest of it off if he looked at her again. He laughed at me.

award" at the funeral.[5] When I was younger, we had a classic case of constantly believing the other was judging us, and we were both right. Lauren's ruddy, trashy grey duplex always smelled like cats and their three Chihuahuas. Cherri and her husband, Jim, yelled at each other across rooms constantly, cursing loudly, infecting us all with their rotting marriage. She and Lauren fought constantly pre-diagnosis, culminating in Lauren running to my house because Jim caught her bleaching Cherri's cigarettes.[6] I thought she was trashy, and I was right. Cherri thought I was pompous, uppity and self-righteous, and she was also right. I gave the kitty litter a haughty glance as I wiped it off the bottoms of my feet.

"There's only two gloves," Alyssa said, handing one out to me in her fat palm.

"Teamwork!" Lauren replied with optimism. We were the marionettes, tugging her hair from above.

Alyssa gave me a rare look of solidarity. Like with any group of three girls, the tides were always changing. Two of us would grow closer, leaving the third one out. While that night was my turn to be the odd man, Alyssa's brown eyes reminded me of a time we shared more. Since Lauren's diagnosis, the dynamic had shattered; we'd been alternating positions as her favorite. Alyssa, a K-Mart Lauren, was the natural choice. We never recovered from it.[7]

5. My parents loved Lauren. Her death was the first and only time I've ever seen my dad cry. He called her "Snorin' Lauren" for her dreadful snoring in her sleep. He said she could keep the whole house awake even through a closed door.
6. Cherri smoked constantly when we were kids, and more when Lauren got sick. I remember seeing her during my deathbed visit. Cherri excused herself to go smoke outside while Lauren desperately clutched at her oxygen mask, taking one of maybe her final ten thousand breaths.
7. In the years since the funeral, Alyssa's regularly posted pictures on Lauren's birthday or death-day of the two of them with me cropped out, writing how much she's missed her best friend, partner in crime, sister from another mister, and so-forth. On the off-season, when the audience isn't quite in the deathaversary mood, she'll choose current pictures of her and her friends at the local Dairy Queen, wishing Lauren were with them. I recognize all the girls in these photos; we went to middle school together. Alyssa stays in our white trash hometown, working at the daycare we all met in, like it is some big gesture, a daily memorial. Like she wouldn't have stayed there anyway. I imagine the alternative excuses she'd give if Lauren never got sick. *I'm just really close with my grandparents; I'd hate to lose any precious years with them... Well, I've got two units left in an associates degree at Los Medanos Community.* I imagine the other circumstances of a healthy-Lauren world. I imagine her getting off a plane visiting me during my study abroad and the smell of her neck as I pull her in. I imagine drunken dancing and stolen kisses in a Budapest nightclub. I imagine eating raw cookie dough, our legs wrapped around each other with familiarity built in a lifetime of love. I imagine seeing her smile one more ti–

My dad gave Lauren her "I'm sorry you're dying" present in the form of a mani/pedi for all three of us the next day. I could already imagine the annoyed looks by the woman doing my nails, one hand clean, the other blackened by the dye. I rubbed the chemicals through her hair, the only part of her body that, to this point, had remained untouched by them. We saturated her curly locks while singing badly to *DJ Got Us Fallin in Love* by Usher crackling through her phone's speakers. I'd never heard it before, but the chorus was easy to memorize.

"What do you guys wanna do?" Lauren asked, placing a plastic hairnet over her head.

"We could play Wii," I replied with the wrong answer. Offering a kid option in tween-hood was the height of stupidity, and I was glad they didn't bother replying.

"We could go on Omegle," Lauren said with a cute quirk of her eyebrow.

"Didn't your mom say we couldn't go on that?" Alyssa asked with a giggle. I remembered Cherri's hoarse, but stern voice. She'd heard bad things about it. Her warning fell on deaf ears, as we all ran back to Lauren's room. I was still unclear on what it was, but when they ran, I ran.

In preparation for video chatting with strangers, there was a process. You start by pushing up any chest you may have, angling the camera right above the ribs. Alyssa's boobs had already reached double D status, the envy of my A3 chest, but Lauren switched bras in favor of something a little more padded, and both changed into V-Necks. Next comes the makeup. They added another layer of mascara and eyeliner each; Alyssa doused herself with perfume. Finally, they assumed the webcam position: laying on the stomach, cleavage out, and coy smiles on. I pulled out a thick book, ostracizing myself with pretentiousness that I would later paint as lack of inclusion when I felt sorry for myself. I felt better than the girls with every skim of a page as I pretended to read the words, but my curious eyes flickered toward the screen in intervals.

The "text chat" option was quickly bypassed for the far favored video chat button, and, with that, we began.

Dick, dick, dick, dick, dick. I had never seen a penis before that night. The girls impatiently scrolled through them with a blush in their cheeks, occasionally slowing down to inspect the larger ones (or, at least the ones captured with an angle to make them look larger). The images filled me with a heavy feeling of disgust. I recalled Lauren's kiss, glimpsing at her now "chocolatey" curls grazing her shoulder, the one with my favorite freckle. Even a glimpse of her emerald eyes in my direction hatched pterodactyls in my stomach. Jacob and Edward's shirtless scenes left me feeling tepid. I thought about this as I glanced over at the girls. I knew that's not how they felt, as they giggled at the flashing images on the screen. I decided to stop thinking about it.

"Oh here we go; here we go!" Alyssa said. Two boys with floppy skater boy hair roughly our age, maybe a couple years older, appeared on the screen. They smiled at my friends, but I lingered just out of view of the camera.

Hey ladies, what school do you go to, how old are you, where are you from, oh just my CDs, yeah I love them, too. Haha, we'll take off our shirts if you do.

Lauren and Alyssa flashed the boys peaks of their hot pink bras, the little Victoria's Secret silver heart in the center of their blossoming breasts. The chat screen changed every few minutes as Lauren and Alyssa giggled, flirted, and moved on. In nearly every pair or group of boys we would ever come across, there was always somebody that favored Alyssa for her breasts just as there was always one that preferred Lauren for her face. The only thing I had going for me was feigned indifference, which piqued in boys a curious chase that would last a day or two.

The boys on their east coast time zone pretended to be tired after realizing under-the-bra was probably not going to happen, and Lauren scrolled to the next stranger. *Dick, dick, dick, dick.* She finally settled on an attractive older boy. He smiled at the sight: young, attractive girls, eager for his attention. He was experienced and slower with his approach, not asking for bras right off the bat like the amateurs before. I watched from out of view. He wore one of those fake smirks men perfect after looking at pictures of models, the ones they think look better than their smiles, even though the grins they hide are the real panty-droppers. He had on a camouflage jacket and a tan hat, screaming "backwoods", which never did it for me, but was sure good enough when I wanted to be the one noticed. My elbow "slipped" into view of the camera, and his eyebrows rose.

"Who's that?" he asked. Lauren, without consultation, moved the laptop camera to capture my whole face. I thought that was it, I was done for, my ugly, ugly face, my baggy t-shirt, my stupid fucking book, my itty bitty titties. He smiled.

"She's pretty," he said to my friends as if I wasn't right there. Lauren got excited and continued to point the camera away from Alyssa and toward me. She still kept herself in the frame.

"What's your name, beautiful?" he asked.

"What's yours?"

"Thomas. Should I just call you beautiful, then, or... should I name you?" he asked. Everything went pale to the haze of a boy calling me beautiful for the first time.

"That depends. What do I look like to you?" I asked.

"You? You look like a Chelsea," he said, so a Chelsea I became.[8] "But, I've

8. This is the first time a man names me, but it will not be the last. When I am eighteen, on a

gotta say, I really want to know what kind of bra you're wearing... you know, for research purposes," he smiled innocently. He dipped his head as if to create a fake blush, like he couldn't believe he said something so daring, like it wasn't a go-to line. His request seemed fair enough. I dipped my toes into the pool.

"It's purple," I said.

"Hmm, are you sure?" he asked. "I don't know if I can trust your professional opinion here."

"I'm not colorblind," I retorted with fake bite, transparent for miles.

"Come on, Chelsea- don't be like that. I'd never ask for more," he said with a honey-smooth southern twang. His eyes, a brilliant pale green, flicked up to his camera. I knew he was no longer just looking at my face; he was seeking something inside of me, whatever part he could tap into: the parts that wanted to show up my friends, to seek validation, to feel a little daring, or to take advantage the anonymity of it all. Would he stop there? What could a boy gain from a bra strap? It was a tempting gateway. Lauren's green eyes looked at me with skepticism, and a deep sigh showed she was growing tired of watching me contemplate. I looked at the boy, tugged my sleeve and brastrap off my shoulder, showed him my bare collarbone, and hit "disconnect". In his place, more dick appeared.

"You could have at least given him your number. He was totally into you," Lauren said nonchalantly, clicking through the penises.

"God, he was so hot!" Alyssa chimed in with envy. I smirked and tried to ignore the queasy feeling in my stomach.

"Yeah, he was kinda cute. His eyes though!" I tried to gush along.

"Very Ian Somerhalder. I was like, 'Boone, you're alive!'" Lauren laughed, a welcome sound at any occasion.[9] The thunder outside boomed and we moved closer to each other. I could feel the soft skin of her forearm brush my own; I closed my eyes for a few seconds, taking it in, letting my other senses dull to sharpen the small nerves pulsing at her touch.

"Guys, what's he doing?" Alyssa asked. I was brought back to reality. Alyssa was

train to Chicago, a married thirty-year-old man from Wales will name me Cassidy when I refuse his advances. He will place his head in my lap while pretending to sleep. I will be greatly tempted to touch his hair. Other names boys will give me: Chelsea again, Natalie, and "Crystal", the last after a stripper on the show FRIENDS.

9. Lauren missed many things in her untimely sickness and death, including updating her Ian Somerhalder references from "LOST" to "The Vampire Diaries". Other things Lauren has missed, in order of what would have been most important to her: the redemption of Justin Bieber in the "Purpose" 2015 era, a *Charmed* revival trailer, and the release of Cheez-It: Extra-Toasty.

still here, Lauren was still dying, and there were still men on the screen that held her attention. I opened my eyes and glanced at the computer, expecting to see a guy with a somehow more unique method of masturbation. Instead, there was a man in his thirties pacing back and forth, shirtless, in a black room. It reminded me of a police interrogation room that you see on *Law and Order: Special Victims Unit*, lit by a small desk-lamp and nothing else. His pale skin shined with nervous sweat, his eyes jumping from the floor to the ceiling as he walked back and forth through the room. My glance followed his up to a noose hanging from the ceiling, and my stomach lurched. Only a few seconds earlier, I was flying, hyper-conscious of Lauren's arm grazing mine, and knowing she felt my skin on hers. The butterflies were replaced with a hard black rock of fear and dread in my stomach. I thought of the tumors in Lauren's belly, shrunken for now, but not forever. Was this what it felt like? A lump in your gut, wiping away anything good you'd ever felt, till there was only it? A furious blush hit my face when I realized what kind of equivocation I was daring to make. No, I had never felt anything like cancer.

The man's pacing calmed, as he slowed to a stop beneath the noose. I took a moment to examine his face. While every part of me screamed this must be a prank, a joke played on naïve children like us, the panic in his eyes was as real as anything I'd ever seen. If it was a prank, this man deserved an Emmy.

My eyes flickered to Lauren's face. She was leaning forward; more interested in this moment than any of the boys we'd spoken to that night. Her eyes locked onto the screen with a morbid fascination, her left hand held to her foundation-covered chin.

"Laur-" I whispered, but she shook her head, silencing me.

The man got up on a stepladder and, with shaking hands, wrapped the rope around his neck. Alyssa yelped, covering her eyes, forcing me to remember she was there.

"Lauren!" I yelled. She shielded the keyboard with her arms, preventing anyone from clicking away from the sight.

The man curled his toes around the front edge of the stepladder, let out a nervous breath, and took one gentle step forward toward his death. His body dropped fast, and the sight of his neck cracking was the last thing we saw when Lauren finally slammed the laptop shut. She had a look in her eyes I had never seen before.

"People die, Nikki," she said with an even tone. She walked to her desk and fiddled with her knick-knacks and picture frames mindlessly, grazing her fingers over the faces of all the people she'd leave behind at an undetermined date and time. One day, all of us, though we did not all know each other, would let out one simultaneous cry.

"It wasn't real," I said with resolve.

"It looked real," Alyssa whispered, shaking.[10]

"People do stupid shit like that. There's no way," I shook my head. My breath came out in hot, uneven bursts. I had to be right; I was always right.

"It doesn't matter," Lauren said. "Forget about it." Alyssa and I locked eyes for the second time that evening, before bonded in our indoctrination to the girl with the chemoed curls, now connected by our love and concern for her. I wanted to reach out and comfort Lauren, but my feet stayed glued to the floor. I looked at her face. Her lipstick was a little smudged, and the black liner had faded into the cracks on her eyelid. A zit on her chin peaked out from where her concerned hand laid earlier. She saw it, the inevitable moment that ran her life.

I think she was wondering if that man was stronger than she was. He got to choose the time and place. Lauren had to lay in wait, doing her best to fit 80 years of experiences of scraped knees, laughter, sex, mistakes, and selfies into the numbered days. Somewhere inside me, I wanted to tell her that her capacity to find her agency in the most hopeless of situations, to keep living beyond breathing, is what made her the finest of all of us. Instead, I stood there, watching, wishing I could touch her shoulder, the one with my favorite freckle.

Choose your own.

Path One:

We flee down to the kitchen, shaking off the scene behind us at the promise of a tablespoon of cookie dough each, which we take off Lauren's mom's outreached fingers. We eat so many Jolly Ranchers that we grow an ungodly second layer of purple "sugar tongue", which we peel off with disgusted fascination in front of the bathroom mirror. We make popcorn, wake Lauren's brother with our laughter, and go back upstairs. We pop *High School Musical* 2 into her pink Mickey Mouse DVD player, sit on the edge of her cheetah bedspread, and sing along to all the songs together. We still have some of the dance routines memorized, and we record ourselves doing them in her closet door mirrors. I still watch the videos years after Lauren dies, crying and smiling to myself about that night together. We all fall asleep on each other's legs and shoulders like when we were kids, giggling into the night. Alyssa will call Lauren a blanket hog, and she will be right. We come back again in months to swim. I help apply sunscreen to Lauren's baldhead, and she hobbles on her walker into the shallow end. Lauren makes

10. I reached out to Alyssa for the first time in four years to ask if she still believed it was real. She does.

jokes about "holding out" until the big How I Met Your Mother reveal, or at least until The Hunger Games: Catching Fire film comes out because that's her favorite book in the series. She wears a large pair of circular sunglasses with leopard print on them, and almost no makeup. She knows she doesn't need it now.

Path Two:

The three of us, shaken and exhausted, crawl into our individual sleeping bags. I picture all the penises in my head; I can't close my eyes without their moving images dancing beneath my eyelids. I picture Thomas, that Southern boy, touching himself to my bare shoulder, and a pool of bile threatens to rise in my throat. I look over to Lauren's shaking silhouette in the dark, my beautiful girl in a hurry to live before she dies. I think she's crying, but I don't want to bother her if I'm wrong. I think of the hanging man, and cry soft tears until I fall asleep to the image of how his penis may have moved as he asphyxiated. I will not see Lauren until our last goodbye, where I'll try and fail to find the words to lift her spirits in a hospital room, her chestnut curls burned to ash. She tells her mom she is not afraid, that she is ready, but upon seeing me walk in, she breaks, and admits it's not true. I tell her I'm not ready either. She says none of us are. I will not see Alyssa until the funeral. She came to Lauren's bedside without me, and took lots of photos. Lauren plans her own wake, making a playlist, food selection, and demanding everyone wear her favorite color, purple. The "celebration of life", however, has an inverse, morbid effect. The lyrics to Katy Perry's "Roar" scream over the loud-speaker as I try my first Dorito's Locos Taco. The speeches are supposed to be about spreading her light in her absence, but nobody smiles.

ANNA DE MARINIS

Sophomore
Major: BFA – Acting
Reading: Poetry

Anna De Marinis is a sophomore BFA Acting major in the School of Music, Theatre, and Dance. Originally from New Jersey, she spent a great deal of her time in the outdoors with her brother and the other children in the neighborhood who were exclusively boys. This now influences her writing, taking inspiration from nature and what it means to be a woman. As an actress, she is also very interested in the human experiences that unify us all and allow us to find empathy in unexpected places.

Nominated by: David Ward

Colonization

They've docked their ships
Set foot on untouched land
Leaving footprints in smooth, dry soil
A marching drum, trampling closer
Heavy breathing, animalistic growling declaring their presence
Setting up camp
Planting their seeds
Plowing the fields
Thrusting foreign flavors and scents upon our virgin tastebuds
Sawing through ancient timber
Tearing up roots
Removing the foliage, our protective canopies
Vicious sunlight beating down
Eyelids ripped open
Mouths hung agape
Their hungry fingers turning over stones, digging deeply into the earth
leaving open wounds in their wake

"Assimilate" they whisper
"Make your home a resting place for my rough and travel-worn body"

How did you find us
Why did you chose us
Oh god how could you lead them here
The most sacred of places torn to shreds by little boys
By pale, greedy creatures who know only how to take

Changing the topography of our land until we can no longer recognize her
Until she is no longer ours
Irreversible damage

We pray for rain to wash away their touch but we find ourselves plagued
by drought
A dry spell that provides no relief from this dusty heat
A fever tormented colony dripping with sweat and disgust
When will this land cease to be enough
How will you satisfy your appetites then?
We beg for them to leave things as they were

"Oh but this is for you!"
"It benefits us both."
"Just give in to change""
"Stop resisting"

So the ground below us relaxes and makes herself pliant
She allows their construction, their dissemination
We protect ourselves with affirmations
It tastes like poison in our mouths

They move south, in need of warmth
Their drums and their marching spread over our country, drowning out the lands very own heartbeat
They take in their work
Pride swells in their bellies
They are satiated
So they jam their flag into our soil
A jagged, bloody, intrusive rod with unrecognizable, offensive colors
Fanged teeth smile as the feeble wind attempts to knock it over
It stands strong

And just like that they're gone
Sails puffed up by the wind
Disappearing into the horizon
And even if years later we were to uproot the monstrosity
The waving symbol of all that was but no longer remains,
The gaping hole where it once stood would never close
Its resting place would scar our beautiful precious soil
A ghastly sight, unappealing to any future travellers
This land has been depleted
What more can one desire from such a place?

Moving in.

I haven't met you yet but
someday
Someday I will
Someday I will step into your body and fill up your shoes running my hands through your hair, whatever color it may be
Perhaps you will feel more familiar than expected
I will look deep into you crystal eyes and see my reflection
See myself as you see me
I will pull at your thighs, take in their strength, drag over your curves, soft or hard, I will worship your shape
I will reach to the sky and feel your height pulling me upwards
I will become your dreams, taking them on as my own
Holding tightly what you hold dearly
Someday I will stare through your corneas, drinking in green and orange
Swallowing the pictures whole, unsatiated by the world around you
I will claw for more with your bitten and bloody nails, dirt and dead cells building a home underneath
I will squeeze into molds unfit for my porcelain skin
Shedding layers as I go
I will grow
I will age
I'll let my tears take root in your wrinkles, framing your eyes and mouth, impounded by decades of smiles, decades of suffering
All you crinks and knots, I will take your weight, bearing them on my hunched and fragile shoulders
I will make meaning of your constellations, moles and freckles, a lifetime under the sun
I will understand your memories, let them make up who I am
I will learn from you lessons
Your mistakes
Your traumas
Your regrets and your triumphs
I will be proud
I will be embarrassed
Someday I will love you
I know I do not now

I don't understand you yet
I let other voices take root in my ears
Other hands feel your skin and tell me how you taste
I am victim to coercion
To opinion
To perspective
But someday
Someday I will love you
Deeply and fully
Unconditionally
And in that moment I will know what it was all worth
Every question will be answered and finally I will be satisfied
Finally I will just be

MALLORY DWORTZ

Sophomore
Major: Undeclared
Minor: Spanish
Reading: Short Story

I am from Grand Rapids, Michigan and I really enjoy taking creative writing classes. I haven't declared a major but as of now I am leaning toward English with a minor in Spanish. Some of my favorite things/activities include: tie dye, music festivals, lava lamps, and Mackinac Island, where I have spent the last two summers working. After college I want to work in a city somewhere and hopefully use my potential English degree.

Nominated by: David Wade

If Tampons were Behind the Counter like Cigarettes

DING!!! I hate when store doors let everyone know that you're there. Sometimes you just want to fly below the radar, undetected, you know? This is especially one of those times. I am clad in muted colors, hat on and hood drawn. It is certainly not the time to remove my sunglasses, despite being indoors. Even armed with protective measures, at the ding of that glass swinging door, the cashier calls out,

"Hello!" how invasive. How rude. He stares right through my $3 shades. *He knows.* Screw his greeting, now he certainly, without a doubt, knows the purpose of my visit: my top secret mission. Why does it have to be a **boy** behind the counter? It truly just adds insult to injury.

A little background: Today started off just as painfully average as any other day. I woke up about 10 minutes later than I should have, my mom put peanut butter crackers in my lunch, and it has been approximately two weeks since I've worn this particular tie dye shirt. This is important. Middle school girls will not allow outfit repetition in less time than that. I went to english and math, same as usual. It was before gym class that everything went wrong. While switching into my ugly sport shorts I noticed it. The unspeakable happened. I threw on a hoodie from my locker and slipped out the back exit.

Startled, I dart into the nearest isle and let my hands drag across the shelf, my fingertips tapping each item as I shuffle forward. Pretending to intently scan the contents around me (Ah yes, cleaning supplies! Just what I was looking for!), I revisit my plan of attack. What I need is held hostage behind the counter by the enemy (that stupid boy). This must be handled delicately, so as to ensure the least amount of embarrassment for me. I pull out my phone and look up the cost, finding that the cheapest box is said to be $3.97. The thought of waiting there at the counter, helpless, while he counts out change causes little beads of sweat to start nesting above my Cupid's bow. I can see the box burning a hole in the counter... HELL NO.

"Exact change it is!" I whisper sneakily as I dig through the front pocket of my backpack to find four crumpled $1 bills. *He can keep those three pennies.* There really is something to be said for my generosity. Stalling, I use the edge of the shelf to straighten out each one, each dollar I mean, being sure to iron out every crease and crinkle. I take a deep breath and stroll up toward the counter. I had rehearsed my line all the way here so as to appear cool-as-a-cucumber,

“What can I do for ya?” he asks, accusingly. Wiping the moisture from my upper lip, I exhale and summon the words,

“T-The little purple tampons please.”

“Okay,” he says, turning around to retrieve them. I stay on high alert. I may have stuttered, but I refuse to sink further, “That'll be $4.21.” Oh no, *sales tax*. This is a waking nightmare.

“Ok-kay cool,” I reply as calmly as possible. I'm cool-as-a-cucumber, remember? “Here's $4.” I hand him the flattened bills already in my hand, and drop to the floor to begin my descent into hell: searching for loose change in a thirteen year old's backpack. I dig my hand into the abyss, scratching at the bottom of each pocket, desperately grasping for that 21 cents. I swear, and I'm not being dramatic, this experience is taking years off of my life. *Breath slower* I have to remind myself as the sweat returns to my face, “AH HA!” I spring up and let four coins spill onto the counter, two nickels, one dime, and one penny. They are covered in residue from loose pieces of gum, but there it is, exact change. I snatch the box and casually speed-walk out of CVS. *That wasn't so bad.*

DANIELLE FALLING

Sophomore
Major: Environment and Creative Writing
Reading: Poetry

I'm from Grand Rapids and enjoy writing about the moon, among other things. I'm a student in the Residential College and enjoy swimming laps, cutting hair, being a radio DJ, the campus farm, and painting; not because I'm especially good but because they are nice to do.

Nominated by: Sarah Messer

The Going is Paused

I

His hand lingers on the doorknob
the going is paused
but we both know
as soon as he turns his cheek
our moment has frayed.

A milkweed pod cracked open
millions of thin white shivers
tumble out into the wind
and he goes
his fingers do the turning.

The door it's not even open yet
somehow already closed.

I close my eyes in the next room,
my hands folded like two doves
hovering near my chest.

II

goodbye
'god be with yee'
we send our loved ones with god
adieu adios
wearing a robe of finality
ma' al-salāmah
and so they go
namaste

one to the next
we exchange ciaos
so to have two equal bookends
of salut or shalom
to protect us from
truly lending our living
to goodbyes.

III

The sun is shining
we've been together all day

a day is both eternity
and instant

our faces are stoic
stone magic pools

your lips press to my cheek
I push and pull at your hand

we, two mirrored magnets,
spring apart and clatter in projection

and the sun keeps shining
on our distancing hushed footprints

IV

I pull you close and smell every meal we've ever made
lingering in the slope of your neck
now stronger and steady
it is me doing the enfolding
like how you taught me
phantom figment thumb wars over a pot of soup
fill me with warmth
as a heaping spoon of chili powder
I squeeze the one million tiny hugs from your body
as half a lemon to balance the sweet
and "say goodbye, love you"
sprinkled like salt
for the last time
for the thousandth
and hope that you find the leftovers
I left for you in the fridge.

V

You are
nowhere
were here
now where
did you run
off to?

power plant's
water vapor
cloud vanishing
from instant to instant
you are slippery
and do all the slipping
I wasn't even holding on

and now where
you were here
now nowhere.

VI

Our language will grow disparate
as two diverging species
it will be strange to catch up

I get out of the car to stretch my legs
and even through the unrolled window
I'm going to miss you

because when you spin really fast,
the world spins around you
and it makes just as much sense as before
except it's moving and everything has changed.

in this town saturated with memories
little ribbons of kindness are scattered about
and each goodbye feels a little more goodbye
and a little less see you later

you turn the key and I am frightened for a moment
you roll up the window and I check your mirrors
you lock the car doors so I wander away,
you know the desire to run flows through me like a river.

VII

My dress is too flowing
for the briskness of winter
so I do the leaving
you do the staying.

I hear my burgundy heart thump thumping
in my toes and elbows
my heart tells me things
like how to keep an ice rink between my eyebrows
and where to put marble memories for safekeeping.

My heart is chanting with a thousand doorbells
and in the reverberation I catch an echo
of a whispered maybe
saying "turn back
undo this silly going"
but with a dip I continue my leaving
with a blink you continue your staying.

This is not ready,
warmth shifting never is.

I stop the dryer before it's done
pull the molten cake from the oven
the center will sink as it rests
on the stove, a last green breeze
sliding along the crater's curvature
–unknowing.

VIII

I ask of you nothing:
this might be the last time
last spring, last summer, last autumn,
last winter

it's impossible to see which will be last of this turning

so I'm riding my bicycle until the wheels pop
gonna lay under this maple tree until the bulldozers roll up
I'm sitting here with you at the train station
until you are nothing but a blip of smoke on the horizon

buried and departing
my vision blurring
throat salty thick
with the coming of the going

some people weren't meant to leave
but since divergence is the secret
second strong nuclear force of the universe
I engage with the dissipation
and the new empty spaces in my sponge chest
the spreading sends me postcards
and I wish time could move out of order
for this one instance
so your train could reverse into the station
and undo this snapping of gravity.

IX

she cut her hair and threw out her favorite shirt
she took down all the photos from her walls
and painted everything "chantilly lace"

she stopped drinking coffee
she replaced that habit with alternating days
of crushed ice and hot lemon water

she started wearing copper lipstick on weekdays
she switched all her jewelry from gold to silver
and made a new personal email address

she started writing in all capital letters
she booked a ticket to Omaha
even though there's no one to see there

she stepped out of her old work boots
she blinked into someone new
I've not had a backwards glance to spare since

X

Stretching the time between meetings
like a slab of pink taffy

sweet and sticky
the pulling makes me sweat

maybe you'd say something
if our tectonic divergence

moved in an anthropomorphic fashion
but we are pulling teeth and taffy.

I look up, put my hand to my temple, and squint
over the long slender piece of candy floss

you must be across this sudden ravine
the distance makes me wonder over saccharine

I want to wash off the tacky
and forget why I was clinging to strings

letting go sometimes,
it isn't much of anything.

XI

I am curled on the shower floor
a porcelain deluge of tahitian
waters cascading down my back
if there are tears they aren't mine
the dream I had of you on the river
between the unliving and fully dead
you said, "Don't reach for the jewels in the riverbed."
I trail my fingers over the clear water
and wish on invisible coins
you said, "I was so tired."
and I finally unconvince myself
of the reason for your departure
not Bermuda or Rome or Arizona
I wake up
I dry off, still from shaking.
My mouth a walnut
pursed with trying to keep you
but you said not to reach for the jewels
so I let you drift down the river
silver light vibrating from your hair,
back turned to me.

XII

scrunch of lemon juice
I rub my eyes and pinch at my lips
rolling around a lead ball in my mouth
there's a chain link fence between my teeth

scrunch of spoilt milk
you taste of looking out a window
while biting my sand-filled balloon inner cheek
the underside of my mouth is rusty iron

scrunch of jasmine tea tannins
I stumble brashly along the ridge of parting
unable to rid from my puckered mouth
this soured feeling

XIII

Bye Forever.

Breath comes into my lungs
and you won't be coming back
the ugliest glass in the cabinet
shattered all over the floor
goodbye is the broom
I can finally sweep it up
and won't cut my fingers
thank god.

XIV

Long ago you opened up
a cavity in my chest
and took from it a ticking watch.

Then the eager wind started blowing
and your feet felt its pulling
plum sky, dimpled stream

I watch you vanishing
but still feel a fragmented ticking
in the empty where my kept time used to sleep.

I have faith that you hold the watch
in your embroidered breast pocket
that it's warmth occasionally keeps you

up at night thinking smoothly
with your fingertips
tracing forgotten weeks into the watchface.

FAREAH FYSUDEEN

Sophomore
Major: English and Philosophy
Reading: Non-Fiction and Fiction

Fareah is a sophomore studying English and Philosophy. She considers herself a novelist, though that might be too generous a title, considering she's written many halves of novels but has yet to complete one. Hence, currently working on a *novella*– a win-win situation. Fareah loves immersing herself in artwork, in friends and family, in social justice work on campus, in the mundane, day-to-day activities of life. Her work is deeply inspired by her background as an Indian-Muslim-American and the tension between personal and politicized identities. She is interested in exploring the quiet thrills and aches of being human; she is stunned daily by the beauty of what she cannot understand.

Nominated by: Greg Schutz

A Letter To My Body

You start with the Hijab. In the same way that an artist marks off his page with painting tape, or a carpenter sketches an outline before plunging the blade into wood, you clearly demarcate yourself in the folds of the scarf. One clean O. Beneath it, your intellect, senses, beauty. Within it, everything that is *you.*

Almond-shaped eyes built upon almosts: almost big, almost captivating, almost ingenius. Eyes are not the windows to your soul. If so, they are poor excuses with crusty shutters and blurry panes. Still, if one looks from the outside, they are perhaps the most attractive part of your face: your nose is a full, round-edged triangle, your cheeks full with no edges. Your lips are dark and ample, each one a different color: the shade of watered-down prunes on top, and the heart of a strawberry on the bottom. Your dentist told you that your jaw was misshapen and apparently asymmetrical, which accounted for the strange lopsidedness of your lips. They looked much better when not forced to meet. And so that's how you sat: lips slightly parted, each lip a different color, front teeth just visible through the window. When you smiled, all your gums showed–big, shiny, and purple–and the triangle of your nose became a kite-shape as it scrunched into laughter. All your features were swimming in the warm, bronzy, dark blanket that is your skin. It is clear as a white water lake. You are always aware of its color, everywhere you you go, especially in your white-male-bearded philosophy classes and your fair-Pakistani-friend parties and your grandmother's remark that the Michigan winter had lightened it just a little. Somewhere down the line, the acute awareness of its darkness transliterated to a declaration of pride. The sun glowed beneath your skin. Stars lived and died within its pores.

You draw yourself a little taller than you are. Really, five-foot-two-inches-slash-three-inches can be interpreted a lot of different ways. You either grew or shrunk half an inch every doctor's appointments depending on which nurse measured you. If you were just a little taller, perhaps you could command a room with your mere presence, but being five-foot-two-inches-slash-three-inches makes that kind of immediate acquisition of power a definitional impossibility. You are, objectively, by most accounts, of average height (but trying not to be).

You are probably wearing an A-line dress in this portrait, so you will not see this; upon closer inspection, however, you can tell that your thighs are quite large, drum-like, water-falling from the mouth of wide hips; your waist is dramatically smaller in comparison, and an admirably. You have curves, but please don't look too close–you's trying to hit the gym this summer, so this portrait is technically incomplete until then. You will probably consider this portrait a work-in-progress for the rest of your life.

Overall, you are of underwhelming stature and appearance. You have, historically, been able to charm some select people into believing you are beautiful. But you're just a mound of flesh as we all are—just suits of skin and bones trying desperately to navigate this zero-gravity outer space of judgement, prejudice, friendship, love. A body is nothing but the life it holds; so those people that believe you are beautiful, intelligent, passionate, ambitious, good-hearted, talented—maybe, I think, have the clearest vision of you. And when you stare at yourself in the mirror, you are reminded of the web of history that has carved your curves, painted your in earth-dirt armor, tree-topped your silky black with a piece of cloth, and you think, the God that made the sun, the moon, the stars, and all of the seven heavens—He has breathed inside Me. *I am, in all accounts, an expression of the divine.*

Letter To My Sister

Dear Aalleyah:

Enclosed is the first Hijab I wore to my first day of seventh grade (it's a bit tattered, and I know you won't ever wear it because you'll think it's ugly—but still, it's supposed to *mean* something). I could stop here but I won't.

You're the most beautiful person I've ever met. I'm not exaggerating when I say that your beauty strikes me in ways you will never know. I know we are sisters, and there may be some expected jealousy between us at you being quite a great deal more beautiful than I am—but I am filled with so much pride when I see you, I'm sure my heart is going to burst like the plumes of an overstuffed feather pillow. I love how dark and rich your skin is, even if our particular subcontinent of the world won't value it; I love your large, slightly upturned eyes, though it's unbearably annoying when you roll them, which you do almost all the time; I love the delicate blooming of your smile, your smirk, the contorted faces you make when you're trying to be funny. Beauty was a distant abstract until I realized yours.

And then the much-anticipated decision came this summer: Would you start wearing the hijab? Would you wear it to your first day of high school? I was almost certain you wouldn't—you didn't seem confident enough in your own skin, you were always concerned about other's impressions of you, the whole family was not sure if you performed your daily prayers or if you were lying about it. But you did it. How? Why?

Aalleyah, wearing the hijab takes a level of tenacity you won't fully understand until after you put it on, until you've worn it for *years*. Until you have to tell your white college roommates that they have to inform you before they have guys over. Until walking home at campus past midnight feels indescribably frightening, and you have your index finger quivering over the "send" button with 9-1-1 dialed in. Until you're sure no man will fall in love with you because of this hijab—this bandage to hide the wounds of your bleeding ego. Putting it on the first day will feel like you've conquered something. And the second and third day will feel like that, too. And maybe the first two years. But the initial conquest will wear off and you're left with America, and private beauty, and God. Sometimes it feels like it's not enough. It'll take years before you discover these are the only things that matter.

I wonder if you wore it because of me. Of course this pains me—a choice for that reason would be too grave for flattery. I don't want you to feel like you should have to because I did it. You're desperate to impress Amma, even though you don't act like it. I feel like sometimes I've played up the part of being the idealized, highly accomplished older sister a bit too dramatically, and left you to look like the shallow girl who likes K-POP and spends two hours deliberating before posting a picture on Instagram. There's a mystery and complexity to you that no one in our family seems to understand. You're a storm no one knows how to tame. I see the wedge between you and Amma and I can't help but feel as though I'm driving you two apart.

Wearing the hijab is discovering and nurturing a relationship with yourself. There is nothing in the world like it. It is hard, and gruesome, and there are tears. In the beginning, it is all romance and excitement, but it soons devolves into reality: you question your beauty, you question if people want to be friends with you, you question, what is so *wrong* with wanting to look beautiful? There is nothing sinful about being beautiful, or wanting to be so. But you are a great deal more than that, too.

You are powerful and independent and God has placed himself inside of you. A divine light. A celestial spark, with or without the hijab. The hijab is simply a tool for you to fan your flames, to rise to greatness, to be the best version of yourself. It is the *jihad* of the heart that makes it so sweet; if you can overcome social convention and defy the expectations of an entire society, then surely you can follow all your dreams.

I love you so, so much Aalleyah. I want to be your best friend. I want everything in the world for you. But sometimes I need to remember that you'll discover the world yourself, and not through anyone else's eyes, and especially not through mine. I won't send this letter to you because you'll learn it all yourself (does that mean I don't have to talk to you anymore? God, I *hope* so. Insert your infamous eye-roll here).

Paradise lies beneath your feet. Hold your head, and hijab, up high, Ally.

Your Akka,
Fareah

CHARLES HARRIS

Junior
Major: Communication
Reading: Poetry

Charles has hopes of being a not only a rapper but a pioneer for change within the entertainment industry. He has started his own collective, soon to be record label, New Renaissance Music. It gains inspiration from the Renaissance time period and also the Harlem Renaissance and aims to be the next leading figure in this time of growth and creativity as it relates to music and create his own renaissance in this generation.

Nominated by Lorenzo Diaz-Cruz

I Lost It.

Being alone is borderline addicting,
Actually, I take that back it's totally an addiction
Cause we barely scratching topic on the surface I of non-fiction
Trynna be the hero, but always feeling the villain
Always feeling like no matter what you do, you never got control
If bad decisions, were academics then I'd be in honor roll
Cause instead of textbooks, I was learning how to roll and not learning how to cope
Trynna save myself, but I'm running out of rope
Cruise line full of people I'd rather be on that boat reminiscing
Leaving all past versions of me off in the distance
If I keep messing up, the golden child will be one of the figures
Because based on what I'm doing, it's like fuck it go figure
Forget the school work, mama saying it's much bigger
My mama got her masters so it's hard refuting truth,
But I tell her it's so different when she out recruiting troops
We both visionaries, so we never reach a truce
And I got too much pride to ever say she true.

Time to get serious.

If I take this step it's no reversin,
This the only time and place when imma need rehearsing
Really, I can't lie I gotta lotta work to do
Wishing I knew the outcome
Hoping for the truth
Looking to the future and hoping it's with you
What if I told you undeniably?
You the only one when them girls be eye to eye with me
Deep in my mental, I can't get you off my mind you see?
Love is a forever thing I found that with you
You the only one, tell me who better than you
The list is kind of short, it's a one to one
But did I realize too late, or maybe too early?
Ya boy so young that's why I'm underperforming
For you and only you, I'll give a perfect performance
Acting like I'm fine with you being around all the time,
but only you know how it's killing me deep inside
I let you take a peak,
And baby I can't lie,
my soul ain't for the weak
But you conquer it every time,
You seen the other side, so divine
When the flowers bloom it remind me of the summer time
Or rather how I spring to attention when your name get brought up
I just need one chance, to show you how I love,
But maybe it's out my hands
And maybe I'm out of luck, this is, bigger than me,
this is, out of control
But I swear to God you and the music what make me whole
I'm at a point in my life where I've been blessed to know my wife
And I ain't old enough to drink
but when I said be the greatest, man ain't nobody blink,
so, what that tell you how I think?
If I want imma get it, but damn, who are we kidding
you'll stop me in my tracks, when I need to run it back
Moving too fast not thinking about repercussions

This is more than a passion,
More than summertime madness
Being in your presence hoping the time don't pass
I need every second and opportunity
Second place myself, girl, I hate what you do to me.
Beautiful monster.
Twisted Fantasy.

VICTORIA HELRIGEL

Freshman
Major: English
Reading: Fiction

Victoria Helrigel is a freshman at the University of Michigan, planning to major in English. She enjoys many forms of creative expression: writing, drawing, and watercolor, mainly. She currently writes for an on-campus magazine, Mentality.

Nominated by: David Ward

Brevity

After death, we have twenty seconds of brain activity, a phenomenon documented by science and art alike. The heart stops, and the brain and its synapses begin to die, expelling their contents, memories, feelings, dreams. This is life flashing before your eyes. Twenty seconds. This is brevity.

I imagine my brevity will begin where I begin. Not with birth – I don't remember that. I think my brevity will begin with my first memory, my first experience with death in two parts.

Part one: the car accident. The car flipped before I could comprehend, then I was dangling as a marionette with my car seat belt as my strings. I unbuckled myself and crawled over the ceiling, looking up at what used to be the floor. There was a house in the distance like a small flare on the horizon. I sat on the bumper of a firetruck and stared at it, wondering who was inside, wondering if they were looking at me and wondering, too.

Part two: the funeral, our main destination while I was staring at that little house and the fire in its windows. The car accident made us very late. All I remember is my mother picking me up, both arms twisting around my waist, so I could look into the casket. There was a grey ghost inside, and he smelled like dust and medicine. I was made to lean into the coffin and kiss him. He was cold.

Twenty seconds for an entire life. First day of school and the boy who puked on my shoes. He cried so hard he threw up. We were never really friends after that. Learning colors. I was a good reader – picked it up real easy. Green eggs and ham. I didn't eat it. Guacamole in class. Cursive in the third grade. I played my guitar, Smoke on the Water on one string, and everyone clapped. I broke my collar bone – had to wear a lame sling. No one signed it. Heads-up-seven-up during recess when it was raining outside. I shut my thumb in a car door. The nail turned purple and fell off. A wooden box the size of my grandma and a photo and lots of flowers. Moving, the first time. The new town had seven elementary schools. We used to have one, and it was the same building as the middle and high school. I'd never seen so many people.

First day of fifth grade and I was nervous. It was the day after Halloween, and I hadn't gone trick-or-treating. I had been driving four hours away from home to this place. Everyone kept asking me what I had dressed up as. I lied and said, "A witch." Spanish. Everyone else had been learning Spanish since the year before. I knew *nada*. Recorder. I had never played that before. At my old school, there were only maracas. We got a cat. We moved into an apartment. I had never lived in an apartment. Our neighbors were crazy, and I'm sure we were crazy to them, too. We got a new truck. It had cool seats in the back, ones that faced each other. Eighth grade and my friends weren't my friends, anymore. We all acted like we were, though. Moving, the second time.

Back home. A corn field. Not much else.

Moving, the umpteenth time. First day of junior year and the awkward introductions. Everyone thought I was a freshman because they had never seen me before. This town only had three elementary schools, a happy medium. New friends. Driving and my terrible instructor. My first real job and my terrible manager. Senior year. College applications. Waiting. Ugly cap and gown. Cruising down the dirt roads in the country. Driving back alone in the dark from work, busted speaker throbbing in the back seat. Letter of admission. Graduation, sun in my eyes. I sat in the front row on the football field and wore sunglasses with flowers around the edges. Freedom.

First day of freshman year and sitting in my dorm room, completely and utterly alone. Singular. My roommate. Old friends. New friends. Classes and eccentric professors. Late nights and movies and too much food. Standing outside in my pajamas for the first snow of my college career, no jacket, no shoes. Snow looks different to me, now.

If I were to die, today, this would be my brevity, and brevity, while usually resulting in death, is not necessarily the end. Many cases have been documented wherein a patient has been declared biologically dead and lived, despite the bleak diagnosis. Even after a flatline on an EEG, a machine monitoring brain activity, patients who have been successfully revived can recall sensations from the time of their flatline. Cases of near-death experiences are characterized in part by a changed sense of time and strong feelings of elation, joy, ecstasy, and harmony. Most are even disappointed to be brought back to life and look forward to their return to the place they felt they were in near death.

I sometimes wonder if I am in my brevity in this very moment. If I was reliving my life in twenty seconds, would it feel like twenty seconds? Or would it feel like a rambling movie, an endless highlight real, a thick scrapbook with pages and pages of memories that took another lifetime yet to see? And I feel so strongly about so many things, like far-away houses and new snow. While I wonder, I know one thing, certainly: I don't want to leave.

NORA HILGART-GRIFF

Sophomore
Major: Public Policy
Minor: CASC
Reading: Poetry

Nora Hilgart-Griff is a Tennessee-born Michigan native, and a sophomore in the Residential College. Her talents include picking up bugs to take them out of the house and knowing exactly when to pop the toaster for that perfect crunchy-on-the-outside, soft-on-the-inside texture.

She enjoys gummy vitamins, collecting paint samples, and worship music (though her dad wishes she listened to more Kanye), and still ties her shoelaces using the bunny ears method. This whole poetry thing is as much a surprise to her as it is to all of you.

Nominated by: Christopher Matthews

Sang/Sens/Sans/Cent

The word for *blood* sounds just like the word *to feel* in French.
Would you wash your car if you knew it was going to rain tomorrow?
Would you hand off your beginnings if you knew they were all going to end?
Today, I lose my way learning a song that everyone refuses to sing;
stand taller, now.
Hold a vigil for your lost causes--there will be no bones left from the burning for the shamans to interpret,
But you'll know exactly what their singed edges mean.
The word for *without* sounds just like the word *one hundred* in French. It's like the way
absence and *presence* rhyme--but not quite, and yesterday
In class
We watched a video of an ape hugging a human who freed it from a cage; the whole room seemed to find it endearing but my stomach couldn't grasp the charm.
A celestial body, moving and stirring in unison,
We are wardens, yes,
and redeemers too. Perhaps these
Are the necessary constituents of persistence. Most things do come in opposites;
In constant undulation. Still,

I wonder what would happen
If we tipped the scale so violently
that all we would see is light.

Mont St-Michel

It is the angle of the sunbeams
That makes me realize I don't want to die.
It is the way the dust motes seem to throb
With the cycling of the sea.

I realize that twice a day
The ocean swallows this island
But the singing goes on anyway.
It doesn't care that I can sprout wings
And roots at the same time,
But I do.
You are made of what should kill you;
Feather and sky and dirt.

Is this what it is to pray?
This laying of hands, this
Coolness of stone? This learning
To lose what I've already lost?

Dark robes, prostrated bodies,
Salt-spring skin–I suppose
I love this life. Where the air
Is thick with angels. Where the birds
Bob wetly in the mounting, tender tide.

Not Dreaming

1. I've seen five shooting stars this year, and it's only January
This makes me think that something very good is about to happen, or else
The sky is falling out.

2. My boyfriend startles me awake and
I think he's someone else, he asks me
How my dreams are and when my heart stops beating doublespeak
I tell him that I haven't had any. I think it was a lie, but
I can't remember what his face looked like. I can't remember
If it ever really happened at all.

3. Maybe it's common knowledge:
When you're in a maze you can pick one wall and put your palm against it and if you
Walk and walk without ever moving that hand you will
Eventually find your way out.

4. This girl Lucy in high school was telling a funny story; she was trying to get this guy
To do her and
He kept pointing to the ceiling every time her fingers slid beneath his boxers, finally she asked him god? Are you worried about god?
But he was just afraid that his parents, with their room upstairs
Would hear them. And that day our teacher talked about plagues and burning witches and I
Kept looking at the ceiling but we were on the fourth floor and it was only the roof
above us.

5. Despite being enamored by ritual I am an impatient person and
You don't feel it when you nick yourself with the razor. This is what's so difficult;
You only notice your mistake
After trailing wet red footprints on the tile, and
Yesterday
On the street
A little girl pointed to my ankle and screamed.

mutuari

And I am at your door again,

Can I borrow some honey,

Another moth kills itself in the lightbulb on your wall, whispers something Important as it

Fizzles into dust.

I am waiting on a winter lake; there is an ice fisher,
he tells me

I am melting. I can feel it now; all the good things

Have gone to seed, my hands are full

Of honey. I am at your door again; *can I borrow some eggs*; a lie

They are broken across my kitchen floor, no

I have already eaten them. The ice fisher won't leave me alone. He keeps

crawling out of my lake

He comes into my house and takes my honey. *Listen to the wind, for once* he tells me,

Listen to the way it blows through you.

I try to stop him from leaving but I am too busy wondering if this

Is the reason I am always cold. I am at your door again,

but it is Christmastime,

You are too busy and I am too poor

To pay rent to the edge of your porch. The ice fisher, of course,

Is covered in honey. *Stop trying to marry the moon,*

he says,

Everything comes in halves. When I arrive home, the moths have left a gift of rotting eggs,

They are melting, now, and maybe soon the puddles

will be full of fish.

SOPHIA JACOBS

Sophomore
Major: Computer Science
Reading: Poetry

Sophia Jacobs was born and raised in Cincinnati, Ohio. She is a big fan of Biblical and mythological allusions. She is haunted by this formative poem she read when she was 15 but has never been able to discover again. Her hobbies include looking for bunnies in Kerrytown, napping, and watching poorly-reviewed movies with female protagonists.

Nominated by: Erika Nestor

Nightmares

I keep dying.
It's different each time.
Once, I was sucked into a vacuum,
and then I woke up.
A Russian assassin from a British TV show
kissed me
and then tried to kill me
while wearing a violet satin suit.

The apocalypse keeps happening too.
Do you know how many times I have tried to save everyone
from a flood?
A nuclear hug?
The implosion of earth?

This sleep is

tiring.

I can't keep track of faces.
I don't journal after.

I have to check on people when I
wake.
I had received a call.
I watched skin slip off
bones,
light burn
out of eyes.
I check just in case they are dead.
I could be psychic. I don't know yet.

Sometimes my dog appears,
and I miss him.

Sometimes you are there.
We are in a basement that is like your basement
but not it.
You're wearing a red fleece jacket
instead of blue,

and I miss you.

I usually die
in this dream too.

The End of the World at a Party

I hosted a house party when the world
ended, and I found Death himself
in my red solo cup. Of course,
I had wondered before if
the world was doomed.
The seas had risen
and the Arctic ice melted.
Hurricanes came in pairs
and Death bought a condo in Florida.
Every extra bit of warming
had mattered.
I was already on fire
when the backyard grass
flared up like candles,
their red hot tongues
licking the lollipop lawn.
And I, with the attention span
of the ebbing tide
left my own party
to see the stars melt from the sky
and drip onto my forehead.

Two options arose:
Nothing
or life forever–

I chewed my chapped lipsand confronted eternity inside again.
The world is ending I said.
Climate change had caught up,
but everyone kept dancing.
Dancing badly, I might add
out of rhythm like toddlers,
and I loved to dance,
but the ground beneath my feet
decayed. I couldn't dance
on a dance floor like that.
I watched the apocalypse,

my bed and the streets desolate.
Would graves spring forth zombies?
Undeadness seemed too cruel.
I didn't want to eat cold soup
at every meal.
Trees turned to dust,
and I looked at my hands,
the same hands on my wrists,
when ice caps used to exist.
The only honest thing left:
fingernail clippings
on my bathroom floor.
And I readied myself
for Death, crushing my cup
while everyone danced,
and the sun stroked the earth.

Nothing or life forever.
Nothing I thought.
Forever–

Eve, When Asked If She Too Had Been Possessed by Seven Devils

I was hungry, you know – is that a devil? I suppose.
They thought so – my husband, his father,
every bird and worm and blade of grass.
They grew fingers to point at me while
Adam sucked the juice from his own.
Sure, the garden had bounty, but
every meal tasted of dust, berries with no seeds.

The earth opened herself up for me
every misty morning and evening,
but I had worn out watching sunsets –
Mark that as number two.
Standing around bare as dirt
amongst trees and leaves and trees
was not so kind to my wandering mind.

I was chatty that particular day.
Woman's mouth working for herself – I know for a fact
that's the third – saying so many, too many words.
I greeted all the creatures,
not just the serpent twirled at my feet
like a green glimmer of light on the cusp of a wave,
asking me "how was your day?"

Adam talked to God who never talked to me.
No wonder he said I came from barbeque meat.
Number four – blue fury bubbling beneath
the skin, my stomach a cauldron
wanting no more sugar – just spice.
I rubbed cayenne against my cheeks
and began wearing leaves – they called that vanity.

The image of my reach to the branch of that tree
is wrong – it was a bush beneath my feet.
But I possess woman's memory – fifth devil femme.
Even Adam shifted his thoughts accordingly.

God has a devil too, you know:
copying Jupiter, Amun, Zeus – his myths are all boring.
Finally, six – I'm branded with three.

I can't help my heresy.
I've met God – I'm still unimpressed.
The snake held more empathy in one tine of her tongue
than he in his whole heavenly body,
clouds just water packed together.
When I plucked the fruit from the vine,
I slashed my hand through that divine façade.

I looked at Adam and God,
then Adam, then God.
Then the serpent
Then the serpent
Then the serpent
Then me – godlier than all three –
Seventh devil – this knowledge – fruit stuck in my teeth.

JAZZARAY JAMES

Junior
Major: English and Creative Writing
Minor: Art and Design
Reading: Short Story Fiction

I am a writer from the land of Iowa, commonly mistaken for Idaho and Ohio. I aspire to write stories about the wondrous and tragic events I encounter. Studying literature adds to this passion. I am also an artist with a passion for sculpture and printmaking. I hope to write amazing stories paired with sculptures or other pieces of art I love in the future.

Nominated by: Laura Thomas

Stunted

The boy is seated at a wobbly wooden desk a few feet away from Alfred, a large man in a plaid sweater who seems to be watching over everyone. The boy scans the room to see two other girls seated next to adults with white booklets laid out in front of them. The girl farthest from the boy and closest to the large windows, windows with closed blinds that trapped the sun outside, meets his gaze and bites her lips. He notices that her left leg is jittering like she might have to pee. He breaks his gaze as his eyes float up to the banner lined around the room. An elephant, a tiger, and a lion are smiling as they pronounce words. He lowers his eyes to his desk. He wonders where the lady that sat him down went off to when she left the room. He inspects his desk closely. Pencil marks of old hearts and letters, letters that probably spell out names, the boy cannot be entirely sure, line every inch of the desk. He places his hands in the cubby beneath the desk and feels sharp pencil shavings and crumpled up papers.

Footsteps creep up behind him. The bottom of a white dress with ships and carousels printed in blue appear in his peripheral. He looks up to see a black woman with a blue ribbon tied around her afro walking past. She sits down across from him.

"Hello, my name's Mauricia. What's your name?"

The boy looks back down at his desk. She waits for him to respond.

"And your name?" she repeats.

He leans forward to tap the ground with his left foot. His movements shift the weight of the of balance desk. He lurches forward. Her long arms reach across her desk to his and stabilize him. He scoots back in his seat again and grimaces at her.

"That's okay, I don't need your name right now. I'm here just to do a little reading with you. You're going to read some words and maybe a few short stories today, is that alright?"

He places his hands back under the desk and fidgets with the sharp pencil shavings. He strokes some and breaks others. Mauricia reaches behind her and pulls out a phone, a pencil and two white packets. She slides one of the thick white packet across his desk. Although she dims the light on her phone he can still see the stopwatch.

"Alrighty, we're gonna read the story titled *The Importance of the Sun*. Right here," she says as she opens his packets and flips to the page. She points to the first words with her pencil. "You can start whenever you're ready," she says with a smile.

He pulls his hands out from under the desk and takes in a deep breath as he lays them on the packet. He looks at the long lines of words. There's a word he knows. There's letters he knows. But then he sees words he's never seen before.

He closes his eyes.

Suddenly he feels himself falling and rocking the overwhelming current of the ocean. The monstrous water, which is now as present as air, rocks head. Waves like daggers beat him in the chest. Blunt and forceful. His eyes peep open. In the corner the water creeps across the tile, up the desk legs and seeps into his socks. He shuts his eyes again, opens them and the water is gone.

"Right here," she says reaching across with a pencil to the first word of the passage.

He places his right pointer finger where her pencil had just been. His finger follows the letters on the page. "Tttt-hhhu-eee–My feet are wet!" The boy leans back and pulls up his feet to his chair, touching dry socks. He raps his hands around his legs. "I don't want to read!"

There are two other girls on the other side of the room. He cant's see them anymore but he can hear them reading.

"Rita and Josie we-re su-ppo-sed to go home i-m-me-dia-tely after school. Instead, they went to the park. The sun was out and the birds were chir-ping." Samantha's voice rings with the confidence and clarity spotted in every choir soloist voice, a distinctness he admired, despite her few pauses. The boy turns to the girl.

Mauricia follows the boys eye and leans in, staring at him with imploring eyes. She says, "It's okay. It's okay. She's older don't worry about her. I'll walk you through it."

He breathes faster. He wants to throw down the test and run out of the room. Yet, he's anchored to the seat. A rod composed of his father's words from his last outburst at school tether him to his desk. *Ya leave dat seat right there, I'm gonna whoop yah ass. Yah hear? All you need to do is be obedient.*

The boy shuts his eyes. *Yes, sir.*

He grips the seat of his desk, squeezes his eyes and rocks his head forward.

"I don't know. Don't make me! I can't read! I can't do it."

Mauricia leans in as far as she can. "I can read the first word for you. We can sound them out."

"How about you try for 30 seconds and then we take a break with some of those Legos." She points over to the colorful bin of assorted toys. A Batman Lego lies erect before them all. The boy bites the corner of his lip to hold back a smile.

The offer is enticing.

But, the words disappear.

His vision fogs and the words blur into unintelligible squiggles.

A scratchy voice, almost like a whisper, calls him back to the text.

"*Don't Read. Don't Read. Don't Read. REEeeaaadDeh. Deh.*" Slow sounds echo around him. "*Deh. Deh. Deh.*"

Another teacher's foot is tapping the floor. "Cun-Fie-Deh. Confide." She's helping one of the other girls in the room.

"Do you know this letter?" Mauricia says in a pleading voice.

The light in room fades. The overhead light flickers. The words nearly disappear. He doesn't know their combined sounds.

"I know the alphabet!" the boy yells.

He feels a cold touch on the back of his neck. He slaps it hard like an insect buzzing by out for blood. He shakes his head. The letters don't mean anything. "I'm not going to do it. I *can't* read!" He lifts his fist into the air and bangs the desk. The front right metal leg bangs against the tile over and over.

"Stop!" Alfred demands, standing from his desk.

"Stop!" Mary pleads.

Stop! another voice says, a voice that isn't in the room, deep and fervent like his father's. *Stop all dat fussin' right now!*

Alfred stands up from behind his desk. He's a tall black man. He approaches the boy. "Young man, I have a son like you. He says he can't do this or that, but all he needs to do is try. Sit up straight. We're not babies here. We are men. You can read if you let us walk you through it. And, once you can read you can do anything."

Anything? The boy thinks. *But why read when daddy says all I need to do is be obedient and listen.* He doesn't say this aloud. He balls up his fist.

"Listen to me, son." The boy keeps his eyes on the desk.

"Look at me," Alfred demands. The boy keeps his head down.

Alfred pounds his hand against the desk. The boy jumps back.

"Sit up straight like a man and look me in the eyes." The child listens attentively like the stern words coming from this stranger's mouth were his fathers.

"Now, you can get any job you want. You want to be an astronaut? You want to travel the world? Well, you need to know how to read to do those things."

Okay, thinks the boy. The boy sat up and put his index finger back on the paper.

"Your time is up now, but we'll finish assessing you tomorrow. Come over here." Alfred leads him to his desk. "We have some sight words your family should work on with you tonight though." Alfred turns around and picks up a book with a small pig on it. There's a red tag on the spine. "Here, young man. I got a good book for you too. Why don't you have one of your parents read this book and work on the sight words with you at home, okay?"

A special book, the boy thinks. He nods his head with a smile and shoves the zip lock of sight words into his bag. He holds onto the book and presses it against his side.

***

The boy walks home from school with a smile on his lips. The red sign on the street has words. The green signs on the street corners have words. He thinks to himself that one day he will read them. He walks up his apartment porch steps and rings the doorbell number 459 for their apartment. The door buzzes. He pulls back the heavy metal bar on the glass door. Down the hall his mother's head peaks out the door, a gentle smile rising on her plush rosy cheeks. The boy's lips purse as he sees the Applebee's name tag just above her right breast. He thinks of her early morning kisses as she leaves for her first job. She moves toward him to swoop him into the hug he cherishes most.

"Hey, baby," she kisses the top of his head and pulls him back from her chest. "What you got there?"

He remembers the book in his hands and lifts it up to her. "I got a book to read," he says with a twinkle in his eyes. "I gotta practice sight words and read this book before tomorrow. Will you read it with me, mama?

"Nah, I can't. I gotta leave, baby. Maybe yo daddy can read it to yah."

As they enter the doorway of the apartment, the boy hears the sizzles from rice bowling in an open pot. His mouth waters as the smell of smoked honey and sautéed vegetables wash over him. His father's favorite meal. His daddy was always at home cooking ever since he stopped working as a janitor.

"Did yah hear me Harry? The school done gave lil man some sight words. You can practice soundin' those out with him, can't yah?" Melinda goes into the backroom to finish getting ready for work. The boy sits down on the seat closets to the kitchen to watch his father cook.

"I can't read Melinda. I ain't gonna be reading with him if I can't read. Dey stopped me from readin'."

"You've done said that thousand times, baby. But you can learn if you try. Also, ain't no body stop yo' ass from readin' nothin'. We wasn't livin' in no Alabama or Georgia or nuhin. You done stopped yah self. You was skipping school and running out the room." She yells from the bedroom, "Harry, why we got him goin' to school if you don't want him to learn?"

"It's daycare. And he's got to learn to listen and socialize if he wants to use his skills to get a job." Harry moves away from the sizzling stir fry, placing a lid on top of it. The boy catches his father breathing deeply, so deep he leans back, like a hissing tea pot that's ready to burst. Harold makes eye contact with the boy. "Don't you dare read." The boiling water reaches over the top of the pot. "You livin' just fine, aren't yah?" The water seeps over the side of the stove and slithers onto the floor, making its way across the white tile to the hard floor. It slithers to the living room. It inches to the boy's toes. He follows it. "Look at me when I'm speakin to you." The boy bites his lip as the water leans in ready to take him. "Yo' daddy takin' care of his family and yo daddy don't know how to read."

His son holds his breath and then nods. The book slides off his legs onto the ground into the fangs of the water.

"Harold, the rice!" Melinda says as she reenters the room. Harold scoffs and rolls his eyes. He reaches in the cabinet to garb a dish rag and then tosses it murky water.

"Takin' care of what, Harold? What are you takin' care of outside of this house? We're barely livin'!" Melinda walks over and mushes the towel under her left foot.

Harold turns down the heat on the stove.

"Don't do it son. The MAN said not to. All powerful. Cruel for no reason. All that sick man wanted was to put a black man down. HE didn't have no ghost cape, but he might as well have. HE was something evil. HE the reason I never learn to read. HE don't want me to read, my kids or my kids' kids neethah. You can't read and yah ain't gone happen. I swear HE will always make sure of it."

His son gulps.

"No one made sure of nothin'." Melinda walks over to her son and picks up his backpack. She grabs the hardcover book and flicks the water away. Placing it under her shoulder, she takes her baby by the arm and ushers him through the kitchen, past the bathroom to his room. The boy makes his way under the covers and Melinda turns on the night light at the head of his bed. She walks back to his side, resting next to his feet. The blue light kisses her smooth skin and the boy feels warm.

"Okay, my child. What have you got here. She ruffles though his bag. "Ah, okay you got flash cards." She leans the cards down to catch more of the light. "*Who. See. Ball. We.* These are those sight words, aren't they?" She lays them on his lap. "Why don't you practice them for mama while I'm at work."

He looks at the cards.

"Well pick them up, why don't you? Baby, it's alright. They're nothin' to be afraid. Don't listen to ya daddy."

"But mama- "

"Don't mama me. You a smart little whip. You know enough to do enough to sound out these sounds. You don't need yo' daddy." She sucked in a deep breath. "You know Frederick Douglass, baby, right?"

The boy nodded with his head down. His eyes still fixated on the cards.

"Yeah, I taught you about Frederick. Man, he didn't need nobody. Frederick had himself. He knew that the only way to be free was to liberate your mind through knowledge," she points to the cards, "through reading, baby. Frederick didn't need his daddy, or no other man to learn to read. Baby you can ignore what he said."

She picks up the cards and places them into his hands.

Her watch catches her eye. "Fu- huh. Baby I gotta go. But you're gone practice, right?"

He sways and doesn't say a word.

"Look at me when I'm talkin' to you."

His eyes glisten into hers. His lips putter.

"There ain't no reason to pout. Everything good comes with challenge," she grabs him by the cheeks. "Baby, you strong. You're brilliant, you can take a challenge. My baby ain't no different, ain't no less capable than Harriet Bailey's baby. But you ain't no slave like Frederick. You ain't goin' be no slave. You gone read for me, right?"

"Yes, mama," the boy says in a whisper.

"What's that? I didn't hear ya," she says with her hands on her hips.

"Yes, mama," he says louder.

"Okay, good." A smile crosses her face and she kisses her baby on both cheeks. She stands up and heads for the door. She pulls it behind her until only a slither wide enough to see her white teeth and one of her mahogany brown iris is left in the crack. "I love you."

He smiles. In a voice, no louder than the wane of faint note, he says, "I love you too."

He hears his mama yelling at his daddy. He hears a crash against the stove. He hears his daddy. He hears his mama curse. He hears her curse some more. He hears stomping. He hears the jingle of keys, the door, the slamming of the door. He hears the door. He hears his daddy say wait. He hears the door. He hears slow scrapping against the floor. He hears the creak of the windowsill as it slides open. He hears muffled sounds, human sounds like a strong cough rumbling through the chest, heaving. He hears something press against what sounds like cabinet doors.

The boy turns to his cards. He lifts them up to the dim blue nightlight. He looks at the signs of letters and his chest heaves. He shuffles the cards in his hands.

A long shadow passes over the crack in his door. The bathroom light floods out across the planks of the hardwood in the hallway. The boy's eyes fixate on the crack in the door.

Suddenly he hears a bursting thud followed by the sound of gushing water emit from the bathroom. The water pounds the bathtub over and over, like gulps from a mouth. It begins to sound soothing. The boy shifts attention back to the cards that lie in his hands.

"Hmm, hmm," he says with each breath. "Okay." The word *See* rest on the cards. He recognizes the S and the E. He thinks back to the alphabet, his mother slithering her arm and hand. "Snake she said, she said snake. Ssssnake. Ssssss." He smiles and then laughs. His eyes move to the next letter. "E, it's the letter e. E makes the sound eee, right? Eee eee?" Sss-Eee-Eee. Seeee?"

He nods his head and his right eyebrow curls closer to his eye like a bunched-up hamster as the feeling of "yes, I got this" washes over him. He places that card closes to his thigh with the same rewarding feeling that he collected his Pokémon cards from his friends.

"Okay, next word." He tightens his lips and squints his eyes at the next word. *Whom.* His top lip rolls out from the bottom like a baby rolling out of bed as he two front teeth clomp down on his plump lower lip. "Double u. Uh. Wwwuh? H. Aa-che. Uh. Aa-che." He nibbles on the corner soft tissue between his cheek and lips. He clenches his teeth. No memory of his mother making these sounds come to him. He bends his legs into crisscross apples sauce. His back bends like a long ruler stick snuck its way into the center of his spine and bent the rest into a straight line. "Uh."

The light in the hallway shuts off. The boy looks to the crack in the door. The boy hears large steps go off into the direction of his parent's room, down the hall a few steps past the bathroom. His parents wall resting aligned with the wall past the end of his bed and behind his toy set area. Hears his father's dressers rustle for a second. Then the boy hears nothing, nothing but the gushing of water echo out from the bathtub, its sounds as constant as the platter of rain on his window or its loud trickle down the street drain. The boy leans it closer to hear the sounds. There is something active, almost lively about the water pouring from the faucet. It drums against the sides of the tub. It sloshes in a rhythm different than before, or so the boy thinks.

"Daddy?" he attempts to say over the sound. His left knee tightens. He hears no response.

"Daddy, are you there?" he calls louder than before. He squeezes the sharp edges of the cards.

"Daddy?" He says in a scream.

Water slithers across the floor, inching its way forward. The water hits the other side of wall and like a blind cobra finding its way to prey, it redirects itself toward his door. The boy looks at the water with a quizzical eye and his breath hitches in an irregular pattern. The sound of sloshing, of steps in sloshing through a deep puddle makes his way to him. His hands tighten around the cards, bending them in half fist.

A voice washes over him. "*Don't you REeeaddeeh. Deh. Deh. Deh.*"

The boy flings the cards at the door. At first they rest above, gliding on top of the surface, searching for the edges of the water. Yet, before they can, they are eaten.

They lay submerged and mangled.

The light in the hallway turns back on. "Ah shit! I forgot about the tub?"

The boy buries himself into his sheets and turns over in his bed gripping his covers. He grips the covers in tight fist. He feels the book Alfred gave him beneath the arch of his left foot. With one strong kick, he pushes it from his bed. "I can't read." His chest quakes as he imagines being put before that lady again to read those words. Tears soak the side of his check and dampen his pillow. His breath slows, his head relaxes, his grip loosens, and his falls asleep.

***

A creak of the door rustles the boy from his sleep. He shifts around in his warm covers to see his mother bent over in the door way. Her tight curls that had been pulled back into a large puff are loose about her head. Some droop like they've been pulled astray.

She's picking up his cards. She gathers them in her hands and stacks them in a pile. She leans up straight, supporting her back with her left arm, pausing to allow the creaks in her back a second to adjust. "Did you even practice your sight words before throwing them across the room?"

"Yes, mama. I did," he says pulling his covers up to his mouth.

"Mhmm," she sighs rolling her eyes. She shakes her head with her eyes closes. Her lips pull tight against her teeth like saranwrap stretched tight against the corners of a baking pan. Her teeth move up and down ever so slightly like she's holding back something. She releases them and her cheeks droop.

He scrunches the tight muscles of his eyebrows. He doesn't know if he should tell his mother about the scary water, about how it slithered to his room and told him not to read. He bites the thick inner portion of his lower lip and just shakes his head. "I can't read, mama."

Her lips compress, squeezed tight in circle and she shakes her head. "Baby it's time to go to school."

She turns away from him and moves towards his dresser. She ruffles through his top drawer for pants and the bottom for a clean shirt. He sees a yellow top with a blue design. There are fish swimming water. He hates this shirt, but he's too afraid to say anything else.

She tosses the clothes on top of the bed.

"I'm going to get your daddy up. Get dressed." She closes his door behind her with a forceful tug. He flinches with its bang.

He stares at his clothes. He wants to roll back under the covers but he knows his mama would be mad then hops out of his bed.

"Harold, get up." He hears the bed frame of his parent's bed shake. "Harold! Harold, I need to sleep. Get up!"

Feet drag against the floor. The fridge door opens. The boy moves from under his covers and grabs the pants his mother gave him. He pulls the yellow shirt up to his face, its pungent hurting making his lips curl. He eyes the water that flows around the fish, that tug at the orange fish that hops away from it, that smothers the blue fish that rest beneath it. He throws the shirt across the room.

"Lil man, come eat!"

He hops out of bed and rustles through his dresser for a different shirt. He sees his black panther print shirt and pulls the soft gray cloth over his head. He goes out into the kitchen and sees a plate resting on the counter with eyes and toast.

His dad is leaning against the counter with his left hand over his face. "Hurry up and eat. Yo' mama don't want you bein' late."

The boy scarfs down his food. He throws the plate in the sink, grabs his coat and rushes out the door.

The school is around the corner. He doesn't have to walk far.

When the boy arrives at the school, he's taken to the room from before. He is placed at the same desk in the same room. A new white booklet is opened to a passage he still doesn't understand.

"Were you able to read with your folks?" Alfred asks.

"No," the boy says flatly.

"That's okay. We'll just start where we left off yesterday," Maurice says pointing to the first word on his test booklet. It one of the words from his flash cards.

His eyes scan the letters W H O–The letters vanish. Reappear.

The thudding resides in his ear. "*Don't you REeeaddeeh. Deh. Deh. Deh.*" Raspy breaths escape the voice.

The coordinator, Alfred, stands above him. "Come on son. You got this."

Sloshing sounds on tip toes like careful feet in water soaked with squeaks like sneakers creep across the floor. "*Don't REeeeaadeh. Deh. Deh. Deh.*" The last eH sound caresses the boys eye lids.

"Don't make me. I can't read. I can't. There's a man. *THE MAN*. You know *THE MAN*"

Alfred and Maurice look at each other. Alfred moves over to the boy and pats his back. "It's okay, little man. We're the only ones here and we got yo' back."

He is tethered to the table again.

The boy sucks sin a deep breath. He opens his mouth and nothing comes out. The water on the wall creeps toward his desk.

"The water," the boy says pointing.

"We'll worry about that later. Focus on this."

The boy hears loud footsteps and his eyes search around Alfred and Maurice but find nothing. Maurice taps the page again with her pen. "Right here. "

"Come on, little man. It's not gonna kil–"

Alfred's left eye twitches. "Where's the boy?" He says looking around.

No one hears. No one sees. The sloshing feet retreat.

GRACE KENT

Sophomore
Major: Public Policy
Reading: Auto Biography Essay

Grace Kent is a sophomore from Ann Arbor, Michigan studying Public Policy and minoring in writing and digital studies. She has a passion for social justice work–specifically in the realm of higher education policy. Grace hopes to dedicate her studies and career path to amplifying voices of marginalized people in the United States through policy and advocacy. In her free time she enjoys listening to classic rock and playing chess.

Nominated by: Elinam Agbo

Tailwinds: A Memoir

"Tilt your head back," my mom would say, as she washed the shampoo out of the bubbly hairdos my sister Celia and I sculpted in the bath. We dreaded when my mom plucked us out of the warm water and into the cold air, but after she dried us off, she put on our soft, fuzzy pajamas–the kind with the little feet in the bottom–and the shivers soon subsided. After she brushed our teeth and combed our hair, we jumped into the same bed. The smell of Johnson & Johnson's baby shampoo still reminds me of my youth. As a family, we always read together before bedtime. At first, our parents read to us. But as time went on, Celia and I shared the reading duties, passing the book around. We laughed out loud to Shel Silverstein's poems and cried at the end of Charlotte's Web. No matter the book, we always sat on the bed together and read peacefully to end the day.

One night, my dad put away the books and said to us, "Tell me a story." Surprised at the change in our cozy routine, I remember asking him what he meant. "Let's make a story," he explained, "Here's a notebook we can write on; each night, we can add two sentences to our story, one from Grace and one from Celia." And like that, my dad's idea developed into our new tradition. Each evening, we read back what we wrote the previous nights. After some time, we had a few paragraphs of a story–a ridiculous, funny, and at times absurd story. Anxious with anticipation, we could hardly wait to read what we created from the beginning–and we laughed so hard our bellies hurt. Even though we added sentences every day that twisted the story in different directions, we also began to notice that what we impacted the story as a whole. Although I did not realize it at the time, it was my first lesson in how to write a meaningful story; it was something more than just stringing a few sentences together. At that age, I did not need to worry about mechanics or sentence structure; mostly, I just wanted to giggle.

The first bedroom I shared with my sister had sloped ceilings, bumpy walls, and smelled of aged wood from the attic behind it. The house, a cozy bungalow, sat on the middle of Beaumont street, where we lived until I turned seven. In the backyard, my parents built a stone bonfire pit, and in the fall, the smell of the smoke from burning leaves would linger on my jacket throughout the season. Our small, friendly neighborhood consisted of modest starter homes. We knew most of our neighbors and considered them friends. Celia and I would stare out our bedroom window each fall, watching the "big kids" walk to the bus stop at the end of the street. When I finally started kindergarten, I proudly carried a pink, princess backpack and walked to the bus stop with the others. Celia waved goodbye with her nose pushed up against the window as tears rolled down her cheeks.

One warm day, the boy from across the street, Nathan, came outside; his curly blonde hair bounced in the sunlight as he strolled over to our house. Celia and I noticed him approach as we drew rainbows with chalk on the driveway. Nathan and I played together before, as he was just two grades older than me. Nathan's father, a fireman, knew my mom from when they attended elementary school and middle school together. I used to watch Nathan ride his shiny red bike back and forth in front of our house, and if I was lucky, he would occasionally look up and smile at me as I stared down from the window. He was one of my first true friends. That day when Nathan walked over to our yard, for some strange reason, I ran back into my house and returned wearing my favorite pink skirt. Nathan then asked me, "How much money do you have in your piggy bank?" I thought the question seemed odd, but I replied, "I think I have sixty-three dollars. Why?" Nathan smiled at me and handed me an old crinkled dollar. "I only have one dollar, but I want to give it to you. Now you have sixty four."

The next summer, my mom got a phone call from the hospital. The woman on the other end of the line asked her a few questions. I could see my mom's face lose its color as she struggled to hold back the tears. My mom turned away from me and Celia so we would not see her cry, and she hung up the phone. We soon learned that Nathan's family had been in a tragic car accident, which killed Nathan and his parents. Nathan's older sisters, who were also in the accident, survived. Given my age and inexperience with death, I could not understand how something so unfair could happen; I could only think of those blonde curls in Nathan's hair that bounced in the sunlight and his bright smile. He gave me his only dollar that summer afternoon, and his kindness stayed with me. Later that year, we moved from our little house on Beaumont street. Nothing felt quite the same after the car accident. We left behind our friendly neighbors and quiet street, but I never forgot warm baths with my sister, bedtime stories with my parents, and most of all, Nathan.

Time passed quickly after we moved from Beaumont street, but I stayed in my same elementary school and progressed through the grades like the rest of the kids. One day, a thin man with a wiry, gray beard came to our class and introduced us to the game of chess. His appearance was that of a wise man, and he offered chess classes before school. My dad, an avid chess player himself, encouraged me to join the Chess Club. In the beginning, the kids who played chess were considered "cool"; however, by 4th or 5th grade most kids found new interests, like "wall-ball" or valued the extra hours of sleep, more than another chess lesson from the wise man. Although the Chess Club fell out of fashion, the game never grew old to me. Growing up, I enjoyed chess because it allowed me to spend more time with my dad, a geek for brain games who never turned down a good game of chess. We owned a large, wooden chess table where my dad and I sat and played each night. I loved that chess board because the pieces felt large and heavy in my hands. I formed a habit of rubbing the soft green felt on the bottom of each wooden piece as I pondered each move. There, I taught myself to close my eyes and identify each unique piece by the shape of its wooden carvings in my hand. Sometimes, after I made a foolish move, my dad would look up at me with a sly, "game over" kind of smile and allowed me to take the piece back or rethink my move. As I got older, he permitted "take backs" less and less, and I had to live with my mistakes. We kept a running tally of our games, and the score on the whiteboard where my dad and I tallied our wins and losses tilted heavily in his favor. Later that year, I realized our chess games served as more than just nightly entertainment. At times I fell badly behind and wanted to quit, but my dad told me to fight back with what I had left. Other times, I would move impulsively or impatiently, without considering the board or thinking about the consequences. As I grew older, the metaphors and lessons were unmistakable. The game consisted of many subtleties that I found paradoxical. I learned that what appears to be a loss in the moment can result in success later. From my nightly matches with my dad, I discovered that sacrificing one apparently insignificant pawn could lead to the possibility of success later in the game, just as one setback in my own young life had the potential to lead to greater success later in life. I just needed to persevere and learn from my mistakes.

Lessons in perseverance motivated me as my elementary school career came to a close. My mom echoed the same principles I learned in chess, as she taught me how to become a runner. She had been a competitive runner since age seven and she wanted me to experience the same excitement for running that she did. She encouraged me to sign up for my first 5K race, which she warned was longer than I thought it would be and had a large hill towards the finish. In order to prepare, we trained for weeks by running loops around the streets in our new neighborhood, but I struggled to find the excitement she wanted to share. One street, Bethany Circle, had a particularly steep hill. My mom always made sure that our loop finished with Bethany Circle, and we would prepare for the feat by telling ourselves, "If you can do Bethany Circle, you can do anything." As the weather got colder, we pressed forward. We covered our ears with headbands and put on our knit gloves. My mother and I ran side-by-side through the neighborhood and breathed in the frigid air that seemed to paralyze our lungs. Even though I wanted to walk up the Bethany Circle hill many times, with my mom by my side, it was never an option. She told me that hills allowed me to catch people in the race. She said, "Imagine you are a fisherman. Cast out your pole and snag the person in front of you. Reel them in slowly as you run up the hill." I used this tactic when she ran alongside me in my first 5K race, and I felt amazed at how many fish I caught on that hill. When I crossed the finish line, I experienced the salty, sweaty taste of success, and I knew there would be more races in my future. I ran the entire race without stopping, and I knew it was because my mom believed in me. We ran dozens of races together after that. I even kept my paper bib from every 5K I ran, each a trophy for our perseverance. But most importantly, my parents taught me to believe that things like "Bethany Circle," a game of chess, or so many other challenges in life can be overcome with hard work, dedication, and a willingness to pursue the talents that I have been given, for which I am so grateful.

Now that I am in college, I am beginning to more fully understand the complexity of life's "challenges." In the spring before I began college, I met my dad at a coffee shop near our house where he liked to read the *New York Times* while I did homework. This particular day, he handed me an article to read called, *To Help Tackle Inequality, Remember the Advantages You've Had*, by Sendhil Mullainathan, which I kept. The article addressed the issues of economic inequality and the uneven distribution of wealth in the United States. Mullainathan asserted that although the problem is quite obvious, there is little agreement on how to close the rather wide gap between those who have and those who do not. "Do we need to level the playing field so that people born to modest circumstances have a better chance? Should we be trying to instill a stronger work ethic in the United States?" But his use of the metaphor "headwinds" and "tailwinds" when thinking about privilege is what captivated me the most. "Most of our time and energy goes toward overcoming the challenges immediately in front of us. Headwinds demand attention because they must be overcome. Tailwinds may evoke a momentary sense of well-being and gratitude; but primarily, they free us to focus elsewhere, on challenges that must be overcome." I sat in the coffee shop that evening and thought of the many tailwinds in my life that propelled me in the right direction. Mullainathan's article talked not just about policy and political divide; but about looking at life from an unfamiliar perspective. He reminded me that even wealthy or privileged people with loving families can look back on their lives and remember the things that stood in their way. But he also reminded me that we do not often enough look back on our lives through the lens of humility. I gripped the article tightly, because it consumed me with overwhelming gratitude. I began to understand that my successes in life are not only attributed to my own hard work, but they are also aided by significant tailwinds, such as my supportive family, exceptional educational opportunities, and financial stability. I no longer took for granted our polished wooden chess board or my daily runs with my mom. This small, sudden realization motivated me to think more compassionately about others who lack the tailwinds from which I have benefitted.

As life progresses, I will add to my story piece-by-piece, like I did with my sister and parents, until I eventually come to a point where I am satisfied with my accomplishments. Or perhaps I will never be satisfied. Mom taught me to conquer the hills and to keep my mind positive. From my dad, I learned that every match requires two players, just like success in life requires help from others. As I travel through life, just as I advance my pieces across the chessboard, I will remember my dad's advice to not be afraid and to make bold moves. Now, when I look at the tally marks on the whiteboard, I understand better that the word "checkmate" means more than simply winning or losing–it means that I played the game. For me, it also means there will be other opportunities to learn, reflect, and improve–and maybe even a chance to even up the tally on that whiteboard someday. From Nathan, I learned to give what I have. And from from my parents, I have learned to graciously accept what I have been given and to never take for granted life's warm baths.

EMMA KILLEEN

Senior
Major: Fine Arts
Reading: Non-Fiction

Emma Killeen is a senior in the Stamps School of Art and Design with a focus in graphic design. Growing up in the suburbs of Chicago with a permanent book in her face, Emma writes mostly for fun and self-expression. When she's not working on North Campus until the break of dawn, one could find Emma walking through the Arb with headphones on full blast, perusing the frozen aisle at Trader Joe's, or taking a power nap. Upon graduating this Spring, Emma hopes to pursue a career in advertising and will miss U of M dearly.

Nominated by: Erika Nestor

Housekeeping (excerpt)

An excerpt from short story: **Housekeeping**

Like she had every day for the last fifty years, Marie had let her coffee go cold. The stuff tasted like mud anyways. She'd coyly sip at her lukewarm cup during her fifteen minutes off and then head out for a smoke. The plastic yellow chair where she'd always sit had become chipped and sagging with time but Marie didn't mind, it was just nice to get her calloused feet off the ground for a few blissful moments. While she sat, she made a mental list: Room 212, 421, and 302 had all just checked out, floor six still needed their sheets and towels, and the main bathrooms needed a quick run through. Oh, and there was a stain in 231 that required tending to. Marie took a long draw from her cigarette and stamped it out on the pavement. Slowly pushing herself out of the hard chair, she sighed. Her rough hands fanned over her starchy white apron and stiff chartreuse dress. It clung to her plushy waist and hanging breasts, biting tight at her neck. With no prevail, she pulled at the itchy white collar.

Worn down with time, her black Reebok sneakers made no sound as Marie trudged down the hallway to find her cart. Her back, hunched from years of scrubbing at toilets, was especially sore today. Her usually strong arms felt weak and her eyelids heavy. As she made her way down the hall Marie could hear snippets of life coming from within the passing rooms. A baby crying, a woman laughing, a phone ringing, a bed thumping. Like every day, Marie wondered where these people were coming from and where they were headed. She imagined entire lives for the people behind these doors, both glamourous and tragic. Sometimes as she was cleaning, she would pretend to be one of them, a visitor at the hotel for a night or two and then off into the world to some exotic location or quaint cottage home. She never let her mind wander too far though, for her daydreams only made reality sting more.

The "Do Not Disturb" sign was always a slap in the face for Marie. What it meant was another room added to her to-do list. It also meant another couple sound asleep inside, living the life she wished she had. With a sigh, she moved on to the room next door. After three unanswered knocks and one rehearsed "housekeeping!", Marie let herself in. The stench from room 212 pummeled Marie as soon as she cracked the door. It was like a mix of old cheese, sewage, and sex. Like most guests, they had left their towels scattered everywhere, the was bed ripped apart, and there were wrappers on top of every table and surface. It had seemed as though these particular guests were holed up here for about a month, surviving off of the hotel's room service menu. Stacks of crusted plates and oily cups lined the floor. There had to be about twenty serving trays strewn about the room. There were countless stale coffees and thick creamers, rock-hard breads, egg-coated dishes, and old, soft fruit. Maybe this was the reason for the silverware shortage in the kitchen below? Furiously pulling on her elbow-high rubber gloves, Marie knew she had her work cut out for her.

ANNIE LEMBERG

Senior
Major: Psychology
Reading: Fiction

Annie Lemberg is a fiction writer and poet studying at the University of Michigan, Ann Arbor. Her work is heavily influenced by the autobiographical, drawing on topics of chronic illness, sexuality, and love in a physical body that can be as much a challenge to inhabit as it can to understand.

Nominated by: Patricia O'Dowd and James Cody Walker

Fourteen

I did not think Spencer Shane was cool just because he smoked cigarettes. He liked cool music, too. And he played the drums, and he let me play his drum set sometimes, and he didn't think I was cool just because I was the only girl at school who had tits yet.

Almost every night that summer, the summer after eighth grade, we smoked in the Church of Latter Day Saints parking lot. Spence thought it was so funny because mormons are all pricks who don't even drink coffee or anything. He totally got irony, and that kind of thing.

We'd walk through the high grass next to the road and get fat, hot bug bites, so I wore tight jeans despite the sticky humidity. Spence used to say I looked cute when I wore those jeans. I guess he couldn't see me sweating in the dark.

"If my parents caught me, they'd ground me, for at least a year," Jason said. He was a short, skinny boy who held himself curled inward. He always wore a bright green baseball cap, and I suspected it was meant to distract people from the rest of him. He was my best friend Serena's neighbor. When we were little kids, the three of us'd spend the summer having water balloon wars. The thought of mentioning something so dorky now was mortifying.

"If my dad caught me, he'd for sure hit me," Pat replied, his thin lips parting to release a dark gray cloud into the glassy sky.

Spence hooked his arm around me where we sat, hunched in the grass below his friends. Beside us, mosquitos frenzied around a dirty orange-ish light mounted to the side of a shed. I breathed in the scent of boy deodorant and late summer heat.

"Bullshit," Spence said. "If your dad cared, he'd've beat up Jesse like a million times already." Jesse was Pat's older brother, and a bonafide delinquent. "What about you, Joanie?"

"Me? Oh, my God," I said. "My parents'd kill me."

"No way," Pat scoffed, showing his small, pointy teeth. "They wouldn't *kill* you." He said *kill* like he was pretending to be a girl—the stupidest-sounding girl in the world.

"C'mon, don't laugh at her." Spence flicked dying embers onto the pavement.

"So what about you?" Jason asked him.

"What?"

"What'd your parents do?"

Spence stood up and shrugged. "Who cares."

"Oh, come on!" Pat whined. "You're not going, are you?"

"Yeah, we are." Spence grabbed my hand and lifted me out of the grass. I had nearly half my cigarette left—my last one—but I tossed it away without a thought.

Spence and Pat checked shoulders as we walked past, and I knew it meant they were fine. That was just how boys talked.

*   *   *

Jesse was the slimiest fuck I'd ever met—which, I guess, is probably why he sold us loose cigarettes. He had a rusted-out blue Jeep, a ratty beard, and a beautiful red-headed girlfriend named Lindsay Buckley he'd been cheating on since the seventh grade. Legend was Jesse had her name tattooed on his ass, which Pat swore was true (though I think Pat would've said anything his brother told him to say). Therefore, Jesse was *cool*.

I didn't get it. But when Spence invited me along to meet him, I didn't say no.

It was a Friday in September. Fallen leaves and litter swirled around our feet. The second week of high school, and already we were making shady trades in the school parking lot. Nobody said it, but we all felt bad—just the kind of bad we thought we ought to be.

Jesse was parked in the farthest corner of the lot, his Jeep still running as he leaned out the open driver's side door, radio blaring some heavy metal song. He wore a lopsided, brown leather jacket and posed in it like he thought he was an action star.

"Who's your new friend?"

"She's not my friend," Pat replied. "She's Spencer's."

Behind his own back, Spence grabbed my hand while Pat and Jesse made the transaction.

"Spencer, you got yourself a girlfriend?" Jesse asked while Pat hid the cigs in his backpack.

"Yeah," Spence said. "I guess."

You *guess*?

"Huh. She's cute. I guess." Jesse grinned. "You haven't fucked her, though, have you?"

"You know I'm standing right here, don't you, asshole?" I stepped toward him, rolling up my sleeves: my best impression of someone older and more intimidating.

"Woah," Jesse laughed. "See, she's got a mouth." He pointed at Spence. "You should use that."

"Fucking creep," I spat.

"Shut up, Joanie," Pat snarled. "That's my brother."

"You want my advice, Spencer? One and done." Jesse made an "okay" sign with his grubby fingers and repeated himself, each word falling deliberately from his curled lips. His jagged smile was the same as Pat's, only wider. "One. And. Done." Then he shut the car door and pulled off, leaving us in his dirty, gray fumes.

"Yeah," Pat jeered, throwing his backpack over his shoulder. "One and done!" He stalked off, shaking his close-cropped head and sneering at me with those little teeth. Spence looked back at me for a moment, and I could see something flicker in his wide hazel eyes, magnified under his thick, black-framed glasses. Then he dropped my hand to follow Pat.

"You're going *with* him?"

"C'mon, Joanie," he groaned. "You can't talk to Jesse that way."

"I *can't*?"

He jogged up to Pat. I gritted my teeth and ran towards home. Nobody was gonna see me cry.

* * *

That Sunday I turned fourteen. Around the kitchen table with my parents, evening light through the bay window thin and gray on the pink walls, I tore silver foil away from a shoebox: the combat boots I'd asked for. Mom urged me to try them on with her typical pep—*Give us a runway walk*—and I dragged my feet across the crisp, white-tiled floor. Dad didn't say much at all, his mouth hidden behind a bushy mustache; he just lit the candles. But later, I could hear him downstairs, calling her names and pacing the living room with his bullish footsteps.

They were always like this, acting as if everything was fine until I was just out of sight—as if it made any difference. I think we'd need walls at least ten times thicker to drown out the way Dad yelled.

Mom was quiet as a mouse, and she cooked better than anybody's mom, and she never went out past eight at night unless she was running errands for Dad, so I don't know what the hell was wrong with him that made him call her grimy names like *whore*. But Mom never asked me for help. And once he was done shouting at her, she never mentioned it to me. I thought she might've been embarrassed, so I tried my best to pretend I never noticed the fighting at all.

When Serena arrived for my birthday sleepover, we talked about anything and everything else.

"He sounds like a jerk right now," she said, after my third dramatic rendition of how Spence'd pissed me off.

We were close to falling asleep, lightly touching foreheads with a half-empty popcorn bowl nestled between our full stomachs. We were watching the first season of *The X-Files* (again), and the inside of a walk-in freezer on screen beamed icy blue all over the white ceiling, paling the black-and-red smears of band posters on my walls. Mulder and Scully were stranded at the North Pole with three scientists, and one of them was infected with an evil alien worm.

"What if I love him?" I asked.

"Well, do you?" Serena's purple eyeliner twinkled in the frigid TV-screen light when she cocked her head to look at me, the ends of her short black hair scattered across her cheeks. Her heavy, dark eyes had always made her look solemn, even when we were little girls.

"How're you supposed to know?"

"I wouldn't know." Serena sighed.

Serena'd never had a boyfriend, and I could tell that hearing about mine frustrated her. She was more concerned that she and I no longer painted our nails, made playlists or screamed Diet Cig songs in the bathroom as often. I wondered whether she was secretly glad Spence might be gone soon.

But Spence wasn't like that all the time. I knew things about him that he told no one else—not Pat, not Jason, *never* Jesse: the way his parents fought, the movies that really scared him, the little brown box of seashells that he kept in the back of his closet. He let me hold them, and I touched their pearly insides so tenderly. They were delicate as the insides of ears.

I closed my eyes. Serena plucked the wide glass bowl out from between us, set it on the floor, and put her arms around me.

"Maybe you love him," Serena said.

"Maybe," I whispered.

"You're fourteen, J."

"I can't believe we're in high school."

"I guess we're getting old."

"Is this how it feels?" I asked.

On the first night of my fourteenth year, Serena and I fell asleep intertwined.

* * *

Spence and I didn't speak in school the next day. Instead, he dropped a note in my locker: *Oak and Maple. 12:30. -S.*

It was the same corner where we'd often met, but always with Pat and Jason in tow. The sight of Spence, alone, kicking pebbles under the yellow cone of a streetlight was oddly funny.

"Hey." I could tell I'd surprised him when he turned to face me. I wondered if he hadn't expected me to show.

"Hey," he breathed more than spoke, approaching me with his hands planted deep in his blue-jean pockets. Spence was tall for our age and not quite grown into it, so slender like boys can be. Hanging his shaggy head, he was like a flimsy stalk of wheat. I couldn't stay angry. "I wanted to show you someplace new," he said.

He led me a few blocks away, through a small thicket of evergreens and over a short wall. Beyond the wall was a wide lawn, dotted here and there with pink blurs of flowerbeds. I realized we must be on the grounds of Oakwood Academy, the fancy private high school in our town.

Following Spence through the grass in the dark, I got my shoelace tangled in a bunny fence. A fat moth whisked softly past my face. One lamppost stood, glowing, above the cool, wet grass like a tall stranger.

When we reached a clearing, he stopped. A half-moon of stone benches was strung around a big white credenza—the kind of place they have weddings, I think. We sat on a bench, and I felt the edge of its chill through my jeans. The road wasn't far, but the rumblings of passing cars felt distant.

"I'm sorry," he said quietly.

"For what?" I asked.

"My friends."

Looking at him I recognized, once again, the boy that I wanted him to be. I couldn't love the mean, spineless boy in the school parking lot, running away with his narrow back turned—but I might've loved the humbled one waiting for me to kiss him, his blond hair turned pale as pewter in the almost-dark.

"Happy birthday," he said. From his sweatshirt pocket, he produced a brand new pack of Camel reds, still wrapped in shiny plastic, and a skinny, black eyeliner pencil.

The way he held them stunned me. It was the same way he'd held his seashells: so carefully and sheepishly. You could tell he was handling more than just objects. I stared momentarily before I reached out to take them.

I rolled the pencil between my fingers in one hand, and felt the unexpectedly light weight of the cigarettes in the other. "Where'd you get these?"

"Don't sweat it," he said.

"Jesse didn't make you do some fucked-up shit, did he?" I pressed.

"No, Joanie. Nothing like that." He looked me in the eye, and I looked hard into his, trying to read every green-brown filament though the microscope lenses of his glasses. I trusted him. I kissed him.

On the second night of my fourteenth year, we parted hands on Oak Street. I walked the last two blocks home with light feet in my new boots, renewed by the white splash of each porch light that touched my face.

* * *

It was the third night of my fourteenth year that became a problem.

There was thunder that night, but it didn't rain. It was just hot—the kind of hot that made my lip sweat and my bangs curl. I laced up my new boots. I smeared on the eyeliner Spence had given me.

Squeezing out the basement window at 1AM, I flopped into the crispy, half-brown grass outside like a fish. When I stood up I saw the clouds, almost red against the deep purple sky and the heavy, yellow three-quarters moon.

The woodchip path through the woods was no secret, but late at night it felt like one. Every kid in town knew it led to the spot—the spot that every cute, little suburban town has—where you went to smoke weed and buy handle-pulls of Crystal Palace off senior boys on Saturday nights. The spot was *cool*, and that's exactly what I wanted this night to be.

When I reached the mouth of the woods, I opened the pack of cigarettes Spence had given me and broke the plastic seal to reveal two neat rows of perfect, styrofoam-white filters smiling at me. Their warm, familiar scent floated up my nostrils. I ran a finger delicately over each of the cigarettes, soft and papery, before selecting one from the middle and lighting it up.

I'd envisioned this moment all day in school, and all evening while I'd pretended to study algebra, waiting for Mom and Dad to fall asleep. Puffing casually as I strolled, my shredded Green Day shirt wrapped around every curve I'd grown into so far, I imagined fourteen must've looked good on me.

As I turned to cross the wooden footbridge over the creek, I startled. There was the red glow of embers pinpointing the air—someone was leaned against the railing, the smell of weed mixing with tobacco.

"Well, look at that." Jesse laughed.

"Look at what?" I was suddenly furious at him for tainting my night.

"What're you supposed to be?" He looked me up and down, from my sweat-smeared eyeliner to my shiny new boots.

"Fuck off." My quaking fingers betraying me, I clenched a fist.

Jesse sauntered toward me, the easy swing of his arms taunting me with cool calm. The screeching of cicadas, invisible in the trees, saturated every breath of the wet night air.

"You know why they're so loud like that?"

I didn't say a word.

"It's 'cause they're fucking."

"I don't believe you."

"Yeah, it is."

"It's not."

"No?"

Jesse lunged and put his big, hairy arms around me. He smelled like tobacco and wet dirt. Then he stank like rancid meat. I hadn't thought–I'd just stuck him with it.

He shoved me back and I fell on my ass. When I looked up I saw him crying, holding the side of his face. My cigarette was at his feet, crushed. His eyes looked just like the smoldering ruby butt, with tendrils of smoke curling out of it like fur rising on haunches.

"*Cunt!*" he moaned, cradling his wounded cheek in his right hand.

And then he ran, kicking up wood chips behind him, disappearing down the shadowed path, the crash of his boots fading into cicada screams, until the only sign he'd been there at all was the stench of scorched skin that lingered on the thick, humid air.

My feet were leaden as I walked home. I sucked down another cigarette. My throat ached. In my head I pictured it red and swollen and throbbing.

When I squirmed back in through the basement window and plunged into the cool cement darkness, my skin felt even slimier with sweat and grease than it had in the oppressive heat outside. Hair clung to my neck. I slithered out of my clothes and snuck upstairs in my underwear, feeling suddenly stupid in my C-cup, rainbow bra.

As I passed the kitchen, a thin beam of light from the open dryer, overflowing with a load of brightly colored dish towels, penetrated the dimness with an alien blue glow. I couldn't understand the sight of it. It didn't look like my house at all.

* * *

Jesse wasn't in school the next day. I looked for him around every corner I passed; in the senior hallway; at Lindsay Buckley's locker. Instead I found her alone, brushing her long, copper hair in a small magnetic mirror.

At lunch, I sat on a high brick wall and looked for Jesse's rusty Jeep in the crackled gray parking lot, checking between every faded yellow line, but the Jeep was nowhere. I thought that maybe I'd somehow dissolved him, turned him to ash and scattered him to the trees–or maybe I'd only imagined him in the first place.

"You gonna come in and eat?" It was Serena, standing on the pavement below me.

"Not hungry," I called back.

She sighed and scrambled up the cold, red wall to sit beside me. I thought she looked so cool with her fluffy black skirt bouncing around her, as she climbed without so much as scuffing her purple tights. I always hoped other kids thought I was brave because I acted tough and hung out with boys, but sometimes I wished I was brave in the girly way that Serena was. I was too embarrassed to wear dresses and glittery eye makeup—I worried I'd look like a little kid dressed up in an older girl's clothes.

Serena's dangly silver earrings twinkled in the commotion of her dark, bobbed hair. "You okay?"

"You heard anything about where Jesse is?" I asked.

She scrunched up her small nose. "Jesse? What d'you need him for?"

"Just wondering if he's sick, or whatever."

"Yeah, you'd like that, wouldn't you?" Serena laughed, and aimed little mock punch at my ribs. I laughed in return and stuffed my fists into the pockets of my hoodie, pulling it tight around my chest.

"Is it about Spencer?" she asked.

"Kinda," I mumbled.

"I don't know why you wanna hang out with those stupid guys anyway," Serena said, crossing her arms.

"I don't think they're stupid," I retorted, even though it wasn't entirely true.

"Prove it," she taunted, to which I had no good response.

Jesse was gone all that week. With every new day, his absence felt blacker and hotter to me like a hole burning through paper. Of course nobody asked me where he might be—how would I know, anyway? Actually, nobody asked about him at all. Truancy hardly clashed with his image.

I should've been glad; I never wanted to see his ugly Neanderthal face again. But in all the silence surrounding him, something pushed and pushed against the inside of my chest, but couldn't emerge: something that felt like the truth, but was not a sentence I could speak; something that felt like the memory of his hard green eyes pressing right into mine, though I wasn't sure I'd ever really seen it.

* * *

It was a Sunday. Spence and I were alone in his room very late that night, or very early the next morning, depending on what you want to call it. My parents assumed I was asleep at in my own bed.

"Spence?" I whispered.

"Yes?" He sounded almost afraid to reply, as if his voice might've broken some delicate and essential piece of the moment's machinery.

"Should—should we have sex?"

We were listening to The Strokes to cover the sound of our conversation, and touching hands feverishly, each of our fingers bobbing and weaving between the other's. I liked the way they looked together.

I wasn't a prude or anything; I'd thought about this before. We weren't in middle school anymore, after all—going out with a guy meant something different now.

And a guy'd never love you enough to get your name tattooed on him if you didn't put out. I knew that much.

In my imagination, I'd never played out exactly how things might look. I never pictured the glowing red light of Spence's PC tower staining the wall beside us, or the surprised expression on his face, or even myself spread out on his navy bedspread. Mostly I imagined what would happen afterwards.

We'd step outside, and each have a cigarette. I'd feel like a woman in a movie—like I was projected twelve feet tall in Spence's backyard, the autumn moonlight hitting us all orange and sideways.

And sometimes I imagined his hands. I thought of him gingerly peeling the lid off his brown box of seashells, the first time he showed them to me; I thought of him handing me my birthday cigarettes in the garden. That was how he'd use his hands to touch me, I thought.

But in reality, Spence reached his hands behind my back, and I couldn't see them anymore. I didn't know what I was meant to feel but I closed my eyes and hoped this was it.

At my suggestion, we had a smoke after. It felt like the thing people were supposed to do. I smoked mine down to the filter, watching the red-hot core move down it in a column, imagining it burning all the way to my lips like a fuse and setting me off.

Spence walked me home, and he kissed me goodbye at the end of my street.

"See you tomorrow," I said, though it was certainly morning then. I'd see him again in a few hours, at school, my eyelids falling shut in first period.

"Good night," he said, before he turned to leave.

I wanted to tell him that I loved him, but not as much as I wanted to hear him say it to me.

Tucked into my own bed, my light-up globe kept total darkness at bay, bathing my sheets in familiar ocean blue; I'd gotten it as a Christmas gift when I was three years old. I called Serena, even though we always texted and I was sure she'd be asleep.

The phone rang and rang. Then a robotic voice meant to sound like a woman told me I'd reached Serena's number: *Leave your message after the tone.* I hung up the phone but I clung to it between my breasts—just in case she might call me back, although of course she didn't.

I just wanted to hear her voice, any voice besides the one in my head that sneered relentlessly, *One and done, one and done. One. And. Done.*

* * *

Serena was wicked mad at me. It'd been three days since I'd lost my virginity, and I'd been avoiding her without saying why. She'd sent me a text message like an English essay, a whole thesis statement and three body paragraphs on how I was being a bitch and keeping secrets.

I didn't mean to ignore her. I just didn't know how explain how Jesse had touched me and made me feel like Mulder and Scully stranded at the North Pole full of alien worms, or how Spence had touched me afterwards and somehow made me feel nothing at all.

It was like someone had pulled my plug and drained me. It was like the nuclear apocalypse of my feelings. It was like the only thing left inside me were cockroaches, and it didn't even tickle as they crept around my hollow insides. So instead of telling my best friend about it, I went to Jason's house to play video games.

"God dammit!" Pat shrieked, throwing his controller at the ground. We were playing Mortal Kombat–a two-player game, tournament style–and he'd just been beaten by a girl (again). On-screen, my character ripped off her pink veil, revealing a mouthful of monstrous, razor-sharp teeth which she used to shred the jugular of Pat's character.

I looked over my shoulder at Spence and Jason on the couch behind me. Jason's basement was real small, and all wood-paneled and green-fuzzy-carpeted because his house was old. His mom called it "retro." The boys were sitting as far apart as possible, desperately avoiding even the faintest appearance of cuddling, and their shoulders almost brushed the walls.

"Who's next? I taunted.

"I am," Spence announced, bouncing off his couch cushion and onto the floor beside me.

"I think we should have an all boys tournament," Pat said, pretending feebly not to pout.

"You're just mad 'cause my girlfriend kicked your ass," Spence gloated, tossing his arm around me. He was like a new guy since we'd had sex, always touching me in public and calling me his girl. I thought if we'd done it sooner, he never would've followed Jesse and Pat out of the school parking lot.

"Losing runs in the family, huh?" Jason teased, making himself giggle.

Pat promptly punched Jason in the shoulder. "Shut up," he grumbled.

I felt my hands freeze around my controller. "What're you guys talking about?" I said, trying to sound casual. I didn't dare look anyone in the eye. I just stared at the TV screen.

"Jesse totally lost a fight," Jason said. "Like, a for real fight." He sounded thrilled by the thought of it.

"Whatever!" Pat yelped, collapsing onto the couch beside Jason. "The other guy must've been, like, humongous. And he fought dirty, anyways."

"That's why Jesse's cuttin' school," Jason said smugly, adjusting the brim of his bright green hat. "He's got a big black eye and he's totally embarrassed."

Spence was engrossed in the character select screen. Looking at him from the side, I could see the protruding curve of his thick glasses, bending light in a hundred directions at once that made the world inside them look strange and swirly to me. This conversation meant nothing to him. My throat felt bad, real bad again—like I'd smoked one too many cigs in the hot, hot humid woods.

"It's *not* a black eye," Pat said with a scoff. "You don't know *anything*, Jason."

"Oh, shit!" I exclaimed. "I just remembered—I gotta be home for dinner."

"It's only five," Spence said, puzzled.

"Early dinner," I said, tossing my backpack over my shoulder and running up the stairs without looking back. Spence had started kissing me goodbye everywhere I went. I just couldn't take it then. "See ya!" I let my words tumble down the stairs behind me. I didn't really care where they landed.

*   *   *

I ignored the feather-light taps on my bedroom door until it opened, ribboning the dark with yellow light from the hallway. I didn't want to see anything. I'd even unplugged my light-up globe.

"Joanie?" Mom whispered. "You're already asleep? It's only eight."

"No," I said into my pillow.

"Somebody's here for you," she said, flicking on the lights.

I sat up in bed to look at Mom. Her all-gray pajamas hung loose on her skinny frame, but you could still tell she was so pretty. She had a perfect nose, and neatly curled blonde hair. But when I saw her standing there, timid even in the threshold of her little girl's room, I realized it meant nothing. Dad could do anything he wanted to her, and nobody would stop him.

"Who's here?" I asked.

When I saw Jason waiting for me on the front porch, I realized our outfits matched: light blue jeans and big black sweatshirts. We were twins except for his green baseball hat, which he fidgeted with while he talked.

"You left this at my house today," he said, holding out my bulky graphing calculator, unmistakably covered in peeling dinosaur stickers. I'd had it since the sixth grade.

"Oh, jeez. Thanks," I said, taking it from him, careful not to brush his hand.

"Yeah..."

I didn't understand why he was really there. I didn't understand anything. I just wanted him to go away so I could cry.

"Serena's worried about you," he said suddenly, looking down at his feet pulling the brim of his hat down low.

"What?" I said, dumbstruck.

"She asked me if you were doin' okay, so I thought I'd come see ya," he explained. If he was trying to look me in the eye, I wouldn't've known. I stared down at the chunky black calculator in my hands, as if it might suggest something for me to say.

I swallowed hard. "I didn't even know you guys talked," I said.

"Well, yeah...not so much anymore. But yeah. Like, she's my neighbor."

This was the feeling that made me never want to talk to anyone again: like I was digging around in my brain for what I was meant to feel and not finding anything at all. I think Jason could tell I was feeling it too, because he just kept talking.

"Y'know, I heard about what Jesse said to ya. And how Spencer and Pat ran away–like idiots. I think they're idiots. I would've told Jesse to shove it."

Finally, I looked up at Jason. I thought it might've been the first time I saw his whole head of messy, rust-colored hair. He had his hat in his hands, drumming his fingers softly along its bright green brim. He was so shrimpy and hunched-over he was almost concave.

"Jesse'd kill you if you did that," I said.

"He's just big 'cause he repeated the seventh grade," Jason said, grinning weakly.

I smiled. "Thanks for the calculator. I better go."

"Yeah," Jason said as he replaced his baseball cap, obscuring his pale blue eyes in shadow. "G'night, Joanie."

I stepped inside and locked the front door behind myself. For a moment, I didn't feel so utterly untouchable. I wouldn't be able to remember exactly how many days it had been since my fourteenth birthday for some time, but I remember now. It was only seven.

I thought I ought to call Serena, since she was so worried. But when I got back into bed and gathered the covers around myself, I couldn't shake the thought of myself being cut open longways, throat to pelvis, and bleeding out frozen blue light. I wondered what two fourteen-year-old girls could really do for each other. I wondered if a moment's feeling changes anything at all.

Jesse came to school the next day. I saw him from the end of the senior hallway, leaning up against the blue lockers, the way boys do on TV when they know they're cool. He had a hot red scar on his left cheek, and Lindsay Buckley was kissing it.

LIAM LOOMER

Senior
Major: BFA - Acting
Minor: Playwriting
Reading: Excerpt

Liam was born in Ann Arbor, and has lived in Michigan his entire life—a fact he can't wait to change. Although he studies acting, his main passion is writing for screen and stage. As a writer, he's most concerned with writing about themes surrounding mental health, and promoting diversity and inclusivity through his work.

Nominated by: Jose Casas

FALL

"We could slip away, wouldn't that be better
Me with nothing to say, and you in your autumn sweater."
- Ira Kaplan

autumn is the superior season.

the leaves show their age
and the trees harden
preparing for abrasive chills.

like a small child, i recall the colors:
orange
red
yellow
purple
saturate the world with brilliant splendor--
a dull observation.

air refuses to settle
coarse wind brings with it
an invigorating cold to the face.

have you ever looked at yourself in the mirror and realized how ugly you are
how you're not as charming as you think you are
how alone you are
but that's okay

it has to be okay.
i don't complain. i state facts.

in the stillness and purgatory between near sleep and the hell of waking, have you ever felt like you were falling and jolted yourself up again? have you felt the feeling of weightlessness and the dread of imminent impact? it happens to me about once a week. its at these moments when i'm most alive--eyes wide, heart thumping, sweat pooling, total awareness of my surroundings.
everything's okay. it didn't happen.
my head falls back to my pillow and i remember that nothing interesting ever happens, and the appearance of interest is just an illusion caused by my brain fucking with itself.

it's called a hypnagogic jerk, or hypnic jerk.
hypnic jerk.

i want that to be my nickname.

i don't do well with heights.

i stand thirty stories up
a height i can only guess
by watching mites dancing below.
the thick sheen of glass prevents forward, ill-advised action. my dull heart quivers. i can feel my momentum before me, my chest hurtling towards oblivion
a galvanized mush of bone and gore and concrete
everything's okay. it didn't happen.
i stand safe
slack-jawed
clammy palmed
anxiety churning the blood.

when you fall, does your body meet the ground or does the ground meet your body?
or do they meet each other
two contrasting beings attracted
both yearning for the other's release?

my body needs to reconnect with the earth it came from

in those moments at night when i'm about to earn my nickname, i imagine that i experience what leaves must feel as they fall from their once-trusted positions.

gentle arc, riding the air, nimbly tossing and turning

time becomes eternal
what do you think of on the way down?
what can't you think of on the way down?
whose face do you remember last on the way down?
it only lasts a few seconds

the leaf lands gently, collecting with the millions that had fallen before it

is there a morbid comfort knowing you're not alone for once?

look back up at the great distance from your old branch:
how terrifying that must be to fall away from everything you've ever known.

oh shit oh shit oh shit oh shit oh shit oh shit oh shit oh--
everything's okay. it didn't happen.
at least the view was beautiful

DROWN

"The calm,
Cool face of the river
Asked me for a kiss."
- Langston Hughes

stand above the rushing water
bough of the tree bends, creaks
could i be the next Ophelia
crowning myself in the rush of the river?

drowning is the perfect metaphor for the depressed brain
waves upon waves of doubt crash against a once resilient shore
a grand resort reduced to a shanty town
the lacquer and sheen of false greatness eroded
the inadequacies and failure visible
a torrent, a tempest, a tsunami|
batters the solitary island
fractured into thousands of unidentifiable islets.

when you play with the ocean
be wary of the undertow
sometimes the sea forgets its strength.

i love swimming but pools terrify me. You heard right. i can't bear the sight of me without a shirt on. the body of fifty year old man left in the bath for too long: saggy yet bloated, all fat no muscle. thank you genes and general laziness.
ten years old, running to the long line for the diving board at the public pool
a smile
a genuine one
rare now.
step up onto the board. Ready for a bombastic cannonball.

a Voice from the crowd: that kid's got fat tits
smile gone.
must have a good breast stroke
step off the diving board.
grab the first towels seen.
can't look in a mirror without seeing fat
thanks random pedophile.

hold my head under the water to see how long i last
bubbles erupting from my mouth as even oxygen decides to abandon me
break through the surface, the tension unable to hold me back, begging with gasping breaths to be accepted again

Virginia Woolf
                                        her pockets lined with stone
did she regret taking air for granted when she submerged?
                                                                                                    what held her under the water?
                                                                                                    the rocks
                                                                                                                    or her thoughts?

HANG

"So Judas threw the money into the temple and left.
Then he went away and hanged himself."

is it culturally insensitive for me to like piñatas?

as a child i remember cinco de mayo in spanish class
going outside to see a papier-mâché horse hanging from a tree
suspended in splendor with its orange, red, yellow and purple
(again, the dull observations of youth)
gather around, enjoy the spectacle of a culture far removed from my own
eyes, light blocked out

spin around, whirling into infinity
stick in hand, weapon brandished
beat the lifeless entity until the candy falls out
rush to gather up and feast upon the entrails

i can only think of disturbing parallels
piñatas are sort of fucked up when you think about it
but so is human nature

i remember seeing my teacher walk outside with the sacrifice
sitting inside with my coloring books and math boxes
seeing her tie a string around its boxy neck
setting the noose upon the highest bough
releasing the figure and returning to her students
leaving it to swing pendulously from the rooted structure

it's one of the few things that could hang from a tree and not be horrifying

CHRISTINE MACKENZIE

Sophomore
Major: Psychology, Creative Writing, and English
Reading: Poetry

Christine A. MacKenzie is a sophomore majoring in psychology, creative writing, and English. She loves to write poetry and articles related to the body and mind. In the future she plans to become a mental health therapist and continue to publish her writing.

Nominated by: Laura Kasischke

soured milk

i kept shakespeare on the tongue from the time i could lift complete volumes of his work on my lap and let the shapes of the words flow through my fingertips / flick over my tongue / but i never needed to hear them for most of my life / until now: "there is nothing good or bad but thinking makes it so" now i have the taste of sour milk stuck in the muscular pores of my mouth / cheeks the dried skins of lizards / the roof bricked red and hard / that's how we are when a few words are all we need to hear / and everything else goes out the other ear / that there are no shoulds and musts / but decisions to be made / because we are our bodies / the pain curving down our spines / the faint hunger pressed between our lips / the blush on our noses and cheeks and when and where it happens / even when we're told to be much much more

in fields of sunflowers

1. the trachea ruptured in big fists and small fists scratching in yours
the nails outgrown on her right hand cracked with white dirt like road salt

2. she had spread raspberry jam on her raspberry tongue
and spit all of their sweet seeds back on your lips

3. the metal knife is buried under farm dirt

4. the fields of sunflowers used to be a place
she ran barefoot and yelled out to the sky

5. the jar filled with wetness has grown green moss

6. the nails grew a millimeter

7. shadows fall from the leaves above
and fracture her pale skin

8. there is a light bulb in her pocket
blackened over its curves

9. a yellow sunflower opens
from the rings of her trachea

blank holes

tell me there's more to it than the coloring
of our cheeks with powders / vodka shots
smiles stretched over the redness that folds /
unfolds more than warm piles of laundry
that we fold / unfold to be tucked all pretty
into wooden drawers no one looks inside
or really sees / i mean what is constant forms
blank holes in our brains that we fold / unfold
each day & night even a butterfly with the
bluest sheen could land on our wrists and
fold / unfold its wings for all time even then
there would form a blank hole in our vision

our creations

all of the milk drips out of our swollen bodies
into mouths into bellies the same as when we
strip off our clothes onto white sands and all of
the sun drips off our silken skin to break out
the roundest seeds dormant beneath dead feet
to break out shoots of green purple & yellow
carpeting the world with the bending of elbows
intertwined in more elbows or flowers curling
their mouths towards bodies heavy with milk
when walk onto a green haired hill the sharpness
of a single blade of grass torn between a fingertip
becomes the child *into which i pour all the milk*

how to stop

tell me what it takes to feel more than emptiness
could i simply fill the stomach full of yellow daffodils
or the lungs with a nest full of baby birds / what does it take
to feel like more than a collection of body parts / could i simply
collapse in hot fields of grass / and bury myself in the warmth
of the dirt / is there an answer that could be said aloud / what does it take
tell me what to do and i will do it / tell me to pluck clouds
out of the heavens / and swallow them whole / and i will
at least i'd have an answer / but don't you dare tell me
to smile and pretend that i'm better

ADAM MAGISTRO

Sophomore
Major: NAME (Naval Architecture and Marine Engineering)
Reading: Poetry

I am a Naval Architect/Marine Engineer from Morristown, NJ. I grew up around the water and have a passion for all types of ships. My Grandfather is the inspiration for much of my writing on war as he served in both WWII and Korea. I attended the United States Naval Academy before coming to Michigan and am currently in Air Force ROTC.

Nominated by: David Wade

Ships

Cresting
through the
waves transporting
goods and life. But also the
ability to rain down destruction.
Power is in the eyes of the beholder
Yet it is also determined by those. Behind
the scenes. A ship symbolizes the way of life
of man, endless seas, endless, opportunities.
The sea open
us to a whole
new world that
scares us yet enthralls us The deep blue absorbs us and CO_2. It regulates us, our earth, our
everything. The sea is life. The steel skin shivers and shrinks in the cold, girders twist
and turn. The ship screams when its being pushed and purrs when it is at the
speed it likes. A ship has just as much personality as its crew. For men
and women of the sea, sailors, merchants, traders, and explorers
the only fitting way to sleep is to be rocked by the cradle of
the deep.

Shipboard Sonnet

The cruiser is like nothing seen before,
Gleaming from bow to stern radiating,
Her presence there merely settles the score.
Guns like telephone poles stoic waiting.

For electricity to be sent through,
the wires they support, the lifeblood of
society, the enemy fights you,
but yet the cruiser still sits sailors love.

Sleek and slipping through the night a wolf hunting
Sheep herded by the coastline perfect prey
All hands aboard know they are confronting
Prepared to send them to heavens gateway.

When the deed is done the wolf doesn't think
But the crew aboard does they slay the sheep.

Dad

A seashore isn't a vacation without you.
You left us long ago, I took all the blame.
The waves crash down louder I still wonder who;

You were, when I remember your last hue,
Telling me you loved me saying my name.
A seashore isn't a vacation without you.

I still think of us wearing the same blue,
Eyes, shirts, emotions, I trusted your claims.
The waves crash down louder I still wonder who.

My last memory of you is just us two,
Though only one of us is alive, shame.
A seashore isn't a vacation without you.

Dad you left us, to deal with your mess, do;
You know, I am ashamed of my surname.
The waves crash down louder I still wonder who,

Cares, why do I care about, none of it was true,
I see you hanging from the closet frame.
A seashore isn't a vacation without you.
The waves crash down louder I still wonder who.

LILY MORRIS

Junior
Major: Psychology and English
Minor: CASC – (Community Action and Social Change)
Reading: Poetry

Lily is a Psychology and English double major with a minor is Community Action and Social Change. She is particularly passionate about research relevant to human behavior and motivation, and is particularly inspired by the personal narrative. She is inspired by her family and her identity as a Jewish American from Los Angeles, and is a lover of and friend to any and all dogs.

Nominated by: Sarah Messer

I am tired

"Six million of our people live on in our hearts. We are their eyes that remember. We are their voice that cries out. The dreadful scenes flow from their dead eyes to our open ones. And those scenes will be remembered exactly as they happened." – Shimon Peres

I think about my great grandmother
the infamous Hilda
with her babushka and
her timeless misnomers
and a laugh my mom says
could be heard from Minsk

and I wonder if her eyes
grew wider at night
dilated in the abyss
of a dark sky
sprinkled with the stars
that shone without smog

I think about my grandmother
Sylvia without a middle name
with her silver hair and her
sharp tongue
and her one brown eye
and her green eye to match

and I wonder if her eyes
grew smaller at night
pinned as the light
of six million more stars
than Hilda ever got to see
pierced her beautiful eyes

I think about my mother
fearless little Deborah
with her fiery hair
that she now dyes pink

and her cat eye glasses
and her contagious cackle

and I wonder if her eyes
get moist at night
when she notices that
there are eleven more stars
than her mother had to see
and she can't even keep count

I think about myself
five feet and seven inches
of flesh and bones
and the women who raised me
and the hunger for more
of anything at all

I wonder if my eyes
hiding behind spectacles
a near-sighted lens
bore into the sky filled
with light that does not shine

and I notice that
my eyes have been closed
because I don't want to count
the stars in the sky
or the bodies in the ground
or the amount of
"never agains"

An Ode to Forgetting

my mom has a photographic memory
i know this because she used to tell me that
she could read the newspaper when she was three

i do not have a photographic memory
i know this because i used to remember the shape of shame
but now i do not

the walls in our house are covered in art
prints of drawings and campbell's soup cans
because we should just recall the faces of our loved ones

if they are not etched into my
yellow carbon copy brain
then they need not be above my mantle

what is the opposite of a photographic memory:
what my dad has so he can
forget the smell of abandonment

it can be frustrating to try and retrieve
an old name or fact or date or...
or recall where this sentence was going

but i was always better at being naïve than
giving into the fire of an old flame
what's a grudge to drawing a blank

relatives would often coo and admire
how much i resemble my mother
as if her womb was a Xerox machine and i, a copy

how do i tell them that i
do not remember their names well and
i could not read the newspaper at three

and that just because i don't remember the
fifty states or last week's crossword puzzle's theme
does not mean my waking mind has gone idle

my mind might play tricks on me
but like any good card dealer she sure can bluff
closing the shade between my eyes and my mind

NADIA MOTA

Senior
Major: Creative Writing & Literature
Minor: American Culture
Reading: Poetry

Nadia Mota is a Chicana poet from Adrian, Michigan. She enjoys baking cupcakes for her friends, playing bass in her subpar band, and writing stuff sometimes.

Nominated by: Laura Kasischke

nuclear fusion

we imagine that the universe could hear our voices,
sonic waves sent out through the stratosphere and
up to the makeshift heavens – loud, fiery stars
beating themselves against the dark, making some-
thing of the empty. we circle them with what we've got:
soppy declarations of love, messy but absolute;
those things we don't realize are true until they
spill on the carpet, a stain made acceptable
by the irreversibility of splotchy creation.
because this we've formed: our self-made stars,
these fluorescent stitches illuminating the rain-slick
streets. how a voice can travel across the flimsy
fabric of space and time, some 93 million miles
away: *i made this light, and i'm giving it to you.*

ode to selena

we stand in the makeup aisle at walmart
trying to find the perfect shade of red.

our mothers give us whatever change they
manage to gather from the bottom of their purses

and think of all the almosts: they watched
your death on waiting room televisions and

crossed their hearts, one day they would give
their baby girls your first name. these girls will

grow up with cumbia rattling in their hips and
Blue Moon twinkling in their eyes – we, the

daughters living with your memory. we spin across
every dancefloor like it's the astrodome stage.

we cut our bangs with safety scissors over bathroom
sinks and leave every place with a lipstick smudge,

giving the whole world a kiss as we go. we pray with
our grandmothers' rosaries that it will remember us

when we are gone. we live in the wake of the past.
in the world of our mothers, and their mothers too.

we cry on bedroom floors to "I Could Fall In Love"
and mourn all the things we could have done.

ghazal filled with potholes

back-of-the-bus kids bump on shredded red vinyl over busted seats,
breathing out their worries to the fogged windows on trusted streets.

they laugh, careless and young with friends they grew up with. after school snacks
and secondhand shoes, laces untied. games of four-square disrupted streets.

bills spread on the table, pushed aside for a dinner plate. words like
insurance and *overdue* spill like salt. a look out to the cars and rutted streets.

the free lunch program can't feed silence, the empty inside their homes.
closed doors. electricity cut. they venture out into trusted streets.

a flick of ash in an alleyway, kids cough on air rusting their lungs.
snow falls like a crumbling cigarette sucked beside a dusted street.

they ride borrowed bikes, swerving tires around potholes and plastic bags.
the neighborhood bumps from the bass of a white car in a busted street.

they say that the streets see everything. the broken bones, the growing old.
first dates. first deals. closed fists and eyes sweep the glutted streets.

dim headlights disappear from the pavement, an emptying no one fills.
heavy hand on a thigh. an emptying no one sees but these gutted streets.

they see what they shouldn't, only let it show in undereye circles and
talk in whispers about what it would be like to leave these rutted streets.

fill the potholes on dead-end avenues with fear, with sharp gravel and
bloody knees. no one seems to get out; we keep walking on rugged streets.

NOVA NIETLING

Freshman
Major: Undeclared
Reading: Lyric Essay

Nova Nietling is a self-proclaimed cat whisperer born and raised in rural West Michigan, and she rarely left the region during her life prior to college. Her hobbies include reading, writing short stories, and drawing cartoons. She either has a very refined sense of humor or an absolutely awful one, given that the only person she knows who shares her tastes is her little brother. Please bear with her until her reading is done.

Nominated by: Annika Pattenaude

On the Modern YouTube Camera Boy

Y'all know those boys who cultivate themselves?

Like, two hairstyles: the classic long sides plus bangs of the early 2010s and then that more recent middle pyramid thing, where the bangs are gelled up into a solid wall that's perched across the crown, often managing to look sorta puffy despite being a human-Lego hair hybrid.

They're skinny to skinny fat (which basically means they can pull off a jawline), sometimes a bit of bicep mixed in. They're white Americans for the most part. They've got good voices and cadence. Normal faces—which can easily appear handsome if you're in an observation affair. From the few I've met in person, they wear Axe like it was sandalwood during the plague

Anyways, they're camera boys. They film themselves sitting in a chair for 6-15 hours each day, 3-7 days per week, as they play whatever games are trendy. Or maybe they compile reviews/commentary on random stuff, sometimes in the form of video essays. They make lootbox or card pack opening videos, which are sometimes paid for in viewer donations. They do giveaways and sponsorships. They've all got Patreons and channel-themed merchandise. Vlogs galore in between the main stuff, maybe a few podcasts. If they're not exclusively streamers, they're sure to post daily, with each video being at least 10 minutes long so to optimize ad revenue. Clickbait is omnipresent, though not quite at Buzzfeed levels. And they do their best to cultivate a sense of closeness with their audience (the majority of which are minors), inserting viewer interaction wherever they can.

"Oh, but the meat of their personalities!" you could say—and I want you to say. "Surely that makes for a wide range of content!" Well, the camera's got a way of scaring them into their baser elements, and it narrows the scope in a few predictable ways. What most of it boils down to is one universal sentiment, the tourniquet god of entertainment: *funny is good; I want to be funny.* And while that's not exclusive to them by any means, they still show it more clearly than any washed-up comedian I've ever seen. Thus, their personas take from some combination of four routines in the Jungian ether: overreacting to everything that merits reaction; being creatively judgmental and unimpressed by everything subject to review; referencing a collection of "funny" or suggestive topics, usually obscene; and making a point of one's own self-awareness, clinging to the supposed novelty of a fourth-wall break.

So we have these little people-bots toiling around on their far-off stages, shouting at the void and picking up dust as a snowball does snow while rolling down a hill. To most observers, they're despicable. Even to me, they're kind of despicable. But there's a sincerity here to this lowly, convictionless guile: they *think* of themselves, so clear and so hopeful. After all, they brought themselves up from absolute nothing, probably without any outside involvement. Growing their channel is an ambition like entrepreneurship, like following a dream away from conventional security; what they sell is themselves, and it's a highly personal task. Through this outlet, and this outlet alone, they become that rare breed of people who really, truly think they can get somewhere in the world. It's the American Dream of children living off their lemonade stand, and it's kind of incredible.

TESS PERRY

Sophomore
Major: Cognitive Science, Computation and Cognition
Reading: Fiction

I am a sophomore studying Cognitive Science with a focus in Computation and Cognition, however I am hoping to gain admission to the School of Information and specialize in Data Analytics and User Experience. After I graduate, for a few years, I hope to work in the technology field for a fashion company before applying to Law School, or maybe I'll skip all that and just open a doggy daycare. In my free time I'm usually painting, watching a hockey game (a little too intensely), at Osaka eating sushi like a sumo wrestler, or unsuccessfully trying to force my friends to go on a hike with me.

Nominated by: Oluwapemi Aguda

Jasper Like the Park

The moon clung to the air, like an obstinate child who refused to get off the seesaw to let the sun have a turn. Proudly illuminating the coastal town of Cannon Beach, Oregon, the moon must have been offended when the morning overcast started to roll in at 3 am. Minutes ago lighthouse level rays casted down on the one thousand seven hundred and five residents. Now, the moon's radiation barely seeped through the low hanging salt infused clouds. The new camouflage left the night bodies uninhibited, encouraging them to explore unforgivingly. Howls cut through the mist, footsteps no longer tried to muffle themselves, and, around 4 am when Arie arrived at his shop, the birds began their choir lessons in a sad attempt to distract everyone from the smothering sensation the overcast cheerily provided.

Long accustomed to starting his day when normal college students have finished theirs, Arie pushed the fountain of dark curly hair from his face and unlocked the back door to his coffee shop, The Arborcrest Cup. Contemplating if it was time to give up the rebellious inches he had gained and return to the comfort of a buzzed head, Arie let the back door swing shut behind him. He stretched out his overused muscles, let out a yawn that resembled a banshees' mating call, and with a lazy flick, Arie turned on the lights of the shop. Without conscious thought, he fashioned his once white, now a muted beige, apron, washed the cheerio and toothpaste residue off his hands, and connected his phone to the speakers that were littered throughout the shop and began playing his "Well Damn Jackie" playlist. With a subdued boogie in his feet, he began to turn on the lights and gathered the ingredients to make the morning pastries.

Wrist deep in maple raisin scone dough, Arie's mind started to drift, as it usually does at this point in the routine. He found himself staring into the unknown, black abyss held back only by the thin sheet front of store windows, and memories of dark sky nights sneaked into his conscious. Uncomfortable, Arie pulled himself away from his sticky canvas. He shoved aside the congratulatory letters for various coffee prizes, none of which he planned on replying to because according to the words drilled into his morals "good work is expected not praised," and found the remote for the TV. Arie flicked past the usual 24 hour broadcasted sitcoms, obscure Hallmark movies, and landed on a local news station that was about to begin its morning show.

The morning routine was now in full swing. Oven heat crept into every corner, making the whole store feel like the inside of a sleeping bag. The low wattage lights gave a warm glow that bounced off the inky front windows, highlighting the low visibility surrounding his shop. The overly scripted conversation between the morning show anchors spilled out of the speakers, and the pecan muffin batter was nearly finished. All at once, this loveliness was halted by the bell that hung above the front door violently being slammed into the unforgiving oak wood, causing its high pitch cry to overload Arie's ear drums.

Unalarmed, Arie remained focused on whisking the batter. He assumed that one of his many friends that frequently take to the streets at night had again picked the lock and wandered in as they often do looking for a hot, more importantly free, breakfast.

"Alright, alright" Arie called from the kitchen with an audible smile, pausing before adding "lemme guess, by the bold entrance I'd say it's got to be Joey."

"No. Not Joey. Try again" said a foreign voice with confidence and unveiled sarcasm.

Definitive, precise information, is what Arie has always needed to operate. Starting as a child, the unknown as left him feeling exposed and vulnerable. He learned to use his six-foot stature and military molded, lethal muscles as a safety blanket. Whether in an active battleground or letting in the night prowlers of a small coastal tourist town, his blanket protects him from any threat the unknown might deliver. It has only failed him once.

He rounded the corner from the kitchen to the front of the store, wary of the unfamiliar presence. However, immediately he exhaled his anxieties. In the middle of the velvet couches and the myriad of boutique chairs coupled with marble-topped round tables, stood a scrawny, young man with sharp, defined features. His nonchalant, curly hair resembled the sand and his eyes, which radiated with life, mirror the cold, grey Pacific Northwest ocean; they were surely a matching set. Guessing a generous five foot eleven and one hundred and forty pounds, Arie assumed he could be no older than nineteen years old.

"Hey brother, how can I help you? We don't open for another hour and a half." A prolonged pause, "But, I have got some scones that should be done in about eight minutes, if you're hungry" Arie offered. The young boy smiled and the scent of cinnamon encircled the two men. Yet, the new guest didn't reply.

"You alright there?"

"Sure, sure just taking in my surroundings. Haven't been here before," the guest offered, as he paused to take Arie in fully, with a thoughtful bob of the head and narrowed eyes he added, "Yeah that'd be nice." He walked over and extended his hand he added, "Jasper. Like the park."

"Arie."

"Where'd you want me Arie? Here?" he said indicating to a forest green leather couch in the corner.

"No, back here, in the kitchen. I'll give you breakfast and a show," Arie said while turning his back on Jasper but focused his eyes on the reflective table tops to watch his back.

Arie gestured to the only seat in the kitchen, a wobbly stool right under the TV that was strategically placed there so that people have to stand and work in order to watch. He returned to his muffins while the irrelevant anchors banter filled in the silence. Arie whisked a little more aggressively than needed, letting his muscles flex for the new visitor. As archaic as it was, in the field Arie always felt the need to show new recruits his unmatched strength. Dominance needed to be established early among the lieutenants, and old habits die hard.

"So are you Arie the big friendly baker or what?" Jasper inquired with a laugh people only dole out to old friends while he motioned to Arie's physique. Arie felt like this was one of those rare, unexplainable encounters where the polite get to know you behavior could be skipped, and genuine personalities can immediately present themselves. He liked Jasper, the same way he liked the younger recruits who showed promise. But he didn't want to make this fact too obvious. The kid already seemed overly confident to him.

"Yeah," a smile escaped his lips, "Yeah I guess I am. You're pretty scrawny to be a burglar, don't you think?"

"I don't rob," Jasper snapped. Then he looked down and started to shake his head. With each left to right rotation a smile spread larger, the type you see on a mischievous child. "And I didn't break in. The door was open, lights on, TV playing. Any normal person would assume you were open for business."

"Normal people aren't up and wandering around at this hour."

Arie now noticed the odd juxtaposition of Jasper. He was clean. Face clear of adolescent spots, hair held a glossy shine sponsored by a routinely added conditioner, his nails were perfect semi-circles with no dirt under them, cuticles cut and all. He has time to groom himself. But, his clothes were all wrong. He wore a brown leather, fleece lined jacket with no noticeable shirt underneath, and navy pants that reminded Arie of the one's electricians or plumbers fashion, and he even had clunky worker boots to complete the handyman look. All were two sizes too big on Jasper's slim frame and were covered in a layer of dirt.

"You wanna let me hang up that grubby jacket before it gets its essence all over my shop?"

"No go on that captain. I'm bare-chesting it underneath. Anyway, I was about to ask you two questions."

"Really, Two?" raised brows, "Ambitious. Alright, shoot."

"First, where are the scones? Second, I agree with you, normal people aren't up at 4:30 am like us. So, what's abnormal about you? Why are you up?"

"Wash your hands and you can take out the scones from the oven using the glove beside it," Arie instructed while nodding his head to the sink, and began to put the batter in muffin pans.

"Where's my second answer" Jasper countered while hopping off the stool and rolling up his sleeves multiple times to expose his hands.

"Well, this," he said while gesturing to the pans near him, "I own this place and am too cheap to get a baker"

"Nah, I don't accept that I want a real answer."

"Real answer?"

"Yeah, why is a big man like you in here playing Julia Child?"

"Watch it or you'll lose your scone privileges," Arie warned which caused Jasper to innocently put his hands up laughing in a childish manner, but raised his eyebrows indicating he was expecting an answer.

"Alright, I served in the military for seven years. Worked in the field, drove a lot of tanks," Arie explained while dropping his glance from Jasper to his work. He hoped his new friend didn't notice the deliberate act.

"So you opened a coffee shop while on leave? You know, most guys go on benders and fuck a lot of girls. But, no no not my G.I. Julia Child here." A pause, "Or did you quit?"

"You want to get thrown back out there?" Arie said with uncalled for aggression that made it clear he would follow through.

"Sorry."

With new focus the two worked on their tasks, pulling scones from the oven and prepping the muffins. The elements must have felt the tension in the little shop on S. Hemlock Street. The overcast sank even lower to wrap itself around The Arborcrest Cup in a successful attempt to eavesdrop. This caused the low wattage lights to reflect off the glass that held back the dark morning air, making the space uncomfortably bright. Quickly, the new beams of light, in addition to the rising heat from the ovens, no longer gave a cozy sleeping bag effect, but the impression that one's face was wildly too close to an iron. The men sweat as the smothering, inescapable smell of cinnamon grew and encircled them tighter, like a noose. The early morning silence increased, to the point where it became a roaring buzz in their ears filling every crevice of their conscious. The elements were smoking them out, driving both of them to a point of eruption. It didn't take long until one of them broke under the conditions and gave the overcast the secrets it wanted so desperately to hear.

Cannon Beach was a small town, where personal business was synonymous with public news. Finding someone new to talk to was an appealing concept to Arie. Since he moved to tourist town, he was nearly as desperate as a boy on prom night to tell someone why he opened the shop.

"I used to spend my leaves like that. Got sort of a hero complex. Particularly when you're good at it. And I was good. Especially at driving those tanks. I was back on leave about a year ago. I was driving back from a night out in Portland. I shouldn't have been driving. I mean I wasn't drunk or anything, it was just late. Around 2:30 in the morning. I remember the moon was so bright, like a water downed sun." Arie paused and shook his head to dislodge the image. "Irrelevant. Anyway, I thought I was invincible, you know, I drove tanks for the U.S. Military. I can drive home. But, I started to fade. I was on a back highway mostly lit by the moon. I reached to get my phone to call a buddy to help keep me up. I took my eyes off the road for a second. When I looked up I was in the wrong lane and headlights were coming straight at me. I swerved. I heard the car hit the rock wall on one side. I kept going. I dropped out of the military. Moved back here. Opened this place." With manicistic, low laugh he added, "some hero."

Frozen with respect, Jasper didn't say anything initially. He admired Arie for giving him a real answer. He was about to offer him consoling words when the morning update came on, and the moment felt like it had passed. A story about taxes rising came and went. Then the perky, blonde reporter, who was about to begin a story on a nearby auto shop stealing customers spare tire, was interrupted. The breaking news banner flashed on the screen, along with the unsettling beeping. The reporter, clearly not comfortable with doing anything besides readings her provided script, began to stammer:

"An inmate from Clackamas County Jail has escaped early this morning." Arie already knew where this was going, finding someone to talk to doesn't come that easy. "His name is Jasper Rhodes. He is a seventeen year old convicted of gang-related murder serving a twenty-year sentence. Rhodes used an electrical failure as an opportunity to escape. He killed one guard and inflicted serious head wounds to an electrician before stealing his clothes. Rhodes is armed and considered to be highly dangerous. If you see this boy, please call 911 immediately."

Arie didn't have to look at the TV to know it was him. He also didn't have to look at Jasper to know he was pointing the end of a barrel at him. It was actually borderline comical, looking up and seeing Jasper one hand pointing a gun at him, the other still in an oven glove holding a sheet of scones were a little dry, this imperfection bothered Arie.

"What are the odds we are both killers," Jasper said with searching eyes. The two little Pacific oceans hoped to find anything but fear and disgust in Arie. Instead, the retinas watched as Arie slowly turned off the TV and turned to face him, leaning against the counter with followed arms on his chest.

"I guess we are the same Jasper."

"Now come on. You know that's not true G.I. Julia Child. You're a good guy" he said using his gun to gesture to the muffin pans by Arie. Jasper's heart was pumping for a 300 meter dash. He didn't want to lose the respect and acceptance Arie had just shown him seconds ago, he needed someone to show faith in him. "You chose the hero path, I chose the other. And I got caught. Now I'm trying to figure my way out of it. Maybe I can end up like you, but for now, it doesn't look like I'll get that lucky." Jasper dropped his glace with Arie to the floor and added, "I don't think you can just jump paths."

Arie started to interject, but Jasper cut him off. His eye were now harsh, a tsunami had began, and he emotionless said, "now, I have a third question. Are you going to let me leave?"

Seven years of military mentality flooded Arie's brain, overriding his senses. He began to visualize ways to apprehend Jasper's weapon and turn in the enemy. But, Arie's safety blanket failed him for the second time. His muscles reacted on their own free will suppressing Seven years of training. He turned his back on Jasper, dropped to his forearms on the counter and put his head in the palm of his hands.

When Arie got up, he noticed one thing missing and one left behind. One dry scone taken and one gun gifted. The overcast had cleared.

ABBEY PHILLIPSON

Freshman
Major: Linguistics
Reading: Fiction Short Story

Struggling with a condition that often leaves her bedridden, Abbey has always found creative writing, specifically screenwriting, as an excellent outlet and hobby. She is enjoying her freshman year joining clubs that help kids and adults with disabilities. This pushes Abbey one step closer to achieving her dream of becoming a social worker for kids with disabilities!

Nominated by: Samantha Bares

It's Me, The Nasty, Heartless, Stone-cold Bitch

It is surprisingly very easy to crash a stranger's funeral. I mean, if you think about it, nobody is at the door checking IDs and punching in your social security number. There are no bodyguards and the family rarely orchestrates a private service for the door. But to say that there is no need for these things is a bit of a leap – there's people like me in this world. The budget regarding a death is rather small in comparison to other major life events – that is of course if you count *death* as a *life* event – but nonetheless, a funeral is no wedding; though the cost of a coffin could cover the bill for the dress, the custom name tags, the centerpieces, and there'd maybe even be some left in the budget for the nice cutlery. But, no, there will not be a guest list. But I will say, once you've gotten through the door, prepare yourself for a social *mess.* First there's the guest book: Do you write your real name? Your name backwards? Do you fake a hand tremor so you don't have to write at all? What if someone stares at you funny? "How did you know my Aunt Elizabeth?" they may ask. Personally, I prefer to fake a hand tremor and deploy the "tilt head slightly and smile without teeth" tactic. It' simple, easy, and believable. But beware - if you slip up in any of the key social areas, they will probably think you're there for the pastries and the lemon infused water offered on the table with the obituaries. Perhaps some *are* there for the sub-par raspberry tart laid to disguise the fact that there's a four-day-old dead body in the room, but most of these people are *actual* family members. But not me. In fact, there hasn't been one funeral where I've eaten a pastry, especially not the raspberry tarts. I think they're rather disgusting and I prefer moist desserts.

So why, might you ask, do I attend funerals for any reason other than a loving obligation? Well, to put it quite simply, my mother thinks I'm a nasty, heartless, stone cold bitch. And I think she might be right.

I dropped out of college after my sophomore year to "figure myself out". I was never the college type and I knew it from the get go. The thought of living in the same place where I wrote essays and failed exams made me want to live where there were no walls, no ceilings, no boundaries. But the more I thought about the idea of having no limits, the more confused I became. Maybe I *liked* structure. You go to college, you get married, you start a family. It's a foolproof plan.

I would have made it through, if it weren't for the one day I decided to take my headphones out during class to improve my already failing grade. The professor was on another tangent that, prior to this particular one, I had blocked out with my Aerosmith playlist that kept me sane during his lectures. The professor spoke with his hands, explaining that we live inside a house, inside a town, which is inside a country, inside a planet, inside a galaxy, which is inside space. But at one point, it stops: there comes a point where all structure is lost. The chain dies. Though I'm sure this was intended to be food for thought, it didn't settle well with my stomach. I dropped out the following week.

Now, after months and months of waking up with kinks in my neck from sleeping on the basement couch of my mother's house, my mother accused me of "not even trying" to get my life in order and be a good person.

So here I am, at Harrison Jay Sullivan's funeral, trying.

I parked my old silver Chevy Cobalt in the third to last parking spot in the corner of the lot of Fredson Memorial and Cremation Services. I found that if you park in the last corner spot, it looks suspicious, I guess on the account of the fact that no one chooses to do that much walking nowadays. On the other hand, parking too close to the front draws attention. So I've made it routine to park in precisely the third to last parking spot. I walked with a steady pace toward the steps of the entrance to Fredson's in my funeral shoes: bright blue crushed velvet flats, to be exact. This may seem funny, as I am trying to blend in as much as possible, but black isn't really my color, and who made it a law that you *must* wear black to a funeral? Does there really need to be a dress code to make the day any more bleek? Regardless, I felt blue was acceptable for the shoes – the color of tears, I suppose.

However, I knew I wasn't going to be doing any crying today. I have been to forty-seven funerals and not once have I shed a tear, sniffed a sniffle, or felt any sort of heartache.

One of the first funerals I attended was that of Miss Louise Malcolm, aged sixty-two when she died. It smelled of pipe tobacco and cheap watermelon lozenges in the lobby, but the coffee was pretty good. A bit cold, but good. The stream of the hot liquid sprayed a little when I pushed down on the dispenser lever. Good thing the carpet was forest green polyester. For a moment I thought that I'd be doing the establishment a favor by spilling so much they'd need new flooring. I strolled into the viewing room. Family members were taking the pews, which were otherwise wooden and bare. Louise, it seemed, had outlived most of her immediate family members except her stepdaughter. And she didn't even die of a sickness or of old age. She was hit by a speeding Honda on a residential road in front of her four year old grandson. Driver took off for Mexico. *Shit happens*, I thought as the crowd of people pulled out their travel-sized Kleenex packages. Their cries didn't make sounds, which I appreciated, until the four-year-old grandson was prompted to go up to the casket and see Grandma. "Wake up Grandma, wake up!" The young boy wailed. It didn't phase me. I wished it did.

I thought maybe if it were the little boy who had been killed instead of Louise that it'd be different, but it wouldn't have been. I supposed that the reason that everyone burst into hysterics upon the little boy's meltdown was not because they were reminded of Louise's death or even because the little boy missed Louise. In fact it had nothing to do with Louise at all: it was simply because the little boy was *naive*. He didn't understand the way the world worked and that his grandma wasn't coming back and that she wasn't anywhere but in the ground with the worms and that the bad guys don't always get caught and that the man who killed her didn't care and that there will come a day that no one will care about you either. The world stops giving a shit about you as soon as you begin to understand it. We all secretly miss a time when we were dumber. Somebody cared for us. But you can't unlearn the truths of the world once you uncover them.

But still, for whatever reason, I persisted. Curt Lorris, a father of twelve-year-old all girl triplets, killed in a car accident on the way to his daughter's sixth-grade band concert. The most petite of the sisters played "Amazing Grace" on the clarinet after they closed the casket. The room roared with heaves and sobs. Many people had to leave, I was not one of those people. Alice Peters and Peter Peters, aged ninety-one, died after Alice was admitted to the hospital for another cancer flare up. Her husband Peter laid by her side and they passed together. Alora Tuskey, killed from a genetic condition that the mother had passed to Alora at birth. Everyone could feel her mother's guilt engulf the room. I couldn't. I picked off my nail polish with a pen instead. *Natural selection*, I thought.

I don't know why I kept going, or what I was trying to feel. I just continue to think that each one will be different. *Maybe this time*, I tell myself, as I stand on the wrap-around porch of Fredson's, about fifteen minutes later than when the service was due to begin. I waited on the bench outside, but I thought surely there'd be family here at Mr. Harrison's by now.

I've often thought that this is how it'd be at my own funeral. The parking lot would have plenty of vacancy, the coffee would go cold, and there'd be plenty of raspberry tarts leftover to use for the next service. I hoped Mr. Harrison had a better fate than I.

A plump woman in a cyan sequined dress said to me as she erupted through the front doors of Fredson's.

"Howdy, Young Miss, hope we didn't keep you waitin' too long!" A plump, southern sounding woman in a cyan sequined dress said to me as she erupted through the front doors of Fredson's.

To avoid the riskiness of the conversations that could take place under the company of just one person, I decided to head back to my Cobalt sitting in the third to last parking spot under the sun, the black interior baking. As I turned the corner, a large van rolled around to the front entrance. Twelve or so men and women dressed in vibrant colors pranced out of the automatic side door, laughing, smiling. The patterns of their clothes and the sparkles of their earrings danced in the sunlight. They too, entered the service.

Surely I was in the wrong place, but my confusion couldn't override my curiosity. I stayed put in my boiling car, watching as dozens of people all dressed in clothing that looked like Jackson Pollock paintings. Not a single color the same, but their faces were identical – ear to ear smiles. I bet I could see every tooth.

I don't think I've ever smiled like that. I never had a reason to. The solution to all the woes in the world seemed so simple to everyone but me: just smile! Haven't you heard? By sharing this universal expression, humans are offering peace and expressing that we're all in this together; however, when someone like me, the emotionless, silent type who seemingly never smiles, enters the room, everyone looks on with confusion and unease, as if they're trying to deduce what's wrong with me. I don't blame them. I look at myself the same way.

I was intrigued by their smiles. I felt invited in a way, a feeling I rarely get. I decided that hundreds of people would be rather easy to blend in with. I strolled back to the entrance, where I was welcomed with a nod and a pearly white smile given by the same plump lady and jazz music seeping its way from inside to the doorway, inviting me in. I was greeted by hundreds of people, shoulder to shoulder, looking more like a Skittles factory than a funeral home. I stood out like a sore thumb in my black dress, but for some reason I didn't care to blend in. The place erupted with laughter and music. I took a stroll around the room, having to nudge my way through the crowds, and was stopped in my tracks by canvases bursting with color on easels scattered about the perimeter of the room. My eyes were fixated on them.

I had tried to be an artist once. I was in elementary school. I wasn't very good. I couldn't even color inside the lines until I was in third grade, but still. I wanted someone, *anyone* to just put one of my pictures on the fridge or say "good job". But Alas, I did not do a good job and the stainless steel would have been ruined by my wild colors. But not here, it wouldn't have. Art was welcomed here.

I was broken from my stare to the sound of a microphone tap.

"Is this...can y'all hear me?" The plump woman spoke, as if she didn't have a microphone and needed to speak up. It was calming in a way. She opened the mic for people to speak.

When asked "how was the funeral?", most people respond with "oh, it was...you know..." and people do *know*. There are clues hidden in the answer, though: people don't talk about the funeral home, the brand new hearse or how they liked the voice of the funeral director. They talk about how it made them *feel*. That feeling is usually like a lonely, lifeless tomb: suffocating, confining, cold, sterile, and lifeless. I was sick of it. I was immune to that feeling. But here, I felt almost immortal. Untouchable.

As people began to leave, the remaining group just became louder and happier, making up for the absentees. It seemed like a sort of unspoken rule that if someone left, you must become proportionally louder. I had surely overstayed my welcome, considering I wasn't welcomed at all in the first place, but it felt like I was, and that was something. I headed for the door.

"Thanks for coming, Miss." The plump woman said to me as her soft hand with silver nail polish turned me around at the door. She handed me a small canvas with a painting of a bowl of fruit, sort of looked like the kind of art where most people would say "somebody really made a fortune off this thing?".

"It's one of Harry's most recent pieces." She said to fill in my silence. I deployed my soft, no teeth smile. Routine. It felt off this time.

"I–I didn't know Harrison. But he seems like he was a great guy." I said, hesitantly. "So I can't accept this. I–"

"Please, take it, he would have wanted you to have it." "But I didn't know h–"

"I know." She said through a smile. She began to walk away after planting the canvas in my hand "The outfit gave it away, dear. Love the blue shoes, though! Oh, and take some of these raspberry tarts while you're at it!"

It's funny because I didn't know any of these people, I didn't know Harrison Jay Sullivan, and I most certainly didn't know anything about him. But for some reason I truly did feel like Harriso–Harry–*did* want me to have his painting. He really did. And here I was, standing out like a brown M&M in the sea of Skittles, crying. It was me, the heartless, nasty stone cold bitch, with a raspberry tart in my hand, crying.

EMILY PINKERTON

Senior
Major: English and Art History
Reading: Poetry and Short Story

Emily Pinkerton is a senior (graduating in December of this year) majoring in English and Art History. She's from Austin, Texas, but she doesn't have a southern accent. You will never catch her saying "y'all". After she graduates, she would like to complete an MFA in Fiction. She laughs at her own jokes.

Nominated by: David Ward

Cedarbrook

The dawn light blanches you,
cold bones upon rock,
your arms driftwood on a frozen beach.

Blue envelops every part of you,
seeping in under the door,
through the cracks.

Your sleeping form is unnatural here.
We're exposed in the limbo of your room,
colors washed out
and limbs untangled.
My skin is cold in the places you touched
me only hours before,
warm and frantic in the darkness.

Unwelcome in this house,
in this citadel of a long-dead god
I slip to the ground,
pale footsteps
shots through the silence.

Sour heat explodes where our eyes meet, briefly,
those aching whorls,
sapphire pools,
my blue-eyed beauty.

Bleary is the forbidden morning,
the shrouded,
starving love.
Marigolds in single file
motion to slink up the path to Cedarbrook
where I will be ensconced
in the uneasy sleep of the unwanted.

Warning Shots

Something is nudging me out of myself.
Crow's feathers crowd my mouth, blue iridescent and self-defeating.
The air I breathe isn't my own.

Home is a warm rain; home is a steady mind.
It never rains here, in this land of frozen breaths and bitten tongues.

Spring remains hidden, burrowed under the sleeping frost.
The wilted murmurs summon the truth, wishing it awake:
Seafoam-colored whispers about yourself.

The shadows seem to move towards me, detaching themselves from the wall.
If I get close enough I could dance with them;
Intertwine my fingers with them.

Is that music or simply the soft touch of a friend?
Fingers in my hair, lulling me into peace.

The words are burbling up now, threatening as bullets.
How do I tell you that I love you?
In this sweetest melancholy all I can do is wait.

Blackberries

He didn't shy away from the beating of the clocks.
Their faces pale and glowing, mouths open
as if on the brink of speech–muttering secrets.

He took time to love, slowly, in the accelerating dusk:
a still-lingering gaze even in the half light.
That golden-syrupy sun began to hold its breath,
not even then did he slide, quickly, back into himself.

He stood then, solid, a refuge.
A heart forged by dragonfly wings.
You can still feel them trembling, sometimes.

He knew the smell of sweet–
interrupted by a pocketbook.
Interrupted by the ever-beating tide,
that cruel march of time, slipping.

He ripened with the late summer fruit,
las moras debajo de la sombra.
Warmth striving against the bleeding of the dark.

He left by the echo of the moon,
that sycophantic duchess
trailing faint sparks of red-orange luster
glinting from her coattails.

Loveless

You are a product of who you know.
And I don't know you anymore.

Tensions stretch taught over poised muscles,
the sisterhood

that took a fundamental corner of your soul,
filled with broken nails, blonde hair, cocaine.

All you are is a cold sweat,
shapeshifting in my room, watching.

I loved him. You know I love him–
skin on skin, caressing him on the silver screen.

Your undeserved love, my underserved shame.
Blame me, bottom tier, tarnished.

You met me on the front that day,
bloodied and sunburnt and shaking,

you still held fast, my friend, to that revenant.
That curdled, wheezing hate.

We are a cauterized wound I sealed,
free of fear and loathing.

The truth is, I don't think of you.
I don't think of you at all.

(I'm sorry.
Was it my fault?)

(Listen.
I didn't mean to hurt you.)

(God I'm sorry.
I can't control my brain.)

(I'll be better.
You're right.)

(I promise
I'll fall in line.)

(Please. I'm sorry.
Do you miss me?)

We need to talk.
I'm not angry.

You don't have that
power anymore.

Glass Ships

"The corn is tall this year."
They won't find you for another five weeks
baking in the cicada heat of the Iowan summer.
"Look for the vultures circling."
That's where you're hidden, they whisper
between gulps of panic and hog-heavy air.

"The corn is tall this year."
And the dogs were still in your basement
when they realized you were gone.
"No signs of a forced entry."
is hailed as canon by small-town cops.
They don't know you never made it there.

"The corn is tall this year."
The sky opened up that night, a crack in heaven
to wash away your scent, your dried blood from the grass.
"The reward is $300,000 for Mollie's safe return."
But all you are now is scraps of fabric and bones,
a bleached fossil of men's silent warfare.

"The corn is tall this year."
Your death transformed into a ballad
of the scared, the unwilling, the nationalist.
"Don't use her death for a political agenda."
your father sang. Your soul left on glass ships
disentangling silver ghosts.

EMILIA PRADO

Senior
Major: Psychology and Creative Writing & Literature
Reading: Short Fiction

Emilia is a senior from the village of Hesperia, Michigan. If she had to name the sitcom of her life, it would be "The Misadventures of a Mexican White-Girl." This senior is always trying to find the middle ground in life. Trying to decide if she wants to call her mom for the casserole recipe or the homemade fajita spice mix. Failing to remember if that proverb is supposed to be in Spanish or English. Seeing how she can get her majors to work together. Hoping it all works out and she can live her dream of being an editor and novelist.

Nominated by: Christopher Matthews and Patricia O'Dowd

Dirt Demons

I remember when I saw my first dirt demon. All my life I'd been raised on stories about the dirt demons that hide in fields of corn, rye, hay—anything tall enough to cover their dusty backs. Everybody's mama and *abuela* had tales to tell about those dirt devils. Never go into the field without your dad or brother or *primo* there with you. I always thought it was a crock of shit. Every summer I was always the one that would dare to go the furthest into the feathery sea of overgrown asparagus behind Abuelo's house. Each summer, Tía Tomasa would threaten us with *la chancla* for our stupid game. I never understood until the summer of my twelfth year, the day of my half birthday, the Fourth of July.

Back in those days, we used to invite the farmer who lived across the field to our barbeque. Papí said we had to, something about showing our respect to the man that helped us. He was a nice man, gave us work gathering apples and pumpkins in the fall and cutting Christmas trees in the winter. He always came with his wife and son who was learning to take over the business. I'd never seen his son do much work, unlike the farmer who never hesitated to give us a hand. Me and the *primos* liked that he gave us pop and Rice Krispie treats whenever he came by. The farmer and his wife came because they liked us...I think the son only came because he liked how Tío Nuno grilled fajita.

It was dark by then, and to pass the time until the fireworks started, we played our game. Asparagus season had ended by mid-June that year, and Papí had yet to mow the old field to make way for green beans. Chachi kept whining, saying she was going to tell Tía and then we would be in for a *pow-pow*. Victor told Chachi she was a snotty little *pendeja* and said she would keep quiet if she knew what was good for her. So far Victor had the record, he'd gone so far that we were no longer able to see his curly head. The lights from the back porch could not reach us at the edge of the field, making it harder to spot the difference between vegetation and Mexico football jersey.

That's when I decided to run in after him. I could hear the sounds of him rustling about back there, and followed them in the hopes I could push Victor down as I ran past him and further into the field. The ends of the asparagus swayed in the stiff breeze, tickling my cheeks, and gently clawing at my braids. I stopped to look around to see if I could spot Victor, but there was nothing but the endless crowns beckoning me in every direction. Finally, I heard the crunching sounds of someone stepping over the dead stalks that littered the ground. I smirked and ran after the sound, determined to rub it in that little *cabrón*'s face that I was going to beat him. After only a few strides my toe caught on a rock half-buried in the earth, and my heart leapt to my throat as I pitched forward and landed face-first in the dirt.

All the air left me, and my mouth was full of dry, sandy grains that tasted bitter from the chemicals we used to keep the pests away. I rolled over onto my back to catch my breath, and that's when I heard someone rushing towards me. I quickly sat up to look around for any sign of Victor, but I couldn't see anything.

"*Ya basta*, Victor!" I snapped. "This isn't fun anymore."

My braids smacked around my head like whips when I heard something behind me, but there was still nothing but the bending asparagus. Something turned in my belly, and I knew I shouldn't turn around, but I did anyway. A few yards ahead of me, were two large red lights. They glittered like Abuelita's precious ruby earrings that she only wore on special occasions– but never for church, you never wear *el color del diablo* in church. These were the devil's color. These were the eyes of a demon.

I stood still, praying to God to keep me safe like Abuelita taught me. If I didn't move, maybe it wouldn't notice me. My hand shot to my mouth to stifle the heavy breaths, I wanted to cry so bad. A white-hot pain shot down my spine, and my visions blurred, but I could still see those eyes. The scream ripped through me just as the first fireworks began to go off in the heavens above.

There was no time to look back to see if it was close, I just scrambled to my feet and ran for my life. I didn't know where I was going, only hoping that I could get as far from the dirt demon as I possibly could. Fire burned through my legs and chest, each breath was a labor greater than I had ever known–and I carried bushels of fruits and vegetables across acres for a living. I would've run forever to get away from the demon if I hadn't run into the farmer's son.

For the second time that night the air was knocked out of me. A thick and heavy hand gripped my shoulder and pulled me back. The plants barely went past his waist, he was like the old maples that lined the edge of the fields.

"What are you doing way out here?"

"I–we were playing–I saw–"

He patted the top of my head, "Shush, catch your breath."

I nodded, glad to be near someone to scare off the dirt demon.

He tilted my head up, "You're a real cutie, ain't ya?"

No matter how many times they ask me, I still can't remember anything but those red eyes. I don't remember seeing Victor in the asparagus. I don't remember what happened after I ran into the farmer's son. They tell me that I didn't show up until I came crawling out of the green sea behind the house shortly after the last firework had faded away in inky wisps across the deep blue night. My clothes were in shreds and sweat cut tamale-colored tracks through the ashen dirt that coated me from head to toe. One of my braids had come undone. It wasn't until I was eighteen that Tía Tomasa told me about the blood.

At least, they told me, I came back. All we had left of Victor was a scrap from his football jersey. I don't think we ever played the game ever again. *Nunca.* I know I couldn't. Not after the dirt demon. Even in the peak of the day, I wouldn't go out into those fields without someone else beside me. Abuelo got fed up with that quick.

When I was fifteen, we were planting asparagus crowns for a new crop next to a neighboring rye field. He told me to keep laying out the crowns while he and Chachi went to get more. I really did try, but *los susurrus* in the rye were the farmer's son's heavy breathing, the fireworks, and Victor's shouting. The truck was barely fifty yards away by the time I caught up to them. I don't know what made Abuelo think that would work. Not after Abuelita had to permanently lock away her ruby earrings—she couldn't bear to see me run away from her.

The farmer moved away soon after that Fourth of July. There were no more Rice Krispies to make our mouths sticky with the sweet goop, just chapped lips split by the warm winds. No more fizzy Cola to send us scurrying across the fields with sugar highs, only bitter iced tea that never failed to get mixed with some dirt that stuck in your teeth. No more Victor to push on my way to get the first *concha* from Abuelita's shopping haul. There were so many *primos*, but even just one less of us was too much to bear.

Everybody's mama and *abuela* has tales to tell about dirt devils. Never go into the field without your dad or brother or *primo* there with you. They hide in fields of corn, rye, hay— anything tall enough to cover their dusty backs. I always thought it was a crock of shit. *Ahora, yo no soy pendeja.*

ELENA RAMIREZ-GORSKI

Junior
Major: Creative Writing & Literature
Reading: Poetry

Elena Ramirez-Gorski is a junior majoring in creative writing and literature. Don't let her fool you, she is absolutely filled with blood and guts right now. She is from Adrian, Michigan and has a terrible secret. When she's not writing or painting she's locking herself in a dark closet "to be alone with her thoughts." She would like to dedicate this reading to her friends, who are "concerned to say the least."

Nominated by: Laura Kasischke

This is for the goth latina bitches

my spooky chicas always dye
their hair from natural
black to unnatural black

their grandmas wouldn't let them read
harry potter because no vas a traer that diablo
mierda en this house, pendeja

the chicas who love their brown skin but
resent that they'll never rock vampire makeup

the ones who cut their bangs too short
over the bathroom sink
before a show

who are teased for listening
to that white people music
but just roll their eyes and remind themselves of
alice bag, the plugz, los illegals,
y que no hay nada más chicana de ser una punk

the girls cursed to fall for white boys
with veiny arms and druggy eyes
who leave the family parties
asking why they have to be so loud

las punks, las locas,
las brujas, las darketas,
las 'otras'

the girls who fashion their own
ouija boards from cardboard and
scotch tape, and sit around it
motionless all night,
too badly wanting to believe
they aren't alone

I wanna be as cool as

That kid who doesn't care about the rain,
Doesn't run for shelter,
Just smirks and says:
You take showers, don't you?
Because it's the same for him.
Because he showers clothed.
Because he's just that cool–
Peel off that denim jacket,
It's just more denim.
Impervious.
Who cares.
Big deal.
And while you are scurrying hysterical
Like some ancient fool,
He is rooted with crossed arms.
Come back in a week and
Find him rusted,
Birds nesting in his hair,
Truly one with the universe.
God. So fucking cool.

Three Catholic girls and an atheist go to church

On Erika Polaski's eighth birthday
her mother took her friends to
Saturday night mass
I remember giggling and
sliding in wooden pews
jumping out of our seats
for communion
making our way back but
Kirsten's eyes were wide and panicked
she held a small wafer in her hand
like an injured bird

All of us gasped
Whispered
Just eat it
Don't eat it
I'll eat it
Give it back to the priest
Go to the bathroom
Flush it down the toilet
Throw it away
Bury it
Burn it

We scrambled to get rid of a body
The body of Christ
Kirsten decided to put it in her pocket
Kept him there all night
Turning to paste
In her clammy fist

Love song for la Llorona

I have been you, Llorona
in the back of classrooms and
sprawled out on the sidewalk
stringy black hair
sharpie colored fingernails and
chewed up hoodie strings
crystallized with spit
a creature infested with nerves

I am you, Llorona
all women are born wailing
you and I just never stopped
we were meant curse everything we touch
to cry *where have all the children gone?*

I lost them too, Llorona
you won't need to steal me in the night
I'll gladly walk with you and call
mis hijos
mis hijas
mis hermanas
mis primas
mis amigas
sweet scabby-kneed girls
now younger than me
god help us find
all we let die

I feel you, Llorona
let us both be
women inconsolable
on New Year's Eve
commiserating on the back porch
tears extinguishing the cigarette
between your trembling fingers

I hear what they say, Llorona
beware of the lady in white

the weeping woman
will drown you with tears
let me be so lucky

But I see you, Llorona–
Salt water
song and sorry

Llorona, I cry with you

SHASHANK RAO

Senior
Major: English, Creative Writing and Literature
Reading: Fiction

Shashank is a senior currently racked with anxiety as he tries to figure out what to do after graduation. He has participated in Café Shapiro for the last three years and is excited that he has been invited for one last go around the bend before he leaves.

Nominated by: Christopher Matthews

The Russian Tenant

The summer of 1976 begins with a series of misfortunes. First: the not so terrible news of the death of the widow Pillai, our tenant downstairs, upon being hit by a public bus. Second: my father's announcement that he is to be laid off from his municipal job at the Madras Corporation. Third (and what I consider chief among tragedies): the vasectomy of Baghu, our cleaning man.

"They dragged me and my brothers out of the house in the middle of the night," Baghu sobs. He is seated on my father's favorite armchair. A cup of tea wobbles in his hands. "They said they would give us enough money for a plot of land, but so far they've given us nothing! The only thing I can remember these days is the *snip snip snip*." He begins to cry. My father puts an arm around Baghu and pats his back and kneads his shoulder. My mother straightens a crease in her sari.

"We're very sorry to hear it," she says.

"Please, *please*, Baghu. If there's anything you need, medical expenses, food, clothes, don't hesitate to ask. You have done good work for us. It's not fair what they have done to you," my father adds. Amma delivers Appa a pursed-lip-iron-jawed glare, but he does not catch it. Instead, he sends Baghu back home to rest with two weeks' wages. I do not know what a vasectomy is, but it sounds awful. ("How will I start a family?" Baghu had moaned. "How will I ever find a wife?")

I am very fond of Baghu. In fact, I think maybe I am a little bit in love with him. I sometimes kept him company while he swept the front steps, making silent fun of passersby. He is still young, though he doesn't know exactly how old he is ("Maybe I'm twenty-four, maybe I'm twenty-six. Who knows? My mother lost my birth certificate the day after I was born.") I liked watching his curly hair bob up and down as he swept. I liked seeing him smile, because it was the most radiant smile in the world. Once, I told him he smiled like the sun, which only made him smile brighter.

There was only one person who knew of my affection for Baghu: the old widow Pillai. She would watch us from her bedroom window after a long day of doing nothing in particular, shaking her head disapprovingly.

"You shouldn't be talking to such folk," she warned me from time to time. "You're a girl from a good Brahmin family. He is a Dalit. It is a miracle I have lived here as long as I have with an untouchable running around the house. My friends all make fun of me, you know. And if they find out, your friends will make fun of you, too."

Old hag, I think now. What do you know? You're dead.

"This Sanjay Gandhi, who the bloody hell does he think he is?" Appa fumes after Baghu limps out the door. "He calls himself a socialist, but that word means nothing in his mouth. Who is suffering the most under this Emergency? The poor!"

My father gets very passionate about politics. My mother doesn't indulge him, but I listen. From his tirades I have learned that, in our State of Emergency, political dissenters are being jailed, the truth is being censored, and that Indira Gandhi has dissolved the Tamil Nadu State Government, putting Appa out of a job. And now I am learning that the poor are being sterilized, sometimes at will, sometimes not.

"Enough," Amma says sternly. "You'll give her nightmares."

"That poor boy," Appa continues, gazing out the window, "we must help him. A vasectomy is a very painful thing."

If I can learn about politics during Appa's outbursts, perhaps I can learn what a vasectomy is? I throw Appa an inquisitive stare but Amma intercepts me.

"Cheh!" she spits. "Thirteen year old girls shouldn't be listening to such things. Go, go finish your schoolwork."

That night as I write an essay on the reasons why Ibrahim Lodi, the last Sultan of Delhi, lost the first battle of Panipat to Babur, the first Mughal emperor, I hear angry whispers come through my bedroom's back wall. Our house is old and peeling. Years of monsoon rain have softened its walls. If one wishes to keep private conversation, one must speak in hushed tones. Still, the wispy outlines of speech wafts through the rooms. For as long as I can remember, my days have been rife with susurrations. I put down my pen and hold my ear to the wall, but the sound of pots and pans clanking in the kitchen sink make it difficult to listen. I am able to discern only a few snatches of their argument.

You would sign away the deed to this house if you could

Is it so wrong I felt for him?

Never once have you consoled me like that

I have to find a way to make some more money

We need a new tenant

The whispers stop and are replaced by the sound of footsteps. I scurry back to my desk and pinch my temples, pretending I am thinking intently about the essay. Of all the teachers in school, History Teacher Miss is the toughest. She does not see any value in rote memorization. She has told us time and time again that any monkey can remember dates. It's what those dates *mean* in the context of all that came before and all that will come after that really matters. Right now, I am wishing that I were a monkey. I have only written two of the required five pages, but what more is there to say about gunpowder and Babur's tactical prowess? What has happened has happened and there is nothing anyone can do to change it. My father enters the room. I turn around and am greeted by crossed eyes and a protruding tongue. I laugh and do the same. Appa is the funniest person I will ever know, and when it comes to history and politics, he is by far the smartest. He places his hands on my shoulders and peers over my head to read the opening sentences of the essay.

"Need help?" he whispers.

"Yes, please," I reply. Amma doesn't like it when Appa helps me with my homework. She says I'll never learn how to think for myself if I always count on my father giving me answers to complicated questions. Appa says Amma is smarter than him and me combined, even though she'd never attended college. She just knows things, and even though I do not like to admit it, she is right about everything. However, I am flagging and exhaustion is weighing heavy on my eyes, so I put her out of my mind and let Appa work his magic. Though Appa has a knack for concise and effective language, having written press releases for the city government for close to ten years, he also loves beautiful sentences that briefly withhold their meaning before giving way to the reader's comprehension. He brings me books in hopes that they will help me see the world the way he does. My shelf is populated by names he tells me are "illustrious": Shelley, Eliot, Dostoyevsky, Ambai, Tagore, Akutagawa–these and more all lined up in neat rows. I have started, however, with the tales of Henry James. I don't entirely understand them, but I like the way the words fall on my ears when I read them out loud to myself. I can see why Appa enjoys him. I wonder sometimes if things had gone his way and the world had been more forgiving, if Appa might not have himself become a famous writer. But he is an only child, and his father decided someone had to take care of their ancestral house, which has been in his family for seven generations. Besides, a government job was a safe bet and provided enough income to keep the water and lights on.

"Appa," I whisper, stretching out one of his curly strands of hair. Appa is also the only person I know who sports such thick and twisting curls.

"Hmm?" he murmurs. Once he gets into editing my papers, it is hard to grab his attention.

"Appa," I whisper again, "why do we need a new tenant? Don't you think it's nice without the widow Pillai around to bother us anymore? We finally have the house to ourselves." None of us liked the widow. Even Appa, who liked everybody, struggled to find her merits. The widow was intensely acrimonious. Never had I heard a kind word issue from her crinkled tongue. She commented very loudly on the quality of Amma's cooking when she brought her food on festival days; she remarked repeatedly with searing distaste upon our family's dark complexion though she herself shared our shade; and, worst of all, she sang. Amma and Appa slept with cotton in their ears to keep the noise at bay, but my room was directly above the widow's. Even if I shoved cotton in my ears, I could still hear her go through her set list of bhajans and shlokas every morning at the break of dawn, waking the gods and me with her hobbled voice. I soon began to hate the sight of sunrise. I am not afraid to admit now that part of the reason I accompanied Amma to temple every Sunday was to pray for the old woman's speedy demise.

Appa smiles wryly without taking his eyes off the essay. Amma hides things from me because she doesn't think I am old enough, but Appa is honest with me. Every now and then, he pesters Amma with one of his original quotes when she shies away from my curiosity: 'honest parents breed honest children.'

"We need some more money. Plain and simple. But I promise I'll find an interesting tenant this time. Not one who can't see a bus hurtling towards them." He falls over and sprawls out splat on the floor with his tongue hanging out the side of his mouth. I fall on top of him and we laugh. Appa is a funny, funny fellow.

Within a week, we have a replacement for the widow Pillai. A Russian by the name of Stanislav Vassilyev calls in response to Appa's ad in the newspaper. He is a graduate student taking a year's leave from the University of Saint Petersburg to conduct research on Sangam poetry. He hopes one day to translate the great Sangam texts into Russian.

"Interesting, no?" Appa asks after recounting his telephone conversation with the prospective tenant. I nod enthusiastically. Amma, however, is not so easily swayed.

"A college boy? And a foreigner at that? Whatever happened to the good Tamil Brahmins of Madras—you couldn't find a single one? Oh God, what will the neighbors think when they see a foreigner walking in and out of *our* home?"

My mother has only once warned me against the dangers of the other sex, but when she did, college boys were at the center of her polemic. Such men are never to be trusted, she told me, for they only disappoint.

"He is not a college boy, janum, he is more mature than that, I'm sure," Appa replies, a bit peeved, "and no one else has responded to the advertisement. Besides, I've already invited him for coffee tomorrow afternoon."

I am the first to lay eyes on Stanislav Vassilyev when he knocks on our door that oppressively hot day. Sweat trails down his face and dots his shirt collar. I am most impressed by his size: he is not a large man, but he is tall and lean. His shoulders in particular are a point of fascination. The way they gently stretch the fabric of his shirtsleeves makes me want nothing more than to grasp them as tightly as my arms will allow. No, I want more than that—I cannot say what exactly it is that I want, but is a forceful feeling, a beautiful feeling, an alien feeling that sits in the pit of my stomach like a rich and creamy dal.

"Hello. And what might your name be?" he asks. I lower my gaze. Never before have I had contend with such a reaction. It frightens me. But before I can dwell on them any longer, Amma emerges from the kitchen carrying her best ceramic platter. She has arranged biscuits, murruku, and kola vadai in three neat, appetizing rows.

"Let him in now," she says softly and kindly, very much unlike her usual self. Amma knows better than anyone else how to divide her many faces. To Appa and me, she is strict. To the silk seller, she is stubborn. To the neighbors, she is queenly. To guests and new tenants, she is demure, a shadow passing along the wall.

"Mr. Vassilyev! Please, have a seat," Appa says, striding out of the bedroom. He has coiffed his hair and donned one of the more expensive items in his closet: a teal dress shirt he had ordered from a British fashion catalogue after getting his first and only raise. He almost never wears it. He didn't like the way it clung to his body at first, said it made him feel naked. But when a rickshaw driver and a water boy admired the shirt's make in the same day, Appa came around to liking it.

"Thank you for inviting me, Mr. and Mrs. Iyer. You most certainly didn't have to go through all this trouble."

"It was nothing, really. We only wanted to get to know you better," Appa smiled.

We are all of us enraptured by the Russian tenant. Appa and he unravel minutes into hours discussing the Emergency and the end of the American campaign in Vietnam. Amma sits beside me, bunching her sari between her fingers. Something worries her. She has barely taken her eyes off Stanislav. I wondered if she too is battling the same dark, private thoughts that have been assaulting me all afternoon. Is she imagining the feel of his skin under her fingertips? Is there a gentle tickle treading down her shoulders and back that settled between her legs in a place she is afraid of even looking at? Does she notice as well the growing mound between Mr. Vassilyev's own legs before he crosses them to hide it as Appa and he laugh about this, that, and the other?

For the next three days, Mr. Vassilyev and his shoulders plague my every waking thought and every midnight dream. Soon, I find myself thinking about more than his shoulders—his hair, his hands, and his legs crowd my mind's eye. Mr. Vassilyev—who insists we all call him Stanislav for he would rather not be on such dreadfully formal terms with us—moves in on the fourth day. I decide it is best to stay up that night. It was already a difficult enough task keeping custody of my thoughts and dreams when he was not here. I do not know what new feelings and visions will inch their way into my skill now that he lives just one floor down. I pinch myself, slap myself, hang my head off the side of the bed, flutter my eyes a hundred times. That should do it, I think. But time moves more slowly after dark. My little tricks are not enough to stay the encroaching tides of sleep.

I only remember snatches of my dream: an open window. A lace curtain blowing in the wind. A silhouetted figure in the night. A sigh, a breath, another sigh. And then an urge, a sensation I attribute to urination. But it is richer, deeper than a routine bodily movement. It is tender and warm, like a candle's flame. It hums, building up to a crescendo until I can't hold it any longer. It exits my body singing and laughing as it goes. I wake up and jump out of bed and feel my pajamas for wetness; sure enough, I find it.

I hurry to the bathroom and remove my garments. What have I done? Have I reverted to a bad old childhood habit and soiled myself in my sleep? A viscous liquid sticks to the insides of my thighs. Urine would have run down to my ankles—I don't know what my body has discharged. Suddenly, there under the harsh bathroom light, I see a faint streak of red dribbling out of me. I want to scream even though I am in no pain, but I do not want to wake Amma and Appa. Why are you bleeding? What is this liquid? Why is it sticking? What were you doing in your room? What exactly *were* you thinking about? So I clamp a hand on my mouth to muffle my sobs and sidle out of bed to don a fresh pair of underwear. I hide the bloodied drawers under the mattress, where I will keep them until I can figure out what is wrong with me, and creep back into bed.

The cuckoo clock in the living room chirps three times and just when I settle into my pillow, I hear the gentle thumps for the first time. One two, one two pulsating in the middle of the floor, coming from somewhere underneath, in Stanislav's bedroom. The floor is cool and hard against my ear as I strain to listen for other sounds down there. Is that a breath syncopating the one-two sequence? He must be having a very bad nightmare, I think, he must be tossing and turning in bed like no other. And though I do not want it to, a different thought crosses my mind: what if he is having a dream like mine? What if he is dreaming so violently that the hum he feels is more of a shout that shakes his entire bed? I do not want to imagine the blood and viscous liquids leaving his body. I bury myself under the covers, but still I can hear the thumping. Just my luck: melodies used to wake me in the morning; now, rhythms keep me up at night.

Ubiquitous. It is the word English Teacher Miss asks me to spell and define after finding me hunched over on my desk, sleeping.

"Surely you must know the material like the back of your hand if you feel confident enough to nap through it. Come, come, quickly, tell us what it means."

Show me anyone who claims they can define 'ubiquitous' on their first attempt and I will show you a bold-faced liar. But English Teacher Miss does not seem to think so. With a ruler, she raps my knuckles then sends me outside to kneel on hot sand with my arms held high over my head. She says a little sun will help wake me up. It does not. My eyes grow heavier and my knees burn darker. *Tsk, tsk*, says the widow Pillai in my ear, *already such a darkie and here you are roasting in the sun.*

My friends, however, express concern. During the lunch break, they ask me what is wrong, why I, like their mothers, have bags under my eyes. I hesitate–do I tell them? Isn't this what I wanted: to know? The words fall out eagerly, like water breaking through a dam: "I've been bleeding." The range of reactions overwhelms me. One girl tells me that I am possessed by a rakshasa that will devour me if I don't pray every day.

"But you have to pray in your room, because you're not allowed to enter temples."

Another girl laughs and pats my back.

"You have nothing to worry about," she says, "in fact, if you tell your parents, they'll throw you a party and you'll get a lot of presents."

Later in the day, yet another girl approaches me and whispers: "Look, I don't know what these other dummies are telling you, all you need to know is this: take a rag, fold it lengthwise twice and place it where it bleeds. And make sure you wash it thoroughly once you're done, you'll need it again next month."

I do not know what to make of all this, but I take the last girl's advice. I am careful to tuck the cloth tightly so it doesn't show. The sensation of the extra fabric is hot and irritating and makes me feel unwieldy. And on those noiseless nights from which I can wring out a few dregs of sleep, the touch of the rag reminds me that no peace is everlasting.

History Teacher Miss is also concerned about me. She sends a note home, asking why am I not getting enough sleep. 'Almost every day she dozes off in class' Teacher Miss has written, 'sleep is very important for children her age, you know.'

"What's this?" Amma asks. Her tone cuts me, makes me feel very guilty.

"What's wrong, raju?" Appa intervenes. "You're too young to be having sleepless nights."

If there is anyone in the world to whom I can tell the truth, it is Appa. He is always truthful with me. But I cannot bring myself to say what is the matter. I settle for a half-truth instead.

"I'm having nightmares. I keep dreaming there's something under my bed wanting to eat me alive."

Appa and Amma guess at the cause of my insomnia. Appa thinks I am studying too much and that the pressure is getting to me. Amma thinks I am not studying hard enough.

"She's probably staying up all night reading those books you keep buying for her," she says. "One of them must have scared her, that's all."

The next morning, I find my bookshelf empty. Amma has decided she needs to keep me busy and charges me with greater responsibility around the house.

"Maybe if I wear you out during the day, you'll fall asleep at night," she quips. I do not laugh.

Amma informs the housemaid that laundry is now my domain: its gathering, its folding, its whipping, its wringing, its hanging out to drying—all this under my purview. The work is hard and at the end of it, my fingers are puckered and rough. To whip the wetness out of the clothes properly, I must thwack them against a stone slab on the terrace, five times, six times, seven times, again and again, until they are no longer so heavy with water; then I wring them and throw the clothes in a bucket. Repeat. I am told to do this first thing when I return from school, at the hottest hour of the day.

At the very least, I am granted sanctuary from my thoughts—whip, wring, repeat...whip, wring, repeat. It is easy to focus on such tasks. The actions fill your mind and the body becomes an empty vessel. I do not think about the day I had or the evening that is to come: I concentrate only on the laundry. I forget myself, too. On this hot afternoon, I am only a set of hands whipping and wringing piles of wet clothes.

That is, until I hear the terrace door creak open and I remember myself again, body and all; blood and all; dreams and noises and all. The Russian tenant emerges with a bucket of white garments.

"Silly me," he says, smiling radiantly. "I forgot to hang my laundry this morning."

If English Teacher Miss were here now, I would point to Stanislav and say: "that, miss, is the definition of 'ubiquitous." Stanislav Vassilyev. A ubiquitous fellow. It has been one month since he first moved in and he has made himself very comfortable here indeed. He is there in the morning to walk with Appa to his new job in the registrar's office at the university. He is there in the evening when they return and my mother brings them coffee grinning. He is there on the weekend when my father asks him if he would like to go to the bazaar to pick out mangoes. The noises, too, have become ubiquitous things over the past month. They follow no pattern. It is a cruel game. Sometimes they disappear for three or four days, only to return with added vigor. There was one week when I heard the noises every day. I slept with my hands pressing my ears shut, holding them so tight my arms were sore in the mornings.

Stanislav clips a white undershirt on the line. He has steadily been swapping pants and dress shirts for loose linen kurta-paijamas (Appa bought him three sets of them as a gift when Stanislav announced that he had completed initial translations of *akam* class poems). The Russian says he likes the way kurtas let the wind from the bay lick his skin. Does he notice me staring just a little too long, peering at the places where his bare torso shows through the linen?

"I heard your mother has given you some new chores," Stanislav continues. "*Eppati irkuinga?*"

He practices speaking in Tamil with us whenever he can, to get the accent just right, but I respond in English: "I'm doing well." I regret my terseness immediately and offer to help him hang his laundry.

"Yes," he says, "how thoughtful."

As we hang the clothes on the clothesline, Stanislav discusses the Emergency, its callousness, and the government's blatant misuse of power.

"It is," he says in a low voice, as if worried the wind will catch his words and deliver them to enemy ears, "not so different where I come from."

Where *do* you come from, Mr. Vassilyev, I want to ask. But I hold my tongue. No matter. He begins to tell me.

"Secrets are a daily part of life back home," he says, clipping a towel to the line. Drops of water fall to the ground and disappear almost instantaneously. "Of course, everyone has secrets. Neighbors keep secrets from each other. Friends keep secrets from each other. Lovers keep secrets from each other. Parents keep secrets from their children. I'm sure you have plenty of secrets yourself."

I reach down for another piece of laundry. The bucket is almost empty. I smile sheepishly at him. Yes, Mr. Vassilyev. I do have plenty of secrets.

"I suppose secrets are a natural thing. But they can be very dangerous, especially when your secret is that you're trying to tell the truth without anyone knowing. Where I'm from, people disappear, just like that. I grew up in a small town outside Leningrad and every month, the lights of one house on the street would turn off and never turn on again. The government keeps very big secrets from the people and from the world. No one understands what's happening. Can you help me with this, please?"

We take a long bed sheet and cast it over the clothesline. It fans us with cool, wet air. I have not thought much about the Soviet Union. As a matter of fact, I have not thought much about other places at all. At school, we learn only about nations and kingdoms long past. At home, we speak only of the Emergency.

"After a while, you get tired of secrets. You just want to *know* something. Or maybe you just want to let something be known."

"So what did you do?" I ask, a little breathlessly. An emerald dove coos softly, though I cannot see where it roosts.

"Well, I took a rather sneaky route and started writing poems. Anonymously, of course. I am not so brave. I'd write a poem and hide them around for people to find. Mostly I poked fun at the Party, but a few I wrote took aim at the police.

I spotted an officer finding my poems at the train station one day and his face turned red as a beet when he saw that it was about him!"

Stanislav flashes a mischievous grin. It melts me.

"It's a wonderful thing to let the truth be known. Even if you have to do it secretly."

I can feel myself becoming lighter. Perhaps I need not fear him like I do. Stanislav understands the terror of secrets. He will tell me the truth. I will ask Stanislav about the noises and he will answer me.

"I agree with you," I begin. And then I switch to Tamil. "Say, Mr. Vassilyev. What are those noises I hear coming from your room at night?"

White underwear, dripping wet. His last item of clothing. I do not need to see his face to know that it is blank. The silence weighing down the air is enough. I know that I should be leaving, there are no more clothes left to hang, but he has me in his quiet sway. He lets me go with a chuckle.

"What noises? You must be dreaming."

How I feel after a hornet jabs my neck: hurt, then furious. I want to say to him, "How dare you. How dare you question my sanity after everything you have put me through? All those thoughts, all those visions–I know what I hear every night and I know it is realer than the flesh on my bones." However, I do not.

"Thank you for helping me with my laundry," Stanislav says. I want him to look at me so he can see my angry eyes. He picks up his empty bucket and hurries to the terrace door, but he stops just before he vanishes behind it. "I've enjoyed talking to you. *Poitu varen.*"

And like that he is gone.

Later that day, still stewing in fury, I review History Teacher Miss' comments on my report on the Battle of Panipat. Amma is upset I did so poorly. She wants me to write it again. Seventy-seven on hundred. *Detailed understanding of the characters–insufficient consideration of the wider context.*

There is a set of spare keys in my parents' bedrooms, in the drawer of Amma's nightstand. She believes Appa is too forgetful and would lose the spare in less than a day. If someone gets locked out, they must go through her. I pray no one runs into any trouble tonight because I will be using the keys.

I have thought about it for a very long time. I have weighed my options. My days were filled with visions and revisions of this plan of mine. I decided one week I couldn't go through with it. The very next week, I decided I would. The week after that, I had no idea what to do, and all the while the noises kept on, and all the while I remembered Stanislav's chuckle and him saying "What noises? You must be dreaming." I realize I will have to charge into the dark if I want to see with my very own eyes what I know I hear.

When Amma is taking her bath and Appa is at work, I will steal—no, borrow—the keys. They are a little old, rust chewing the edges. I dig them out from beneath a small pile of small, handwritten thank-you notes.

Thank you for the meal. It was delicious.

Thank you for showing me how to make sambar. I will make it every day.

Thank you for the lovely conversation. I will think about what you had to say for a very long time.

All are signed "Stanislav."

Harmony graces our house. The whispered arguments between my parents are no longer so frequent. In fact, there is an easy cooperation.

Can you pass me the turmeric...

The job is paying well...

...I wish he could stay here forever

For my parents—and for me—this peace is welcome. Happiness is not something they are very familiar with.

I'm sorry.

It escapes my lips. I do not know where it comes from. But I find myself apologizing under my breath once more before slipping the keys into my pocket.

I wait until dark. The noises take their time tonight. Eleven chimes of the clock, twelve chimes. Still, nothing. It doesn't matter: I am wide-awake—there is even a little smile on my lips. Two chimes of the clock. Ah, there they are, the noises, moving to that one-two beat I am ready to crush in the palm of my hand. At first, the thumps are soft, like a cat's padded footfall, but slowly, steadily, they gather strength. The rhythm comes through the floor more ferocious than I've ever heard. I have waited long enough. I slip on a pair of socks to muffle my steps and exit my bedroom. I hear my mother snoring. Appa likes to joke that Amma can snore for two. A funny, funny fellow, my father.

The night breeze soothes me as a calm friend would.

"Go, go," it tells me, "I'll be here when it's all done."

I take my time creeping down the stairs. I take my time inserting the key into the lock. I take my time turning the knob and the lock hardly makes a sound when it clicks open.

I have only entered this room once before, to gather the widow's things after her fatal accident, but I remember it well enough to find my way around, even in this half-darkness. The noises take on a different timbre at such close proximity.

Deep bellowing heaves mixed in with flowing pleasant huffs. I follow the sounds and thuds to the bedroom. A large cloud eats the moon and with it, the only rectangle of light I have to go by. There is a keyhole in the door, sizeable enough for an eye to peer through. And so, framed in a curious lighthouse-shaped lens, the scene unfolds: a formation on the bed, large and dominating, lion-esque; bedposts knocking against the wall, two hands grasping either post; gap in the cloud letting light seep in again; lion's body breaking apart; a head of familiar curls illuminated; word escaping my lips.

"Appa."

I do not know if he hears me, but the movement stops. I do not know if he can see me, but he turns his head and meets my gaze. I back away slowly. Stanislav's voice rises out of the darkness, asking my father what is wrong. If Appa says something in reply, I do not hear it because I am already closing the apartment door behind me, running back to my bedroom. I should not be able to sleep, but my eyes give out anyway. My mind should be full of what I have witnessed, but it is empty. My ears should be alert, listening for the noises' return, but there is none of that—I sleep long and well.

Lies are sweet; the truth is bitter. At least, that's what most people seem to think. I do not agree with most people. I think the truth tastes like a saltine cracker, which is to say it doesn't taste like much at all. It just sits there in your mouth as you try to make something of it. Though I do not see much of my mother in me, I think she and I taste truth the same way.

Amma is in the kitchen next morning, peeling and cutting bitter gourd over an old newspaper.

"Va va," she says without taking her eyes off the bitter gourd. "The little rani is finally awake. I told you those extra chores would help."

My bones ache, overcome by the impact of long-awaited rest For a moment, I cannot see clearly, but when my gaze adjusts and sets itself upon Amma's face, it hits me, nearly knocking off my feet: I have no one left to turn to for the truth. The thought me asking my mother for an honest, unadulterated answer almost forces out a laugh. Besides, what could she know that I didn't? Poor Amma, hunched over a pile of bitter gourd. She is as alone as I am. I shudder thinking about how many secrets I now keep.

Or perhaps there is another way. Perhaps I can simply let the truth be known and we can bear the shock together. I am her daughter, after all. And she is my mother. But I am not thinking clearly. I do not know how to begin. So groggy am I that I don't realize what comes out of my mouth makes no sense.

"What did I see last night?"

"I don't know, what *did* you see last night?"

Amma grins. Appa compares her smile to the Brahma Kamalam, the Queen of Night flower: beautiful and exceedingly rare. When one finds a rare flower, I imagine one handles it with extreme care–in fact, one might be just as happy to leave it quite alone and admire its magnificence from afar. I am tempted to do just that, to drop the matter altogether and add it to my brimming almirah of secrets. Secret thoughts. Secret blood-pocked underwear. Secret viscous liquid. What's one more?

But I can't. I'm sorry, mother with the Queen of Night smile.

"Amma, what do Appa and Stanislav do at night?"

I clench my fist, bracing myself for Amma's face to darken. Destroy a rare flower and you must be ready to face the consequences.

"Why, they're sleeping together of course," she responds without missing a beat, eyes still focused on the bitter gourd.

I stand there, mouth agape. My bones can no longer support my frame. I lower myself to the ground. A puddle of flesh and bewilderment is what I am.

"But why?" I ask, feeling rather dumb when I know I shouldn't.

Amma puts down her knife and sighs. For the first time, my mother tells me the truth.

"Your father and I have an arrangement, that's all. He's happy, I'm happy and things move much smoothly around here now. I'm sure you've noticed."

"But why?" I ask again, this time with anger-tinged curiosity. What lies are we living and how long have we been living them? And why have I, my parents' only child, been cast aside like an afterthought when for the past months, I have suffered the most?

"But what? Marriage is long and hard and just like life, you don't always get what you want out of it." Sharpness returns to Amma's voice as she picks up the knife and begins cutting again. Her incisions are precise and forceful.

"I tried with your father, I really did. I did everything a wife should do and then some–I even learned to love him, how many housewives around here can say that?" Amma scoffs.

"I suppose I could divorce him, da? But what will a woman like me do? A woman past her prime with a thirteen year-old daughter looking for a suitable man, as if I'm nineteen again. This is the best life I can hope for. This is the best life *he* can hope for."

I wish I could say, "No, you're wrong Amma. You *can* lead a better life, we can *all* lead better lives," but I cannot bring myself to believe it. The Emergency, after all, has us all feeling our way through the dark. Nobody's life has turned out the way they expected. Besides, Amma is well acquainted with the saltine cracker-ness of truth and so retains that frustrating quality of being unfailingly correct.

"I flipped your mattress yesterday," Amma continues. She has returned her focus to the bitter gourd, which she is almost finished with. I do not say anything.

"You had quite the pile of laundry under there."

The whistle of a train departing Madras Central Station bursts through the kitchen window flung wide open. I remember hearing once that Ms. Gandhi had taken a vow, back when the Emergency was still new, to make the trains run on time. Who had told me this? Was it Appa? I do not know for sure. The train cries once more, long and tired. So do I.

*

I have forgotten what day it is: Vinayaka Chavithi. It is a holiday from school and the birthday of the elephant god. Amma places wreaths of flowers upon our idol of the Lord Vinayaka. Because I am no longer bleeding, she draws a line of kumkuma down my forehead and does aarthi for me. I receive the blessings of the holy flame. And when Appa and Stanislav return from a mid-morning walk, engaged in a spirited conversation about something I pay no attention to, so do they.

Just before we sit down to lunch, there is a knock at our door. I am the first to open it. It is Baghu. He has come to tell us that he is to be married, and that he is moving to Bangalore with his new wife soon, which meant this, sadly, was a final goodbye.

"Thank you for giving me good work all these years," he says.

"We will miss you, Baghu," replies Amma. She is wearing a red-and-green Kanjeevaram silk sari. A present from Appa to her when he first came around to ask for *her* hand in marriage.

Baghu nods. He looks at me and I look at him. I know I will never hear from him again after this day. But I am happy he is happy.

"Won't you come in and eat?" Appa asks.

Baghu hesitates, but shakes his head. He really should be on his way.

"No, Baghu," I say, placing a hand on his arm. "Please stay."

He looks to Amma who stands behind me, pensive. I look to her, too.

"Of course," she says finally. "Please come in Baghu."

I lead Baghu inside, past Appa and Stanislav who are occupied once more by deep conversation. I wonder if Appa and Stanislav are talking so much because they are afraid of being silent around me. But they, like Baghu, seem happy. We sit on the floor under the elephant god's floral gaze. While Amma prepares the food, I bring out a banana leaf and set it in front of Baghu.

Amma first brings out the rice, dolloping a heap upon our banana leaves. She runs in and out of the kitchen, returning with a different dish with each trip:

poriyal, saaru, kootu, thayir, and bondas flower around the little rice-hill until our leaves are full. We wait for Amma to take her place beside us.

Lord Vinayaka. Remover of obstacles. We say a prayer and begin to eat.

SAMUEL RENTSCHLER

Graduated, December, 2018
Major: Political Science and International Studies
Reading: Fiction

Samuel recently graduated from the University of Michigan and currently works for a church on Washtenaw Avenue. He hopes to attend grad school and become a social worker, writing fiction as a form of self-care and side project.

Nominated by: Elinam Agbo

A Second Dinner

The January wind hurled itself at us, clawing our uncovered faces with angry, icy fingers as we walked through the quiet Kerrytown neighborhoods. No one else was out beside the two of us; there was only the wind and a thin layer of snow left from the night before.

I clutched my peacoat tight around me. I had forgotten my scarf and gloves at home in my rush, and by the time I had walked the mile to Amy's apartment, I had lost feeling in all my fingers and most of my face.

Amy walked freely beside me, bundled in her puffy, blue polyester coat. She looked like a swirl of cotton candy or perhaps blue moon ice cream, her red knit cap a cherry on top. Her cheeks were rosy and her lips were purple from the cold. Her hair fell in light, auburn waves from beneath her hat, indicating she had spent time styling it beyond its usual straightness. Though the weather was terrible, her eyes shone with a smile.

Between the busyness of classes and the holiday break, it had been nearly two months since I had last seen her, and my cheeks hurt from smiling as she shared about the adventures she'd had since then. Through chattering teeth, she talked about her Christmas vacation. She spoke of visiting her grandparents in the Keys, of filling her nights with dancing and cribbage tournaments.

"Forget graduating college," she said. "I think I'm ready to retire right now and get away from all this gross, cold weather." Her laughter steamed in the frosty air.

She beamed as she shared how excited she was for the pediatrics unit she was starting at the nursing school. She gestured as she spoke, emphasizing each sentence and sending falling snowflakes spiraling in new, intricate trajectories.

Through the cold, night air, the restaurant glowed ahead of us, warm and inviting. We cut across the empty street, avoiding the puddles of slush that had been blended together by the spinning wheels of long gone daytime traffic.

She breathed in deeply as we reached the door.

"Mmmm, it smells good." She elbowed me. "Seems like you picked a good one."

I inhaled too but couldn't smell anything. My face still felt frozen.

I opened the door and held it for her. As I did so, she looked at me, one eyebrow cocked quizzically.

"Uh thanks, dude," she said, walking in.

I smiled and followed her inside.

The host walked us to our table, gestured for us to sit with a gold-bound wrist. We sat and, now that we were safe in the warmth of the restaurant, began removing layers. She shed her knit hat and puffy coat. Underneath, she wore a sleeveless copper colored shirt which exaggerated the brown in her otherwise green eyes.

I suddenly felt like I was drowning in the baggy sweatshirt and jeans I had decided to wear. My eyes darted around to the tables around us, to the tight, stylish clothes of the other patrons. Should I have tried harder to look nice?

Before my mind could slip too deep into worry, the waiter arrived, interrupting my panic with, "Hello, my name is Jeremy, and I'll be taking care of you this evening." He explained the specials and left us to mull over the menu options. By then, my face had begun to thaw, and I was happy to note that, just as she had said, the entire restaurant smelled amazing.

"Alright, Mr. Ann Arbor," Amy said. "Since you've lived in this town so long, what sort of food do you recommend for us?" She turned her menu toward me, implying I should point out my suggestions.

She knew quite well that, despite starting undergrad a year before she did, I had never been to any of the restaurants in this part of town. Nevertheless, I played along, pointing dramatically to the options and concocting descriptions for them in a tone that I hoped expressed mock expertise.

She leaned closer, her smiling eyes inches from mine. "You're not as good at this as the waiter was." She laughed. "Let's get the special he suggested. Wasn't that the whole point of coming here during restaurant week?"

Finding it hard to think with our faces so close, I managed a nod.

Her smile broadened, and she leaned back in her seat. "Excellent answer."

The waiter came back to take our order, and the first course – a salad with an acidic fruit dressing – arrived only a few minutes later.

"Wow," Amy said. "This looks delightful."

She pointed her fork at me, trying to force her smile into a serious look and failing. "But, if it isn't as good as it looks, I'm blaming you."

The meal tasted incredible, even better than it looked. Crisp, fresh salad. Mouth watering potstickers. Savory, sauteed pork belly. To my surprise, I even found myself enjoying the mushrooms served alongside the meat.

As we ate dessert, she finished telling me about the rest of her Christmas vacation.

"Almost all of my grandpa's friends golf, and on the second to last day we all went out with them to play nine holes. Right? Well, my mom knew this was likely part of the plan, so she packed little golf outfits for her and my dad."

The waiter walked by our table, dropping the bill off in front of me. I thanked him and turned back as she continued.

"And you know my mom, she just looked super cute in the shorts and visor she brought." She paused, stifled a laugh. "But, my dad must not have been clued in to my mom's plan, because he'd clearly never tried his outfit on before." She stopped again, clamping a hand over her mouth.

She took a deep breathe, continued. "Not only does he look absolutely ridiculous in pastel shorts that are way too short for him, but n his very first swing, they tear right up the back."

I nearly choked on my bite of cake as I imagined her father – a stocky, rugged man – trying to play off a tear in small pastel-colored shorts. As I pulled myself together, she grabbed the bill from beside me.

I coughed and gestured for her to hand it back. I pulled out my credit card and readied myself for her to protest.

Instead, she held it out to me. "Let me know the final total and I'll pay you back half." There was no playfulness in her tone at all.

I paused, looking at the small, leather bill folder she held toward me.

I thought back to when we had gone to dinner together the year before. It had been at the sushi restaurant on South University, a short walk from our dorms. She had tried to pay for the whole bill then, making a joke about destroying the patriarchy one restaurant check at a time.

I remembered she had styled her hair the same way for dinner that night too, curling it slightly so it fell in waves around her face. I had complimented her hair at a party two weeks prior, and she had decided to style it the same way when we went out for sushi.

I remembered walking her back to her dorm, through an evening much warmer than tonight, giving her a long hug goodnight.

I remembered having a difficult conversation later that week. Telling her I wasn't ready for a relationship. Refusing to admit to myself I was just afraid.

I remembered the following summer, both of us working jobs in town, her at the hospital, and me splitting my time assisting in two university offices.

I remembered making up excuses to spend time with her. Setting up times to try new recipes together. Sweeping up quinoa she had spilled. Accidentally buying hot dog buns and cooking oddly shaped hamburgers to make the best of it.

I remembered nights spent joking on her porch. Smiling as she laughed with her roommates. Feeling a sinking sadness at the same time.

I remembered a busy fall semester. Infrequently seeing one another at church or on campus. Sending a text saying it had been too long since I'd seen her, inviting her to try the restaurant week specials with me in Kerrytown.

I realized I had been hoping she would let me pay for dinner, had been hoping a second dinner would be a second chance for something more.

"Hey," she said.

I snapped back to the present.

“I’m just going to Venmo you back. Is that cool?”

I nodded.

“Great. I’m not gonna make my friend buy me dinner, especially at such a fancy, expensive place.”

The waiter brought my card back, and I signed the bill, showing her the final total. She typed a number into her phone, and I felt the notification buzz in my pocket.

We bundled ourselves back into our coats. She pulled her hat over her hair.

We walked in silence back to her apartment. She seemed content to admire the snow as it fell around us, and I couldn’t think of anything to say. As we reached her door, I gave her a quick hug, told her how much fun I’d had.

“Goodnight,” she said. “See ya later.”

She unlocked her door and smiled as she stepped inside.

I smiled back as she turned away, noticing the corners of my mouth felt heavier than before.

I left my coat unbuttoned as I walked home. The wind was biting, but a part of me was glad to feel the cold seep into me. There was still no one else out. There was only the wind, weaker than earlier, and a fresh layer of snow slowly piling up on the empty sidewalks.

NIKKI SILBERMAN

Senior
Major: Biopsychology, Cognition, and Neuroscience (BCN)
Reading: Poetry

Nikki is a senior studying Biopsychology, Cognition, and Neuroscience. She is a New York native and plans to return there to pursue a career in compliance after graduation. Nikki is passionate about sexual assault prevention and works as a facilitator for the sexual assault prevention and awareness center on campus. Her hobbies include painting, reading, and discovering new music. She took her first class in creative writing last semester and is excited to see where it takes her.

Nominated by: Thea Chacamaty

Twenty Below

Bodies cold and blue look to the sky
for salvation; anger is only directed at the sun as they beg her
just to shine once more.
Who smiles when they're told to? Certainly not I nor
most women who walk the streets with purpose and
not an angry soul nor an angry storm, for
it only brings a sigh of exasperated wind from all of us.
On days like these, when wind whips one to pavement,
I wish it would blow by inspiration that hits just as hard-
but I only hear whispers and howls laced with hallelujahs.
Cold lungs shake as they inhale bitter
and exhale woes to the world.
As steps tread heavy, the books on my back hang even heavier
but one day, they will thaw me.
Only memories warm like cups of tea so
I wait for stories to freeze in my mind like ice.
Words may lie and memories too, but the present drags
as long as these winter days until
time is just a smear.
Maybe white lies are better than white snow and here and now;
inhaling truths twenty below will take a toll.
Those drags kill your lungs, they say,
but steps drag too
and bodies cold and blue-
they are tired.
Maybe that flickering sun
is burnt out too.

SAM SMALL

Sophomore
Major: English and Communications
Minor: Creative Writing
Reading: Poetry and Short Essay

Sam Small is a sophomore from Troy, Michigan who enjoys a quality mosh-pit, never has matching socks, and can play every song on expert on each Guitar Hero game. She hopes to one day be an investigative reporter living in an overpriced studio apartment in New York City.

Nominated by: Samantha Bares

where the ocean takes you

the water happily chomped on my toes
so I checked to see if they were still there

one piggy went to the market
and demanded for a refund
I'd prefer a marathon runner,
maybe a salsa dancer,
perhaps a monk?

one piggy stayed home
nuzzled against blanketed skin
until her patience began to fray
an atrophied ambition–
stifled under comfort

one piggy had roast beef
that gluttonous hog
what to do with a surfeiting sinner
who craves a life ashore
is slaughter worse than stagnation?

one piggy had none
watered down by my wages
watered down by our parents descent
until he was submerged by surrender
and emptied into mediocrity

the water happily kissed my toes
and we swam
swam
swam

all the way home

emily & I

"The License to revere, A privilege so awful What would the Dower be, Had I the Art to stun myself With Bolts of Melody!" -Emily Dickinson

Are you the one that knocks on my Head
And tickles the cuffs of my ear
Seducing me with whispers
That induce color, that justify Pain–
Because you know if I didn't I'd erase myself again.
I'm Nobody! Who are you?

You tried your hand on court
A rhythmic flow at each bounce
To try to pass the Clock
But–In the midsts of triumph
Victory hugged you slightly
Your contours were formed–But–
There played a Funeral in Your Brain

You tried your hand in court
To spite angry male snarls who sanction your Wild Nights
You couldn't fight them with verse
Or amicaibally attack with adlibs
You realize, Powder exist in Charcoal– Before it exists in Fire.

You tried to tame your hand
To wire it accordingly
To Rise to Their Requirements
But– it seized all control
And like a Loaded Gun
It kissed you on the mouth
Warning–don't be afraid

AFRAID? Of whom am I Afraid?
Recluse, Virgin, Madwoman
Obnoxious, Jew, Slut
I am afraid I am you.
I am afraid I cannot halt.
Here comes thy hand– May we hold it together?

Untitled

You scan the paper and realize that your mom's hair appointment is at the same time as Jean Val Jean. 24601 is a no-go, nada, goodbye, capuz. You wallow in self-pity on the floor of your bedroom because it feels more dramatic. Yesterday you got drunk for the first time and fell asleep in the fetal position on the prickled follicles of the soft, eggshell carpet–shoes and jeans still attached to your dazed body. *What the fuck are you doing?* You didn't have an explanation so you said you were uh...tired. They accepted it. Part of you wished they hadn't. You shut the door and exhale heavily, a strange headache massaging your temples. But it is today and you want to see Jean Val Jean. You contemplate asking Kristina but you know she'd rather venture for a tank top and jeans, and you're an intellectual and you really don't have time for that. You don't have time to do menial tasks anymore. Biking is also out of the question, because it's a goddamn tundra outside. You're also only thirteen so taking a car is illegal.....but only if you get caught. No, shake that out of your head Vin Diesel, it's not that serious. But somehow, it is. *Hey Sam, I'd like to see Les Mis.* You? Bald headed, only likes Michigan State Football™ and "domestic beer," you? Wears cotton t-shirts with holes and mustard stains, you? Resents his prodigy for trading her jumpshots for monologues, you? You? *There's just nothing better than the sound of the ball trickling through the net.* You decide to pause your silent war and turn to Switzerland– temporarily–and jump into the obnoxiously large minivan. He puts on some music he thinks you still like and it makes you uncomfortable. He buys you popcorn, just this one time, and tells you not to tell Aaron or Brendan because they'll be angry, he *never* lets them do that. You wanted Reeces but you don't object to the word free–ever. You still don't, he taught you that. You watch him sit nervously on your left side, twisting the brass ring on his finger over and over again. You wonder if that's a metaphor for something. He eyes you back, and hesitantly flashes you his yellow teeth. Anne Hathaway Dream's a Dream and he moves in closer. She looks at him, and he is looking at her too. He dreamed a dream, once. You wonder if he dreamed your dream. You wonder if he dreamed he would've still had hair left on his head. You wonder if he dreamed of you at all. You wonder if he's angry you got fat, or maybe just disappointed. You wonder if he loves you because you can't remember the last time he said so. You can hear yourself crying. No, it's not you. It's, *you*.

SOFI SOLOMON

Junior
Major: PitE (Program in the Environment) and English
Reading: Creative Non-Fiction

I am a student double majoring in PitE (Program in the Environment) and English. I enjoy writing, reading, traveling, and yoga. Most of my writing is poetry or creative environmental non-fiction.

Nominated by: Stacy Coyle

Who Let The Butterflies Out?

The package from UPS arrived at nine in the morning, a five-inch-by-five-inch square cardboard box. I brought it inside and handed it to the Program Director, Veronica. She looked at it as though it was the birthday present she had been waiting all year for and said, "It's the butterflies, they're here!" Confused as to how butterflies could be in that underwhelming box, I followed her upstairs. She brought me to an unused bathroom. It had the smell of a hospital, was off-white, around five-feet-by-five-feet, and barely could fit the two of us at the same time. She pointed at a styrofoam board about the length of two feet and the height of one foot and said, "This is where we will hang them for now." I opened the box to find one hundred chrysalises, the hard outer protective layer of the butterfly while in its pupa stage, wrapped in white tissue papers like individual blankets. An index card had the butterfly species names written on it: monarch thirty, swallowtail twenty-five, painted lady twenty, julia fifteen, buckeye ten. Each chrysalis was one-and-a-half-inches tall and one centimeter wide. Each one bulged in width and thickness right at the top of the oval-shaped protective case. The monarch chrysalises were the color of the ocean off the coast of a tropical island, a smooth turquoise. At the bulging point, tiny gold-colored dots lined the width of the front-side of the chrysalis like diamonds the size of a pen's point and dipped in gold for a delicate bracelet meant to be worn only for the highest of occasions. The half centimeter long stem at the top of the chrysalis was black and thin like a piece of sewing string. Chrysalises were wiggling, eager to emerge soon.

We cut off the edges of Q-tips and pinned the half-centimeter left of the rod to a styrofoam-board-covered-by-a-potato-sack. We then hot glued the chrysalises' stems to the cotton-ends, which were supposedly serving as the underside of leaves where chrysalises usually attach to keep out of sight and avoid getting rained on. The space between each chrysalis from left to right did not matter, they could get as close as two fingers on a hand. However, there had to be at least an inch-and-a-half between the rows of chrysalises to give space for emerging butterflies to grab onto the styrofoam-board-covered-by-a-potato-sack directly under their hanging place while soaking in sunlight and pumping enough blood to their wings to soar. Once the package arrived at Sweetbriar, it was only three or four days more until those butterflies emerged.

The chrysalises came from a butterfly breeder in Florida and arrived every three weeks from May to early September. The butterflies are raised and kept in the Sweetbriar Nature Center Butterfly House. I volunteered at the Sweetbriar

Nature Center everyday of May 2018 and saw firsthand the process of raising and maintaining the butterfly population in that Butterfly House. The first shipment of chrysalises were kept in the second floor unused bathroom because it was still too cold to keep them outside. We raised them inside and, once they emerged, brought the butterflies from Sweetbriar's office to the Butterfly House. As May went by and the weather got warmer, we received more and more packages of chrysalises and began to raise them inside the actual Butterfly House.

During the third week of May, I brought a class of twenty fourth-graders visiting the nature center into the Butterfly House free of charge (it typically costs three dollars for kids and five dollars for adults). The Butterfly House was a rectangle with a barn-like-red wooden structure as the skeleton of it and black thin mesh walls and ceiling. The first door led to an enclosed front section for visitors to wait in until the Butterfly House opened. From there, another set of two doors led to the main house. One door to enter. One door to exit. One door could not be used for both, otherwise the amount of people shuffling in and out would leave the door open long enough for a butterfly to potentially escape. The most important rule of the Butterfly House was that none of the butterflies can get out. Once all twenty children were cramped in the waiting area and the front door was closed, I explained the rules of the Butterfly House. "First, please do not touch the butterflies. If they land on you, stay calm and still. If any are on the gravel path, walk carefully around it and come get me. Second, please stay on the gravel path. The plants around the edges are there for the butterflies, so we shouldn't step on them and harm the plants. Third, use your indoor voices inside the butterfly house, we wouldn't want to scare the butterflies by being too loud." I opened the door labeled "Enter" and watched carefully for any butterfly attempting to glide through the yellow plastic panels hanging down over the door to prevent fugitives. After everyone was inside, I carefully closed the door and answered any questions the students had. "Why are they all on the ceiling and not moving? We want to get close to them! We want to really see them!" said one girl. It was an overcast day, and it was still early in the morning. The butterflies always hung to the ceiling when they hadn't gotten enough sunlight and warmth. Nonetheless, the students were still excited by what they saw while watching the butterflies closer down at their level. They ran around eager to find as many as possible. They stood still on the gravel path with their arms outstretched and two fingers pointed parallel to the floor, hoping a butterfly would land on them. Some butterflies were sitting on plants and pollinating flowers. Some were in the midst of emerging from their chrysalis. One had been clinging to the styrofoam-board-covered-by-a-potato-sack for over twenty-four hours with a wrinkled wing. The butterfly wouldn't make it.

On my last day at Sweetbriar, I lifted five different butterflies from the gravel path and into my palms, blew softly on the wings, and waited for them to soar as Veronica taught me. Two of those five left my palms on their own. The other three I placed on a flower hoping it was not the end for them. Every morning before opening we would walk through the Butterfly House looking for those who did not make it through the night to collect their bodies and take them away before visitors arrived. One day, a buckeye butterfly was in the corner laying on its side under a milkweed plant. The wing facing upwards was bent at a ninety-degree angle. A ten-year-old girl tapped my arm, pointed at the butterfly's eyes, and said, "I think he's sick."

The Sweetbriar Nature Center is the only butterfly house on Long Island, NY. When each butterfly dies (most species usually live for only two to three weeks as adults), they're soaked in rubbing alcohol for twenty-four hours to prevent the spread of any diseases from their wings or in their system should they be ingested. They're then disposed of in separate bags within the trash to prevent animals from eating them. Butterflies, mostly for their wings, can be preserved for exhibits, artwork, or as a specimen for scientific research. Rubbing alcohol may not be the best method for preservation, though, as "the alcohol can make them brittle and hard to move around. This can make it easier for your insect to break or become damaged" (Miorelli).[1] This is the reason Sweetbriar puts the dead butterflies in the rubbing alcohol, to make them brittle and not intact, "unusable."

An article on "Monarch Butterfly Garden" mentions the various ways to raise your own butterflies. Similar to how Sweetbriar does it, other methods are easy Do-It-Yourself activities that involve pins to mesh popup cages, taping the stem to a leaf cutting, or tying floss to the stem and taping the floss to a ceiling of sorts (Gomez).[2] Clearly, there is not a lack of butterfly raising. For instance, the International Butterfly Breeders Association, Inc. (IBBA) has dozens of members with butterfly farms. On the IBBA site, each member's contact information and business information is listed. From any of those IBBA members, any individual can purchase live butterflies or chrysalises to be shipped to their doorstep.[3] In the United States, "It's legal to ship certain live animals, including butterflies, through the US Postal Service, as long as they don't require food during their journey and don't make excess noise or smells. "They are shipped in an insulated

1. Miorelli, Nancy. "Collecting Tips – The Awkward Inbetween Steps." *Ask an Entomologist*, 29 Apr. 2015.
2. Gomez, Tony. "Monarch Chrysalis Problems, Solutions, and Normal Development." *Monarch Butterfly Garden*, 20 Sept. 2018.
3. "IBBA Members Contacts." *International Butterfly Breeders Association*.

box with an ice pack. They usually are packed individually in paper envelopes," says Hopper" (Nosowitz).[4] It's almost too easy.

Both the Monarch Biology and Research Lab at the University of Minnesota and the Xerces Society has warned against purchasing and releasing commercial butterflies, though. The Monarch Lab has on their website: "We DO NOT recommend purchasing monarchs from commercial butterfly growers to release into the wild... many monarch researchers believe that the practice of mass-rearing and selling of monarchs is unlikely to benefit the population, and could actually hurt it."[5] Some of those researchers include the Xerces Society, which published a consensus statement on the topic that says, "we believe that releasing commercially produced and continuously mass-reared individuals is unlikely to benefit monarchs, and could actually hurt them, as a result of mass rearing conditions that promote crowding and disease spread, or cause the loss of genetic diversity or adaptation to captive rearing conditions. Large-scale captive rearing and subsequent release can also limit the ability of monitoring programs to understand natural population dynamics."[6] Although there are clearly poor outcomes that can result from mass rearing and raising butterflies, the key to the Sweetbriar Nature Center Butterfly House's success is that no butterflies are allowed to escape--and for good reason. Almost all those who warned against the raising and purchasing of butterflies included a caveat: it is beneficial and supported if it is done for educational purposes or citizen science projects, not to be released into the wild for betterment of the population.

The monarch population is the one of focus for most butterfly-rearing articles and statements, as it is most famed and of concern due to its population plummeting by ninety percent in the past twenty years. It is understandable why many people want to participate in butterflies' survival. Alison Hawthorne Deming writes of her experience while visiting a monarch protection site in Mexico:

> Of the five protected sites, only two are open to tourists, and these, only under the guidance of *vigilantes*, retrained loggers whose job it is to protect the forest from black market logging, disruption, and noise. GUARDA SILENCIO, read the signs posted along the trail– PROTECT THE SILENCE. The remaining three sites will not be opened until naturalists,

4. Nosowitz, Dan. "A Peek Inside the World of Butterfly Farming." *Modern Farmer*, 2 Oct. 2018.
5. "University of Minnesota Monarch Lab." *Monarch Rearing | Biology & Research.*
6. "Joint Statement Regarding Captive Breeding and Releasing of Monarchs." *The Xerces Society.*

> both U.S. and Mexican, have a better understanding of the impact of tourism on the butterflies. As the *vigilantes* led our group through the forest, they leaned down and swept the dirt with their hands in order to clear the path of animals that had fallen in our way and did not have the energy to rise. At first I thought the action was a superfluous ritual--the scattering of bodies on the trail looked dead. But then I saw a man take one of the creatures in his palms and blow on it with his warm breath until the wings loosened and the frail one staggered into the air.[7]

The work of these *vigilantes* and protection sites is powerful; but, not everyone can be the hero saving the monarchs. The phenomenon of Butterfly Houses as insect zoos are open to the public all across the nation. Although there is the biodiversity risk, so long as all are as cautious as Sweetbriar, Butterfly Houses can be a great educational tool. However, there must be a distinction in the roles played by scientists versus citizens. Although places, like Sweetbriar, raising butterflies for educational purposes are beneficial, citizens of the general public should not do the same. Clearly, members of the public concerned with the survival and health of butterfly populations have good intentions; yet, the act of raising and releasing butterflies causes more harm than good. Nevertheless, citizens can still get involved and help with these efforts. Plant milkweed and other butterfly host plants. Continue the education of our youth on the importance of such pollinating species. Support Butterfly Houses, protection sites like those in Mexico, and research centers. We must do everything we can to ensure the continuation and health of butterfly species; however, not everyone can take the same approach. Each approach is valuable in different ways, and a combination of them together really can make a difference.

7. Deming, Alison Hawthorne. "The Edges of the Civilized World." *The Future of Nature: Writing on a Human Ecology from Orion Magazine*, by Barry Lopez, Milkweed Editions, 2007, pp. 143-153.

ERIN STRAUSS

Sophomore
Major: International Studies
Reading: Fiction

I am a sophomore from a suburb of Chicago (Elmhurst). I'm studying International Studies and eventually want to go into law. My dream job is to work for the CIA. My absolute favorite thing to do is travel, so I'll be happy with a career that allows me to experience different parts of the world. Although I have never been a huge writer, my creative writing course last semester was one of my favorite classes I have taken thus far!

Nominated by: Thea Chacamaty

Honey

The room seems to fall silent, but nobody around me appears to stop. Brown Eyed Girl begins to dance through my ears as I feel these large hands wrap around my waist. I turn around, locking eyes with ones of warmth and comfort. It's Charlie. A person that feels so distant from my life, yet is still somehow the most familiar part of me.

The hazel eyes bring me back to a day three years ago years ago when honey trickled off my finger onto my tongue, warming my throat as it traveled down. My thumb stuck to the spoon as I tried to pass it to Charlie. I watched the honey ooze off the spoon as he took his first taste. Nothing felt more like a Georgia August.

Our bee fascination started on my eighth birthday. As little kids, Charlie and I spent hours in his backyard telling each other stories under the peach tree and writing poems about the type of love we were too young to even understand as Van Morrison always played in the background. But we were never allowed past the white fence where his dad worked until we both turned "old enough to understand the beauty of the bees," as his dad always teased us. So when the day finally came for us to cross through the white barrier, I walked down the gravel road to his bright yellow house. Mr. Webber led us in back, where he taught us how to care for the bees and harvest honey for the first time.

For summers afterwards, our lives had been occupied by spending more time with the bees than we did with our own families, and eating lots and lots of honey. Charlie gave me the best gift I could have asked for.

By the end of the day, we had to fill thirty mason jars and bring them to the corner store for the customers whose orders were due for pickup the next day. Instead of working, we sat on the scarlet picnic table and embraced the wind that made the day's heat bearable. Our nerves about starting freshman year dominated the conversation, but I felt settled knowing he would be there by my side. Charlie's skin glowed in the afternoon sun as he told me, "When we're older, the labels on our jars are going to have a picture of us sitting on this exact bench, and a branch from the peach tree is going to hang right over our heads."

His curly locks looked as though someone drizzled honey all over his head. His eyes twinkled with excitement at the thought of the future, reminding me of why it was so difficult to frown around him. The clock inside chimed, signaling that we were going on hour two of talking. But I wasn't concerned because at the end of the day, we always got the job done. That day was no different.

"Charlie, don't forget to come take your medication! You were supposed to with breakfast!" Her voice turned warm when she said, "Hi Emma, sweetie!"

Mrs. Webber's head peeked out from behind the door as she beamed at me. She had always filled in for all of the parenting gaps that my mom left. My mom worked as a lawyer in Atlanta, so her commute alone took a couple hours out of every day. She wasn't strict, but she had refused to have fun or show any compassion after my dad left. She didn't even laugh at the spring talent show when my six-year-old sister, Mia, did an entire comedy skit by herself in front of a gym full of parents and classmates. I doubt my mom realized how much work she had put into practicing for her big night under the spotlight since I was the one who always waited for Mia and walked her home after practice each week. That unbreakable bond between mother and daughter that I always saw in my favorite books and movies was absent from my life.

"I'll be right back. The stupid doctor gave me pills the size of gumballs for that skin thing I was telling you about last week. Meet me over by the hive."

I pulled on my jacket, gloves, and helmet so that all of my skin was masked by white. Charlie ran up behind me with only his gloves on, leaving his suit back by the shed. Wearing the whole attire had always been the most important rule engraved into our heads since day one. He had been feeling rebellious lately. Maybe because we were about to begin high school, so he felt like the teenagers in the movies who ditch class and disobey everything their parents say. I lifted my finger to point to it, but he cut me off.

"This shouldn't take us too long. I'll be fine, don't worry."

Against my better judgement, I let him grab the honey-filled frame. As he turned, he tripped over a tree root but caught himself right before hitting the ground. Bees swarmed the cause of the little earthquake that had just shaken their home, swarming Charlie and clinging to his body like magnets.

Following what we'd been told to do, he sprinted around the backyard, finally making his way back to me. As he approached, I felt relieved to see the surface of his arms again, even though the bronzed skin looked like Minnie Mouse's skirt.

But suddenly, I felt queasy watching his face flush. I could practically hear my heart thump on the ground when I heard his voice. It sounded like a whistle was lodged in his throat as he choked out, "Get my mom."

As Mrs. Webber sped down the gravel road, I explained to her what I had seen happen. Charlie sat in the passenger seat, wheezing with every breath. His eyes appeared to be in another world as we pulled up to the hospital.

My neck hurt when I woke up on the waiting room chair that definitely was not designed for sleeping. The doctor pulled Mrs. Webber aside, but his soft voice overpowered the silence of the area.

"The reaction slowed his heart beat to an alarming rate. The medication he is on is what made the reaction so severe. It could have taken his life. Luckily, you got him here quickly enough that he will be back home in a few days, depending on the speed of his recovery."

A few sleepless nights passed until he finally returned home. After surprising him with a welcome-home cake, I ate homemade chicken noodle soup with Charlie and his parents. The unusual quietness made sense with all of the stress he had been through. But the next day, I realized that his silence had been fueled by anger.

The sun illuminated my room as it rose, waking me up far earlier than my alarm had been set. Toast and jam was my go-to breakfast to take with me on the walk to Charlie's for another day of 'work'. But as I rounded the corner to get into the backyard, I watched Charlie take a full swing at the hive with a baseball bat. He swung again. And again. And for some reason, I couldn't move my feet or mutter a sound when he stormed by me back into the house.

This heaviness settled within my stomach, like a brick had just been placed within me. My eyes got heavy and my throat burned the way it always did when I held back my tears. Weirdly, I didn't feel angry, which I knew because it didn't feel like the way I felt when I thought about my dad. The bees *could* have killed Charlie. But no, it wasn't anger at all. It was sadness. Not a sadness for myself and the hard work I had put into caring for the hive, or a sadness for all of the memories between us that the hive held. Instead, I was sad for the bees and the way they ruined all of the good that they had built up over the years in less than one minute. Was it bad that I felt more sympathy for them than I did for Charlie? I wasn't sure, but all I could think about was that they didn't mean to hurt him.

I slowly approached his room, searching for the right words to say to him. I opened his door to find him lying on his bed tossing a football to himself. He looked so calm, so content with what had just happened.

"Charlie, why would you do that? Do you even understand how much those bees mean to-"

"Just stop, Emma. I don't give a shit about those bees anymore. Even Noah said it the other day–who the hell cares about bees? I'm not an eight-year-old anymore. I have other things I should be thinking about now, like girls. And football. Tryouts are next week, you know."

Of course it was Noah. He was like a god to Charlie, who just worshipped everything that came out of Noah's mouth. Charlie was swearing, too. He never swore. My mind was cluttered with words of anger and confusion, trying to figure out what to say, but Charlie quickly filled in the silence.

"I'm done. With the bees, with everything. And if you honestly care that much about those things, then go ahead and waste your time. But don't try to waste mine."

I turned my back. Apparently, his time was too precious for his best friend. "Goodbye, Charlie."

Week after week, Charlie became more distant. I would understand if he wanted a break from the bees, but it didn't need to include me. I didn't sting him. In the hallways, he only gave a quick nod when he saw me, and I was lucky to get even that when he was walking with his friends. We learned how to stay out of one another's lives. The school was triple the size of our grade school, so it was a lot easier to avoid one another than I had expected it to be. He stuck to his friends like a wolf in a pack, while I was busy adjusting to the fast-paced classes. I saw it happen in movies and books, where the boy turned all mean and cocky around his friends. But to my own, popsicle-loving, comic-reading friend? I guess I just didn't see it coming.

The more time that passed by without spending time with him, the more I felt myself turning against the bees. They did almost take my best friend's life. He was a lot more important to me than any little insect ever could be. Yet, when Mia asked, "How are the bees doing this year?" and I said, "Oh, I haven't paid any attention to them; that was just a dumb hobby for a little while," the words tasted sour coming out of my mouth. It didn't feel right to despise the things that had made me more happy than my own mom ever could. But I also couldn't just forgive them and act like the horrible way they almost took one of the few people I actually opened up to never happened.

When spring showers brought back the vibrant green that coated the rolling hills, I worried about what would keep me occupied that summer. School had allowed me to convince myself that I was too busy for friends, but emptiness settled over me as I imagined a summer without my usual routine or buddy.

Paper scattered the hall on the last day of school, and I found Mia waiting for me by the field. We walked home, but decided to take the long route that afternoon. As soon as Mia opened the back door, I heard his voice. Then I saw his face for the first time in eight years. That face that resembled what I saw everyday in the mirror all too similarly. My dad stood in front of me with wide arms.

"Oh, how I've missed my beautiful girls!"

I felt Mia's eyes watching me, wondering what I would do so that she could follow. I gave him the type of hug I gave to my teacher earlier that day when I said goodbye for the summer–the kind that is loose and ends with a pat on the back because it feels weird to show any type of affection towards a teacher. We chatted to the extent of, "How has school been?" before I realized I was wasting my time and decided to leave. My mom said, "Please be ready for dinner by 6," as I slammed my bedroom door.

Dinner crept by slowly and uncomfortably. He told us about his new job as a banker in Boston, but left out the details of the new family I knew he must have had. After dinner, Mia followed me into my room.

"Emma, why did he come back now?"

"He must think we need him. And that we haven't moved on without him."

I didn't know how to reply further so I just shrugged it off and turned on her favorite movie, *Cinderella*, as she fell asleep next to me. A few weeks went by peacefully, and I started to believe that he was back for good when I saw my mom beam with delight one night as she listened to one of his made-up stories. But as they say, all good things must come to an end.

I woke up to Mia's gentle taps. Shrill voices from downstairs carried through the whole house, and it felt too familiar.

"Go change into some clothes and follow me," I said to Mia. She scurried out of my room and returned wearing the floral sundress I gave her for birthday the previous year.

I genuinely enjoyed the nostalgia that was brought on by walking down that gravel road. It reassured me that I was making the right choice to return and share it all with Mia, even though she was younger than I was my first time.

As per usual, Mr. Webber was in back. He greeted me and welcomed Mia, ignoring the fact that I hadn't been there in over a year. He wasn't the type to care about that. Taking Mia aside, he showed her the ropes and got her started by the next day. We harvested honey all summer long, and my life fell back into place piece by piece. Over the course of a month, my dad turned our home into a warzone. The bees were mine and Mia's source of refuge. I rushed to them when the ringing of voices hurt my ears. I rushed to them when my summer school teacher gave my essay a D. And I *always* rushed to them when I started to think about my old friend Charlie. When my dad finally left the guest room vacant, I realized that the bees were the only ones always there for me. It felt better with him gone anyways.

The next few summers came and went, and Mia and I spent them working with Mr. Webber on the honey bee farm. When I could drive, I started to help deliver jars to different stores and homes. It really became a full-time job. The money I earned helped me get through all of the senior year extravaganzas. My last year in high school had been flying by, but I didn't feel the same uneasiness I overheard girls in homeroom talking about when they mentioned graduation on the announcements. High school had been fun, but something felt like it was missing from the years that were supposed to be some of the best of my life.

And now, that 'something' that I have for so long tried to deny I miss is standing in front of me at our senior prom. Our favorite Van Morrison song floods me with memories of our innocence basking in the summer sunshine. It's too hard for me to push him away, so I sway back and forth with him. His voice is way deeper than I remember it being as he asks me to step outside with him.

I listen to Charlie talk about missing his childhood. I listen to him talk about how his new friends actually aren't as 'cool as everyone thinks they are'. I listen to him tell me about the way his life has changed and how high school has taught him things he never thought it would.

And then I hear him whisper "I'm sorry."

It isn't the type of apology I tell Mia when she catches me stealing her clothes. It's genuine. And it's so heartfelt that I have to pretend not to see his eyes glisten with water as I hold my own back from doing the same.

Up until this moment, I have imagined us making up with an elaborate apology. Yet, I suddenly realize that I don't have time for an apology that demands hours of explanation or a fancy letter. We are almost done with senior year, and college will be here before we know it. All I want right now is to my spend my senior prom just as I had imagined it all my life–right next to the person who means the most to me.

"You'll always be my best friend."

And I honestly do mean that. He messed up, and quite a few times. But he also made me laugh, taught me things about the world and myself, and gave me the friendship a little girl can only dream of. I can't let those bad moments take away from all the joy he contributed to my life. Just like the bees.

Here he is, showing that smile I once missed so dearly. And I don't see betrayal or evil in him. Rather, I see a guy who once taught himself to find the bad in the good; who learned to see the ugliness in something so beautiful. But he learned to outgrow it. And now, all I see in front of me is my best friend. As his arms wrap around me, something pokes my chest. When he steps back, I notice the golden bee pin on his tie as it shimmers in the moonlight.

ALEX TROMBLEY

Sophomore
Major: Physics
Minor: Creative Writing
Reading: Fiction

Alex is a writer from Birmingham, Michigan. He is currently a Sophomore studying Physics and Creative Writing. He mostly sticks to prose form but enjoys writing in as many different genres as possible. Among his favorite genres are historical, realistic and speculative fiction. It has always been Alex's dream to tell stories as a profession, whether by film, written stories or some other method. Besides writing, he enjoys playing music, drawing and, yes, even doing math on occasion.

Nominated by: Akil Kumarasamy

Suburbia

The wind danced between the tall pines in a whistling slalom and settled upon the quiet little town of Sandessy. Today was a day without rain, a rare and beloved experience for those native Sandessians. Though that chill Autumn breeze from the fishhook-shaped lake just over yonder would surely nip at them even through their coats and sweaters, they would be out in force today, enjoying the sun for what small time they were able to see it through the clouds.

Some, like Bill Waterson, would enjoy the day with a far-too-long game of catch so that, for the next few waterlogged weeks, they would be all catched-out. Others, like Frankie Jordan, would play soccer in the school yard, passing to themselves between the invisible feet of their imaginary defenders. Others still would find themselves entrenched in their usual rainy day activities only now with a bit of sunlight streaming through the windows.

Such was the plan of a mister Eddie Dustain, who found himself now in the local, podunk movie theatre next to Suzie Chamberlain. The seats creaked with every small movement and, sometimes, even creaked without. The popcorn was stale and bitter and the marquee still bore the names of the three films they had stopped showing sometime last week. No one had bothered to switch them, or the already antiquated and yellowing film posters inside, for the current showings. Why should they bother? It wasn't as if anyone really cared what was showing, many came multiple times a week to watch the same film they had seen just the day before last. There was no other theatre in town and, in this quiet of a town, there was little else to do.

To Eddie and Suzie (and, indeed, most the rest of the audience) it was not the film that interested them. No, their eyes were directed elsewhere, covertly searching each other for signs of interest. Were her shoulders turned ever so slightly towards him? Was his hand inching over the shared armrest towards her? Was the brushing of her knee on his intentional and do you think that he minded her leg touching him or did he find it irritating? There were so many questions to ask and only an hour and a half to find the answers. So much for the pair to do and, yet, so little time.

It was a dance for them, a dance that had them exasperated by the end of the day but a dance nonetheless. They would recount every tiny little detail to their friends who would pretend to be interested only to complain to each other later about their indecisiveness. For Eddie and Suzie though, they would have nothing else. There was a certain special kind of heaven that could only be found in the chase, that subtle chord of anxiety that was struck with every hand brushing the hair behind the ear and every goofy grin given while leaning against a brick wall. It was that thin and strenuous thread that kept each small encounter between the two so lush and exciting. It was a fragile thing, rice paper kept whole only by the denial of the tears already opened around the edges. Perhaps it was the sweet knowledge that they were worth being chased or perhaps it was the same exhileration a hunter felt when chasing after a hare. Whatever it was they had fallen heads over heels for it.

For now though, it was a dance they did in the dark. They followed the orchestrations of their heartbeats and the flashing lights on the screen. They would peek from the corner of their eyes in the darkness and, if they caught the other looking, they would look away and pretend it hadn't happened at all with a heavy breath and a quick palpitation. Eddie watched as the subtle reflections of the projector danced on her eyes and flooded her pale skin with a slight and quiet blue. It caught upon her dark brown hair rolling down her head thick, vibrant and with the ever slightest of waves. He watched as the light caught all of those little strands that had somehow freed themselves from her carefully constructed ponytail and now danced with the air conditioner breeze that filled the room. He watched that slight definition in her neck as her heartbeat showed through, cast light shades and overtones and how each tiny breath came with a little swell of her chest and he thought about how he wanted desperately to kiss that soft and ticklish part where neck meets clavicle and how he wanted to trail his way, kissing all the way up to her soft pink-painted lips. His thoughts were interrupted by a simulacrum of the sun on the screen and so he turned away embarrassed. What was he thinking just then? They were just friends weren't they? Was he staring just then? She hadn't noticed had she? Oh god, what would she say if she had noticed? But now, as the sun faded away to a diner scene cast in reds, it was Suzie's turn to sneak peeks under safety of darkness.

The first place her eyes went was to his. Perhaps it was one of those tired cliches, but cliches surely had to have come from somewhere right? His eyes were dark and brooding and holding in their greyish blue iris' some odd kind of tired happiness. They were intoxicating in a sort of way; like they had to them some energism which had been locked away behind wall of caution and suspicion. Sometimes, it shone through more vibrantly, that subtle energy and, on those happy occasions, she felt her heart racing just looking at him. There was a fire burning in him that she loved but it seemed to be a fire that he was wary of showing. She only ever got to see it when he fought and when he played sports with the other boys. It was the only reason that she stomached spending time with that rabblerouser friend of Eddie's, Johnny Milligan. He may have brought nothing but trouble but, at the very least, that trouble came with the opportunity to break through Eddie's stony faced facade. She had no idea why he kept it hidden, maybe he thought it made him look cooler, as if apathy was something even remotely attractive.

These boys, all of them her age, were a load of fools. They would, it seemed, do anything to seem "hot" and all that that desperation ever did for them was make them into even bigger assholes than they already were. Eddie may have just been another one of those foolish children, still waiting for that emotional growth spurt to kick in, but for some reason she wanted him still. She told herself that it was that fire that she thought she had seen burning in his eyes but, in truth, she knew it was her own girlishness. She shook the thought from her head, the last thing in the world that she wanted to be was a hypocrite. That was, after all, one of the worst sins a person could commit; preaching something in which you have no faith and giving orders that you yourself slyly slip around. Her parents did that sort of thing often, her father telling her that too much tv was a bad thing right before stealing her place on the couch and her mother telling her that she should never let her self-worth be taken down by a boy but then being unable to tell her father from Christ. They weren't bad parents all things considered, not by a long shot; her friends had it much worse, especially Bobby and Frankie, but that didn't excuse hers from their sins. She loved them, but she couldn't forgive them for their faults. To do so would be like admitting those same faults in herself, something she was never prone to do.

Eddie's eyes flicked over and caught hers before the two jerked their heads away as if struck on the cheek. Shit, had he seen her looking? For that matter, had she caught him looking just now? No, the two teens resolved, the other couldn't possibly have noticed. The game would continue.

Johnny Milligan was out on the prowl, looking for trouble same as always. He had his hands shoved wrist deep in his pockets, fishing around for nothing in particular. His calloused fingertips found the smooth surface of a folding knife. It had an oak handle, he knew, carved with a crude portrait of a wolf. The blade was thick and heavy. His pa had given it to him some time back, a birthday gift maybe. Johnny's pa didn't give him too much and often, when he did, what he gave really had nothing to do Johnny.

Ever since they Johnny's mom left them, his pa had had a hard time remembering little things like birthdays or how old Johnny was. He didn't ask and Johnny didn't tell, both knew they would just wind up disappointed anyhow. That knife was from better times though, before his ma ran off with some fella from out of town. It was his pa's old hunting knife, made for skinning deer and gutting fish and the like. Once upon a time, the Milligans had a been a heartier woodsy stock. This was no longer the case. No, neither Johnny nor his pa did much hunting with that knife. Not hunting deer anyway.

The knife had never drawn blood in either Johnny's or his pa, Sean's, hands. That being said, they loved flashing it with a big grin and, on special occasion, waving it about a bit too carelessly. But never, absolutely never, did they actually cut anyone with it. Not when Johnny was getting his ass handed to him by the older boys on Fifth Avenue and not when Sean got his teeth knocked down his throat by Bobby Waterson's pa, Thomas. It takes a real special kind of psycho to actually cut a guy, a special kind of psycho which neither of the Milligans could claim to be.

Johnny, perhaps, had a bit more of the "real psycho" in him than his dad did. A bit more violence. A bit more anger. The boys down at the station all said so when they thought Johnny couldn't hear them. His dad was a little shit back in his day, they would say, but his kid's even worse. Johnny knew them all by name just like Sean knew all the officers back when he was young and rambunctious. The cells there, it seemed, were a home away from home. If you were looking for Johnny, you went to the precinct first and, most of the time, you found him waiting and bloodied up. That was Johnny, always in trouble and always looking beaten up.

This was something that everybody knew about Johnny Milligan but nobody would say out loud; he was good at starting fights but shit at fighting them. Nearly every fight he was in, he lost. It didn't help him any that he would take on groups of boys five strong on his own. It also didn't help that he picked on anyone he could find that was bigger than him. The secret though, what really made Johnny tick, was that he loved it all. There was nothing better, in his eyes, than getting the living shit beaten out of you. He never told this to anyone and he would feed them their own teeth if they ever accused him of it, but damned if it wasn't the truth. Sean Milligan tried to teach his son to fight many times, taught him to guard his face with his forearms, taught him to throw a proper punch, taught him all the dirty little things you could do to take down a guy twice your size in thirty seconds flat. None of them, though, none of them stuck. Johnny was a boy in love with pain. It made him feel alive, happy. In a sick sort of way, it reminded him of his childhood. His father had never stayed his hand, which was admittedly part of the reason that his wife had left with that slick-suited businessman all that time ago, and Johnny had found on his pa's knuckles something akin to meaning. Maybe not meaning exactly, but something close to it. He found, buried in the callouses, sensation; something he figured was worth living for.

There weren't a lot of those in Johnny's life, things worth living for. He didn't bother too long with school and girls didn't interest him. He didn't give a shit if he was broke or rich or whatever. No matter what it was, it all seemed worthless. He told himself that it started when his mom left. It started long before that but that didn't stop him from blaming her. It was the impermanence of everything that really got to him, the way the rain washed away all the footprints in the dirt, the way people just came and went leaving nothing behind but hearsay, everything. He had no stories of his grandma and next to none of his grandpa, just that he used to hunt deer from out in his cabin. The same would surely be said of him or, worse yet, nothing would be said at all. He couldn't stand the thought of bringing a kid into the world, knew he would just fall into the same mistakes as his pa did. He didn't want to be the type of fella who taught a kid what the buckle end of a belt felt like. No, there would be no more Milligans after Johnny. So what was the point?

Pain. That's what there was. At the end of it all. Just pain, that sweet sensation. Little fires raging on his skin. The taste of your own blood, the cold hurt when you got your teeth chipped up and had their cores exposed to your breath, that electric numbness when you pressed on a bruise, there was addiction there. He didn't want booze, he didn't want drugs, he didn't want the "Big O", he wanted the tingling that spread from a cut when you picked off a scab. Now *that*, that was what Johnny called living. The only question now was where to find it.

JENA VALLINA

Freshman
Major: Undeclared
Reading: Short Fiction

Jena Vallina is a Chicago native and current freshman in the Residential College, contemplating a major in either English or philosophy. Jena wrote her first novel at age 14. It was about dragons, and it was not very good. She hopes to tackle themes such as the complexities of womanhood, family, and mental illness in her writing. When not reading or writing, Jena enjoys spending time with her dog Dahlia, who is the love of her life, and her family and friends, who are also pretty cool. She often considers returning to that dragon novel.

Nominated by: John Buckley, Sarah Messer and Laura Thomas

The Bird's Nest

Ruth had been putting off cleaning the gutters for quite some time now.

It wasn't that the task had slipped her mind, per se, although that may have been a reasonable excuse were anyone to mention to her the situation of the clogged gutters. It wasn't even that she was too busy. These days, it seemed that all Ruth had on her hands was ample time to get things done. Time to sweep the floors, time to pack the Christmas tinsel into its Styrofoam dressing, time to shear the bushes and trim the roses and still, she had time left over to get a manicure. And of course, she had written it down. Ruth never left important tasks to memory. Sandwiched right between "donate old clothes to Goodwill" and "finish *Anna Karenina* for book club" on her official list of things: clean the dreaded gutters. Yet the rain kept pouring, and by the time some impoverished orphan was donning Mike's old jersey and poor broken-hearted Anna had become roadkill on the train tracks, the gutters were colonized by a mutated sludge of debris.

It had acquired a life of its own, the monster nestling alongside her roof. She hated the sight of it, the sticky fleshiness of it like a pulsating organ, the putrid stench which would have been a toxic yellow if it could acquire physical form. It smelled yellow too. Not a creamy unassuming eggshell hue, but neon with its harshness and just as sick-inducing. Ruth hesitated to even poke it with a stick, although she knew her time for wobbling was over. Although a wobble wouldn't be the worst thing. At least, one on a very tall ladder.

Oh, this was all so unlike her. Ruth wasn't unproductive. In fact, quite the contrary. She prided herself on her timeliness and can-do attitude. While other brides slacked off on writing thank-you notes to wedding guests until their silver anniversary came and went, Ruth penned heartfelt letters to aunts Barb and Debra and Mary while on the plane to their honeymoon in Bora Bora. No, Ruth was no slacker. She should have cleaned the gutters a long time ago, when she first started noticing the grime building up and dirty water overflowing from the downspout. But each time she reached for the yellow latex gloves and the trowel and the bucket, she...didn't. She found something else to do, some useless task like polish the wedding china or organize the shoe rack. She tucked the gutters deep within the crevices of her mind, some dusty abandoned shelf she didn't want to look at, saving it for a not-so-rainy day with the secret hope that somehow the situation would resolve on its own.

Stupid. So stupid, yet she had the gall to be surprised when she awoke that morning to a flooded basement and drowned peonies. It should have felt inevitable, the consequence of her inaction, but Ruth was suddenly struck with a sharp pain as though she was the one drowning in the filthy waters. Mike did cross her mind, as she wallowed in her delusions. He would return home from work tonight to his hard-earned house in disarray, and it would be all her fault. He would...well, what would he do to her? He wouldn't strike her, although she wished desperately he would. That would make everything so much simpler, if only he could raise a hand to her. Just once. Not hard. But hard enough to leave a mark. But alas, Mike wasn't like that. He wasn't one of those angry men, who wear their masculinity like a flag. Mike wouldn't even yell at her. He never raised his voice, especially not over trivial matters such as the gutters.

Ruth knows what Mike would do. He'd smile, first of all, maybe even laugh. He'd ask her, in that oh-so-kind voice, why didn't you ask me to do it, because of course I would, if only you'd just ask. And he'd say it in the same voice he said, "I love you," and "Will you marry me?" and "I do." Because to Mike, Ruth could do no wrong. She could clog all the gutters in the world and it wouldn't make a single difference. It was barely a crook in the straight road he walked, leading into that shiny golden bubble of marital bliss which eluded Ruth like the lyrics of a half-remembered song. A song she remembers liking, if only she could recall the chorus.

Ruth climbs onto the ladder, adjusting the hose slung over her shoulder like a pageant sash. She has been weaker these days, on account of her newfound "condition." But she refuses to be dogged down by her sagging body's impulses, which plead with her to lie down and relax. She doesn't want to relax, because to relax would mean to stay still, and to stay still would mean letting the thoughts screaming inside her head to consume her at last. And that just wouldn't do. No, she needed to be moving, always moving, not thinking about everything that is going wrong because to do so would admit that there was a problem in the first place. And there wasn't.

"Hard at work again, Ruth? I swear, you never stop!" Kelly is a neighbor, but she may as well belong to an extraterrestrial species for how foreign her lifestyle is to Ruth. The insidious suburbanite, with her plastic tits and rosy-cheeked cherubs, constantly coos at Ruth about hot yoga and Brita filters and other moronic stuff she supposes are relevant to her interests now. The woman is a goddamn curse, reminding Ruth every day about what she was on the verge of metamorphosizing into.

"Bitch of a storm last night, wasn't it?" Ruth smiles perkily and hates herself just a little bit more.

The real bitch is Ruth. She knows that, knows it in the prune pit of her wrinkled coal-black heart. There is nothing wrong with Kelly. Her boobs were probably real. Her husband was sweet and loving as her own, and her children adorable. A boy and a girl. The quintessential nuclear family. Like a propaganda poster during the Cold War. Ruth supposed she was like the Soviets, rubbing her hands and plotting the destruction of their perfect American Beauty in the background. A true sign of a person's awfulness. Loathing someone's happiness when they never wronged her, when she herself had no reason to not be happy.

Mike looks at her, and he's so in love she wants to scream. And then she wants to dig her nails into her skin, to bite off her fingers one by one, because why can't she look at him the same way? She did once. She must have. She remembers it faintly, those tiny heartstrings plucked like a harp inside of her. But it was so long ago, when they were just kids themselves and marriage and all its side-effects belonged to some crazy and alien ether far, far away from where they dwelled. Lately she's been thinking that they were best left to daydreams; the beautiful kind, the kind you lingered in but could always wake up from.

Her new lover doesn't look at her that way, doesn't kiss her on the mouth or make her breakfast. He wouldn't offer to clean the gutters. His breath smells pungently of vodka, although he swears he hasn't touched a drop. He tells her sometimes, warm limbs entangled under cold sheets, that "the old ball and chain keeps it locked up like it's crack." Ruth hears a lot about the phantom constantly haunting the space between their bodies, before and after and occasionally during their frantic trysts. He must kiss her on the mouth. Perhaps he fears the pheromones in her lipstick will seep into Ruth, turning her into another nagging nuisance weighing him down with Tiffany jewels and double strollers.

The hose spurts a stream of water into the gutters, and out pours the mushy stew of crusty leaves and twigs out onto the pavement. Ruth watches the flow of garbage when

S P L A T

goes the bird's nest, tangle of twigs on the sidewalk, intact if not for the shatter of eggshells in a yellow pink slop. A slab of life, now dead, and Ruth finds she cannot divert her gaze from the carnage below.

Somewhere a momma bird is off collecting food, and she does not know that all of her babies are dead and that her home is gone. It was her fault for leaving them, those tiny fragile eggs alone in their feeble nest, helpless to outside forces. What the bird did not know, was too ignorant to realize, was that the world was an evil place. It is sick, infected by the fatal disease called people. People who see beauty and tenderness and wish for rot. People who see life, who see those precious new lives which are the only pure things left untouched from that black spreading stain, and bring death crashing down in response.

Ruth places her hand on her belly, wondering if the parasite growing inside of her looks like the babies spilled on the concrete. She searched it up once, on a whim. Her baby was no bigger than a little bean. No way could it survive outside her nest. She imagines taking it out, bundling it in her hands, letting it slip from her fingers into some infinitesimal void. A checkmark, posted next to a problem so stupidly solvable it could make her chuckle.

The still-streaming hose drops from her weak hands and washes away all the remnants of the murder but the yolk which settles in the sidewalk cracks. She wonders, briefly, if the sidewalk cracks will always carry the leftovers of her crime, and if it'll remind her each time she kneels down to water the flowers that the rain is still whispering her secrets to all those unlucky enough to pass by.

CIELLE WATERS-UMFLEET

Freshman
Major: Creative Writing & Literature
Minor: Spanish
Reading: Poetry

I am from Greater Grand Rapids, MI, an area that's made much better because my three dogs still live there. I have figure-skated since second grade and am currently on the U-M synchronized skating team. I am also on the staff for What The F magazine here on campus and have written two amazing articles according to my mom.

Nominated by: Sarah Messer

Because You Called

1. dad, back when I measured my age
in the fluffiness of my bedroom rug,
you and mom barged in one day
wielding a paper with black ink stating
that I had sent over one thousand texts
in the last month and demanded to know
how. my cheeks flushed at the time but now
i'm thinking back on it and one thousand
divided by thirty is precisely thirty-three-
point-three-repeating. i said thirty-three things
with one point three days repeating. if
we only get thirty-three sayings a day, how
should we spend them? i seem to be a poor
budgeter. how do you not waste them on
"excuse me" and "what's for lunch?" and
"i love you" so you can blow them all on
"i'm sorry?"

2. it's the future now, and our indulgences
no longer waggle on a paper but rather glare
from a screen. the black numbers are in for
this month, and i'm not the one racking up
the bill this time. in fact, it was you who
dialed the longest-distance call. i was in
ann arbor and you were back in mom's
living room, the july sunset bruising the walls
purple. the line spanned a full two and a half
years. does verizon charge extra for that?

3. upon reviewing the numbers, yes, verizon
does charge extra for that. we might need to
restrain our sayings budget this month.

4. the total cost of that phone call: one marriage,
one townhouse, two feet broiled on the tarmac,
a couple dozen ant traps lodged in the corners
and a bottle of raid for the edges, five hundred fried

eggs and four unfortunate salmon, a string of rainbow
christmas lights I couldn't sleep without, a
draft the length of winter from my cracked
window frame, nine forest spiders who wandered
in and shriveled on their backs, suitcases full of
unworn laundry choked by tobacco smoke, a pair of
shoes from the day i discovered peat, a pound of
mud from the days i still went back, the days
i wished my arms were steak, the days i tracked the
sun from the far end of the couch, the days i slaughtered
and burned for my laptop, the days my arms were
steak, each strawberry ribbon i tied around my wrists,
each pushpin that mistook my legs for a tackboard,
the tissues making the trash beg for mercy, wednesdays
fattened with restaurant meals, fridays clogged with
pandering and five-step farewells to the dogs, sundays
blessed with a packed car, two summers, two winters,
two hours to cram it all into the moving van, one
carpet infused with dog pee, two bathrooms
polished with glitter glue, three cabinet doors
sagging from toddler warfare, maybe seventy, eighty,
ninety bowls of slime, but I lost count at the same
time as my peace and quiet, three weeks' pay bent
into a circle, the gravity of the word "family", a
full nest, a courthouse wedding consummated by
a drive to kalamazoo, half a christmas to make
up for a whole thanksgiving, a tank of gas
diverted to ann arbor and back, five hours of
complaining, one hour of appointment-scheduling,
a high-five and a pat on the back, one decent
mental health day, one night of potential productivity,
two sweatshirts slicked with tears and mucus,
one proverbial cork jettisoned from the bottle, and
a couple cents for the time.

5. i'm not sure any of us alone can foot
the bill. should we all chip in this period?
things are tight right now, but i've still
got the stuff from my birthday lying around.
twenty dollars and indisputable blood.

i'll throw it on the pile for all it's worth
and hope every bit helps.

Bedtime Verse

Even if the night is dark, as nights often tend to be, and
flicking the wall doesn't light a spark, at least I know the

sun will rise tomorrow to fill my room with golden rays
and if it doesn't, if it's cloudy instead, at least the walls

will be muted because my drooping eyes hate when they
shout. I'll wake up tomorrow, at least, either naturally

or to the screeching serenade of my alarm, and don't tell
her, but she sounds like pubescent duck when she sings,

but at least she tries. No matter how early I demand it,
she always performs, and at least she takes pride in her

purpose of checking on me first thing in the morning.
And if, oh dear, if she should falter tomorrow, should

a tickle bubble up in her throat right as she opens her
lungs, at least I can lie in the grasp of my own fantasy

for an extra minute or two, swirl and rock on the waves
of my thoughts. Eventually, at least one will deliver me

to the shore. If nothing else, at least I can rest my body
on a mat of optimism and float away bundled in promise.

KATE WILCOX

Junior
Major: English and Creative Writing
Reading: Poetry

Kate is a poet, a tremendously terrible singer, and quite possibly half-wolf. She is currently working on a collection of poems that use nature to explore the ways we relate to the body in various stages of recovery. She delights in dancing with bare feet, and eating large amounts of raspberries. Sometimes at the same time. She is not sure what the future holds, but knows that it will be full of poetry and hopes it will take her somewhere near the sea.

Nominated by: James Cody Walker

How Would You Make A Snowwoman?

Don't think before answering:
Are you thinking of snow boobs?

They say gender is dead,
but when I say

Snowwoman, somebody says *boobs*.
The lemons are in a silver bowl

On the table the night I first tell you
I want to bind my chest.

You say it's unhealthy.

We are 17 when we drink
green absinthe from your grandma's teacups

You see tigress shapes in the fireplace.
You are 21 when you do it again and again.

But I will not say anything.

When I first dressed in my brother's clothes
my family laughed.

Now they ask if I need more "guy-jeans"
from the store this is what's important:

the icicles crystallized in Dad's beard when he
turns to watch his kids sled,

all our arms looping around each other,
Luke in his blue snowsuit a plump robin egg.

Mom helping us make hot chocolate,
my brothers and I sneaking marshmallows.

I'm trying not to be bitter. This is not for you.
The most sacred parts of me are queer etches

on my skin like freckles. I'm not bitter and it's okay
if you can't read them. I never asked you to.

Woman with Wings Clipped

The tickle of sweetgrass against
pink cheek. You fall into it and I
watch it lap you up, a box of
Free Puppies. All day we kept
saying how good it felt against our
skin – a prickle, a sting, a soft kiss
at the end: This is all we knew of
of pleasure.
And here you are,
sweetgrass folding beneath
spine, curling around arms,
stroking the bottoms of feet,
There are some people the soft
spots of the earth just want to
swallow. As a child, the space
between my shoulder blades
would spasm at night. I was
certain there were wings, despertate,
forced down by
skeleton, red muscle.
I always did like to feed humming
birds, to bring the sweet sugar
water to my lips. With child's certainty,
I jumped off the roof
and
Shattered, spitting
dirt. Sometimes if I lie
beneath someone long enough
their features shift and distort them
into a monster. But when your fingers pull me
down beside you and I go graceless,
a stem stabs into tailbone, I am giddy again.
When I roll closer to you, we'll take
turns splitting each other in half while the
earth coils around our ankles
and knits us back together.

Young Hare Ghazal

Where has she gone? Have we lost the pretty one, the pink-nosed and delicate hare?
Ah, there! – Veiled across another one's shoulders – Even better with no skeleton hare.

Stolen from the field by the hand of Dürer – to sit still on that table and be painted, dear.
And if she squirmed – made stiller, still – We'll take the blood for wine – a redolent hare.

I went to the fair as a child and found them there – rows of wire cages, ribbons adorned.
Winner at the end of the row – Always white-furred and red-eyed – Sweet, celebrant hare.

And If I were you, I'd hide as best I could, or else
They'll find use for you – there's no room for pestilent hare.

Perhaps Dürer only kept her in a cage – Would that be better to hear?
I won't kill you entirely, whispered Dürer – *Only your temperament, hare.*

And what for the other? Will she be taken for paintings too, the weary-eyed, dull hare?
Never, never – There's no room for those like her – We crave a ruby-lipped, elegant hare.

And I, Kate, have not yet escaped – I've only run the blade through my hair.
I'll never be able to pose that way – a perfect feminine hare.

ELENA WILNER

Sophomore
Major: Computer Science
Minor: Creative Writing
Reading: Fiction Short Story

I am currently a sophomore in LSA majoring in Computer Science and minoring in Creative Writing. I have always loved to read and write, and publishing a novel is definitely on the bucket list. In my free time, I play a lot of tennis, spend as much time outdoors or hiking with friends/family as is possible, and of course binge watch Netflix!

Nominated by: Thea Chacamaty

Imogen's Secret

They always used to stare at her as she walked by. No outward aggression, no hostile remarks—it wasn't that kind of attention. It also wasn't any type of reverence or lust that drew their gaze. In the drab hallways of an aged and tired public school, hidden within the maze of cornfields that is Abilene, Kansas, she stood out. It might have been the overalls, a clothing staple which she seemed to own in every imaginable color and which she wore every day, regardless of the fact that Abilene had both very hot summers and very cold winters. It might have been the platform heels, of which she owned only one pair, black and scuffed so badly from all the use that they wouldn't sell for a dollar nowadays. It might have been the wild and curly white-blonde head of hair, the kind you'd imagine would become a toddler but which teenage girls usually iron into flatness. Not her, though. Not Imogen.

I remember when I first saw her. It was the beginning of my last year of middle school, and I had spent ten minutes in front of the mirror that morning telling myself I could make it, only to have the temporary artificial confidence leak out of my bones the second I walked through the door. I had just moved from a neighboring town, and I didn't know anyone—but everyone seemed to know everyone. There were shrieks of long lost friends, arms reaching out and grasping those whom they hadn't seen in months, high pitched laugher of cliques reunited, even the low squabble of a few band members practicing their music. Everyone had a place, everyone had somewhere to be, except for me. I could feel the panic starting to set in, a familiar sensation characterized by a loud and undistinguishable buzzing that roared in my ears. I ducked into the closest restroom, and I went to the sink to wash my hands so that if someone came in, they would think I was actually using the bathroom instead of, well, the truth.

I took a lot of deep breaths looking into that mirror. Like really, really loud and shaky deep breaths, the kind that sound as if you're going to cry. To this day I can still hear how loud those breaths were, echoing off the very walls and sending my body into nervous spasms. It must have sounded like I was dying.

"Are you okay?" The words came from one of the stalls, even though I was pretty certain I had checked to make sure I was alone. I was so surprised that I lurched forward slightly and had to grip both sides of the sink to steady myself. I heard the distinctive sound of a lock sliding, and then the sharp *clack* of a heel hitting the floor. And then *she* stepped out.

The first thing I thought when I saw Imogen was that she definitely didn't belong in Kansas. I was used to the same sort of people, the same generalized appearance that so many of us mimicked. Everyone sounded the same, too, you could hear it when you walked past them, a low monotonous buzzing that I could never get out of my head. I'm sure if you looked real close you could spot our differences, but to my eye, Abilene was a town of greys. Even if you were something else outside of Abilene, that's what you became the second you stepped into it–the second you decided to make it your home. But Imogen's eyes were as bright a blue as her overalls, and her hair was so blonde it was practically white. She sounded different, too. Her voice wasn't a tedious drone. She defied my natural law of Kansas, and so just like many of us would do if we saw a dog walking on its hind legs, I stared at her.

I stared so much that I completely forgot to answer her–forgot the question, even. I watched as she washed her hands, not looking up once to check her reflection or comb a finger through her hair. At the time, I thought I was seeing unbridled confidence in its true form, and I was struck by a pang of jealousy. Not of how she looked, per say, but of how she looked at herself.

I picked up the little things, like how she had a little mark on the top of her forehead, right below the hairline–almost like a tattoo. It jumped out at me, because I actually had one just like it. I was still in this sort of trance when she reached out her arm and wiped a tear off my cheek. I didn't even know I had a tear on my cheek.

"Walk with me to class?" she asked, and I nodded, even though it was quite the assumption that we had the same class, that we were in the same grade, even. But it turned out that we did, and we were. It never struck me how strange that was until now, because there was no way for her to have known. I remember my short little legs hurrying to keep up with her long strides, and the sound of her heels on the hard tiled floor. Most of all, I remember the stares.

Wherever Imogen went, heads turned. At first I felt special, felt as though I had made friends with someone really cool, someone who could make my life a little easier than it tended to be at previous schools. But it wasn't long before I perceived how very *not normal* this particular type of staring was. It was done tactlessly, with no constraints–hell, I even noticed the teachers doing it! When Imogen clacked on by in those loud heels of hers, everyone stopped whatever they were doing–for some this meant halting dead in their tracks–and watched her pass. It was making me slightly anxious again, and I could hear the buzzing in my ears gaining volume. I thought I heard something through the static–something too rude to repeat–but when I looked at Imogen, she didn't seem to notice. And I was not about to bring it up. Fortunately, I didn't have to stay curious for very long.

"Do you *know* her?" a small, mouse-like girl asked me in my next class. She had sidled into the chair next to me when I wasn't looking.

"Who?" I was utterly confused. Imogen wasn't in that class with me, and my mind was elsewhere.

The girl leaned in as if she was going to tell me something very secretive, but her whisper was so loud I'm pretty sure everyone heard. "*Imogen Green.*"

I shrugged and looked at her questioningly. I wasn't ready to give up any information yet, not until I had more to go on. I certainly felt more loyalty to the girl who had wiped a tear off my cheek than the mousy one gossiping in front of the whole class. And yet she leaned still closer, her voice once again carrying in a loud whisper.

"I just want to warn you, since, like, you probably don't know already. Imogen is *not* someone you want to be friends with." At this statement, a boy in front of us turned around and nodded very seriously. "Dave knows," the mousy girl said to me. "Dave used to live next to her, before she moved."

"Don't go near her if you can help it," Dave said, clearly trying to promote his self-importance with the utterance of some ominous warning. I didn't want to make his head any bigger, but at the same time, I really wanted to know what it was about Imogen Green that made people stare.

Dave seemed to be waiting for me to ask it, so finally I said, "Why shouldn't I go near her? She seems plenty nice." And boy, were those kids triggered. Between the two of them, I got quite a thorough history lesson, regardless of the fact that our annoyed teacher kept hushing us. I swear, though, when he sat down at his desk to let us work, he was leaning in closer as if straining to hear the story himself.

"So listen, it all started when we were about seven or eight," Dave began, only to be cut off immediately by mouse girl, who by that time had introduced herself as Caroline.

"No it didn't," Caroline said, rolling her eyes. "It started at the birth of Imogen Green." Dave's eyes got real wide for a second as if he was actually there for the birth of Imogen Green and had only now remembered it. He sat back in his chair, momentarily defeated.

"Alright, alright. You tell it then."

"*Thank* you," Caroline said. She turned back to me, and her voice became all whispery-dramatic without losing any of its volume. "So like I was saying, this all started on the day that Imogen Green was born. It was a Friday the 13th. *Obviously.*" I nodded as if this was indeed obvious. Most of the class was listening in at this point, and Caroline knew it. I had a feeling she would be going for the full theatrical effect, and that meant nothing was guaranteed to be true. But I kept listening, since I'll admit my curiosity was piqued.

"I have it on *serious* authority that right when the doctor saw Imogen, he knew something was off," Caroline continued. "Imogen had all these weird markings on her head, like symbols and stuff. And apparently when the doctor tried to show his colleagues, her hair had already grown over it." I raised my eyebrows, already quite dubious.

"How do you know that?" I asked, because it didn't seem very likely that Caroline had access to decade-old medical records. Dave glared pointedly at me, and a few other classmates who had dropped the pretense of doing work and were actively turned toward Caroline also scowled in my direction. Caroline at least offered a little more explanation.

"My mom's cousin's best friend was the nurse who helped deliver her," Caroline said matter-of-factly. I pondered that for a moment and was forced to conclude that what with Abilene's population of around a thousand people, it wasn't entirely unlikely. "My mom heard it from her cousin that the doctor *swears on his life* that Imogen had those markings on her head."

"And they weren't birthmarks?"

"No! He was a *doctor*. He would know if they were birthmarks." I supposed she was probably right about that one.

"And then, when we were about seven or eight," Dave started up again, but Caroline shushed him.

"I'm telling it, Dave. So when we were about seven or eight, we all went to the same elementary school and most of us were in the same class. Well, we were divided into like three classes. But we all knew each other." Dave nodded in agreement and leaned forward in his chair.

"Imogen was in my class. Dave was in it too. And this one day during recess, we decided to play a little game where we would try to guess what other people were thinking. We all sat in a circle and took turns trying. I *distinctly* remember telling Dave that he was thinking about hot dogs, because he was eating one at the time. And he said that he wasn't."

"Because I wasn't! I was thinking about hamburgers." Dave looked very wronged. Caroline rolled her eyes.

"Oh, yeah. Because you still remember to this day." Dave opened his mouth to protest her sarcasm, but I interrupted him.

"Guys! C'mon. What happened in the game?" Whether I liked it or not, they had me hooked. Caroline looked very pleased with herself. Then she started up again.

"When it was Imogen's turn, she was supposed to guess what my best friend Macy was thinking. And she did. Like, right away. And then Macy started making it hard for her, like random numbers and names and stuff like that. And Imogen still guessed every single thing right. And then finally we all tried, and I even had a turn with her, and you know what I thought about?"

"What?" I asked, bending closer.

"I thought about what a total *freak* Imogen Green was. Because I knew she would be guessing words or numbers or other things and was probably just getting lucky the whole time." Caroline paused for effect. The entire class appeared to be leaning slightly toward her, as if she was some gravitational force pulling everyone in.

"But that didn't happen. Her eyes started tearing up, and she got all sniffly and weird and refused to play the game anymore. And then I knew." Caroline paused again, letting the last sentence sink in before delivering the final blow. "She wasn't guessing at all."

I started to laugh, but no one else was, so I forced it into a sort of strange cough. Even the teacher looked grim, and I could see other kids in the class nodding as if they knew this account to be true. "You must be kidding," I said, waiting for someone to yell "Gotcha!" But no one did.

"You can ask anyone! We all saw it. Her mom came and picked her up after she started crying. We could hear her yelling at Imogen across the playground. She kept on screaming, '*You weren't supposed to show them! How could you have showed them!*'

"Anyway, we haven't seen her since. Her mom shipped her off to some boarding school and we thought we'd never have to see to her again. But apparently she's back. And friends with you." Caroline resumed her earlier skepticism and narrowed her eyes at me. "How *do* you know her?"

"I don't, really," I said. "I just met her today." Caroline looked satisfied, but I wasn't really paying attention. I was rubbing the birthmark on the top of my head, lost in thought.

I couldn't find Caroline in the cafeteria at lunch that day. Or rather, I thought I saw her, and I thought she saw me, but she gave no indication that she knew me and ran off to some group of girls who didn't look particularly inclusive. I could practically hear the mean things they were saying about me.

The familiar backdrop of white noise filled my ears as I realized I wouldn't have anyone to sit with. I slid into a seat at the very edge of the cafeteria, shrinking as much as possible as if I could somehow hide in plain sight. And the buzzing was still there; an ever-constant drone in my ears that was interrupted only rarely by conversations passing by. Absorbed in my own melancholy, I had the misery startled right out of me when Imogen plopped down into the chair next to mine.

"Sorry! I didn't mean to sca–" Imogen stopped mid-sentence and turned to look at me, her eyes analyzing my face, coming to rest on my forehead. Something made her falter; her grin disappeared in an instant.

"You know, don't you?" She said it quietly, timidly, and there was a mixture of both surprise and sadness in her voice. As if the inevitable had happened much sooner than she had anticipated. I looked back at her, and in meeting her eyes something rather inexplicable happened. The buzzing dimmed, and then all of a sudden there was silence. Well, not quite silence. I heard her.

Imogen's eyes began to water, but in that instance I had never felt more weightless in my entire life. I reached out and wiped the tear off her cheek. And then I said what I'd barely dared to think since Caroline told me her story, what I'd brushed off as impossible but which I could finally accept.

I can hear it too.

Imogen's eyes widened as she realized I had never actually opened my mouth. Yet she heard me, and I heard her reply. In that moment, I understood two things. Firstly, there was definitely something going on upstairs that required ...further understanding. But most importantly, for the first time ever, I was not alone. I would never be alone again.

YI QING ZHOU

Freshman
Major: Psychology
Reading: Non-Fiction

I was born in Beijing, China and moved to Montreal, Canada at the age of three. I grew up speaking English to some people, French to some others, and Mandarin to my family at home. As I was constantly surrounded by influences coming from different directions, understanding my cultural identity has always been a challenge. Through my lyric essay, I hope you will enjoy discovering bits and pieces of the things I have learned on my journey. In my free time, I enjoy reading, dancing, playing the piano, walking in nature, and trying different kinds of cuisine. I also love stargazing! And bunnies.

Nominated by: Sarah Messer

Option Three

1.

For nineteen years, she has been standing on an unsteady bridge suspended between two worlds. Every time she gets asked that question, the wind starts blowing and the bridge wavers a little bit more under her feet. She wishes she could say something, anything. But every time, her tongue gets stuck on the roof of her mouth. Her thoughts become turmoil. She is trapped. Their questioning gaze insistently fixed on her finally hauls her to reality. *Where are you from?* They ask again. *Where am I from?* She asks herself. The wind makes the bridge rock a little bit more, back and forth, until the whole world becomes blurry.

2.

After she was born in the spring of 1999, she lives with her parents, maternal grandparents, and uncle in a two-bedroom apartment in Beijing. Because her mom is only given 105 days of maternity leave, her grandmother and twenty-year-old nanny are the main caregivers during the first year of her life. In January 2001, she travels to Canada with her mom for the first time to join her dad in Montreal, studying for his MBA. In April of that same year, after finalizing the immigration documents and fulfilling all requirements, her mom brings her back to Beijing where her grandparents begin to raise her on their own. She lives with them in a modestly sized apartment in the Xicheng District. The apartment consists of two suites connected by a glass-walled walkway. With a towel on her head, she goes in that passage every day and catwalks along the row of plants and clothesline. But her favorite place in Beijing is Yuyuantan Park–Jade Deep Lake Park. She likes to run through the light green canopy of weeping willows. She likes to eat red bean popsicles while learning tai chi with her grandfather. She likes to gather the longest twigs she can find, put them through the holes of a little bridge, squat down, and "fish." Holding her grandparents' hands, she likes to close her eyes and swing herself forward, pretending to fly. For her, this is home. Although she will immigrate to Canada a year and a half later, the question *Where are you from?* is always followed by *China* and a gap-toothed smile.

3.

As first-generation immigrants, insecurities rapidly creep in. Her parents' savings are dropping; they have to find a job. But isolation weighs them down. Despite being Canadian citizens and living in a populated neighborhood, they constantly feel like foreigners. But her dad knows that if they wish for a better future, they must accept where they are now and trust that others will accept them too. *When are we going back?* She asks her dad one day. He hesitates, then smiles. *Canada is your new home, sweetie.*

4.

When her parents enroll her in her first kindergarten in Montreal, she doesn't know any English words–besides *water*, *hungry*, and *sleepy*. But she adjusts very quickly as she finds safety and comfort in her teacher Katherine and her new friend Maria. Maria and her love to make matching bracelets and build Barbie houses. Although both have no idea what the other is saying, they understand each other through their gestures, expressions, and the joyful gleam in each other's eyes. Every day she is excited for school and refuses to leave her Barbie house when Dad picks her up in the evening. She is happy in her new home.

5.

Today you will draw your home, Katherine announces at the start of art class. All the kids set to work: houses, gardens, and pets quickly fill their canvases. She stares at the sheet of paper in front of her. *Canada is your new home*, her dad's voice echoes. She takes out her favorite box of Crayola markers and prepares to draw Maria, the Barbie house, and the snowman she built with Mom and Dad the other day. But then, she remembers her grandparents' smile, the little bridge, the fishes, and the willow trees. She thinks about it for a moment and eventually decides to leave the paper blank. She tells Katherine she is *sleepy*.

6.

She is Chinese by birth, but she is Canadian by law. She looks Chinese, yet lives Canadian. She speaks, acts, thinks Chinese. She talks, reacts, believes Canadian. But even if she knew exactly who she was, people would never agree. In Canada, she looks Chinese. In China, she sounds Canadian. Where can she call home? Is it the city where she was born or the town where she grew up? Is home the house in which she lives or the place where her memories dwell? Every day, this tension makes the bridge sway a little more. No matter how hard she resists, she is tugged and pulled to one identity and to the other. She is not only divided between two worlds but also feels alienated from each.

7.

As she strolls down the aisle of makeup, she hears voices behind her. She turns around and sees two women following her. She distinguishes faint murmurs in French. *Qu'est-ce qu'elle... Regarde-la...* The two women laugh. *Pourquoi la p'tite chinoise nous checke de même... Elle a tellement l'air...* She walks towards them and stops. *Hi uh.. Chinese girl... what uh.. what do you want? Do you need a translator?* The woman on the right asks her mockingly. The woman on the left bursts out laughing. With the greatest patience and composure in the world, she begins her reply. *Non, mais merci pour votre préoccupation. C'est très gentil de votre part. En fait, j'aurais besoin de la base de maquillage juste là, derrière vous. Est-ce que ça vous dérangerait de bouger, s'il vous plaît?* The two women stop laughing.

8.

After a thirteen-hour flight, she finally exits the plane. A huge whiff of hot, humid air welcomes her. At the baggage claim, people jostle one another to find the best spot. Outside, ceaseless honking fills the streets and three cars run a red light. At the convenience store, a group of teenage boys cuts an old man in line. In the subway, people push and elbow each other to squeeze in the closing doors. Waiting on the side for the next train to come, she watches them. They are Chinese, she is Chinese, but why does she feel so different?

9.

She loves the steamed green bean noodles her mom makes on Friday nights, the glutinous rice balls her family eats on Chinese New Year, her grandfather's favorite tomatoes and eggs stir-fry, and the chive dumplings she would make with her grandmother as a child. She asks her mom to pack these foods every day for lunch—until school lunches become FBI interrogations. *What is that? Are you eating worms? Why are you eating slime? Are those eyeballs? Is that dog meat? Why are you eating leaves? Ewww why do you eat eggs like that? Miss, something smells weird!* She will always remember those voices. How they were filled with disgust.

10.

She is talking with two Chinese people she just met on the plane. The two people chat about Han Hong's latest single, the historical drama every teen in China is raving about, and the new electric car policy. She has never heard of Han Hong, has never watched historical dramas, and has never learned about Chinese policies. She is silent and replies with smiles and nods. One of the two Chinese people finally turns to her. *Hey, why aren't you saying anything? Are you even Chinese?* She isn't sure if it was tease or a scorn.

11.

The psychology class ends. She leaves the lecture hall with her friend Grace and another guy friend they just met. All three are Chinese. They all know how to speak Chinese. She prefers to speak English with Grace. She asks Grace what's the reading for next class. Grace replies she's not sure and tells her to ask the guy. She asks the guy what's the reading for next class. The guy asks her to repeat. She asks him what's the reading for next class. The guy interrupts her and tells her to speak Chinese. He says he can't speak English to a Chinese who knows how to speak Chinese: *that's just weird.*

12.

The world only gives her two options:
Option 1. Conform to the stereotypes expected of her.
Option 2. Conform to the "whiteness" around her.

13.

Despite how hard she tries to find peace with her reality and despite how hard she wishes to preserve every single part of herself, the world refuses it all. Maybe she is asking for too much, she thinks. So she chooses option 1.

14.

Option 1. *You must be good at math; you don't need to work hard to get good grades; you really should become a doctor; you wear glasses because you studied too much right; it's surprising you don't have an accent; what are you eating; I'm sure you got A+; wait so you don't eat dogs; Chinese names are so weird; I'm guessing you play ping pong; why can't they just get English names; wait why aren't you doing pre-med; you're just so naturally smart; Chinese people can't speak French at all; do you have tiger parents; their accent is hilarious; where are you from; I can't believe I got a better grade than you; no I mean where are you really from; you're less shy than I thought; are you Korean; are you a communist; even if you don't study you're going to do well; you literally eat rice every day; why aren't you applying to Harvard; do you buy fake stuff; school must be so easy for you; stop massacring our language; don't worry you're Asian you're never going to gain weight; where is your nose; are you related to Wanyi Zhou; by the way your dad really looks like Jackie Chan.*

15.

Every comment is a tear; every remark is a drop. But one day the tear will become a wound and the drop will become a slough. She is angry at herself, at her differences, at the world. But the only option left is option 2.

16.

Option 2. She stops studying Chinese; she packs sandwiches instead of dumplings. Layer after layer, she peels herself off. She contours her nose; she hates math; she slacks off on school. Day after day, she forgets who she is. She throws out her glasses; she gives up piano; she gives up med school. *It's not unfortunate*, she assures herself, *it's self-defense*. And it's working. The more she avoids the stereotypes, the more the world seems to like her. She is so happy. But far away, she hears her grandparents cry.

17.

You're not in China, stop speaking Chinese. Why can't you just get an English name? Eww what are you eating? You're massacring the English language. Do you need a translator?

Stop, she says.

Stop speaking English. Can't you speak Chinese? Why aren't you saying anything? Are you even Chinese? Don't you know your own country's history?

Make it stop, she pleads.

18.

She is tired of not belonging. She is tired of being a perpetual foreigner, of being pushed to one side and the other. The only solution left is to choose a side once and for all, she thinks. But which side? What part of herself does she sacrifice?

19.

In her dreams, she is standing in the middle of a bridge. She looks to the right end and sees China. She hears her grandmother reading her a bedtime story. She sees Yuyuantan Park and her grandfather doing tai chi next to the willow trees. She sees herself fishing through the holes on the little bridge. She sees streets of food stands and smells the aroma of scallion pancakes and *youtiao*. She sees little kids—who also have upturned eyes, olive-yellow skin, a low bridge nose—run, scream, and laugh. When she looks to the left end, she sees Canada. She sees her friend Maria and the joyful gleam in her eyes. She sees their giant Barbie house and their matching bracelets made of red and white beads. She sees the woods next to her house and Mount Royal with a blanket of orange leaves. She sees Mom and Dad building a snowman and herself making snow angels in the backyard. When she wakes up in the morning, she thinks about her dreams and her two identities. She thinks about the bridge and wonders in which end she wants to be.

20.

For nineteen years, she has tried to close the gap between her ethnicity and nationality, between who she believes she is and who others expect her to be. But today, she stops trying. Every day, she realizes a little bit more that the cultural differences she has learned to hate are the very differences that have shaped her worldview, her values, and her individuality:

I grew up eating chive dumplings, using an umbrella on sunny days, and stirring eggs with chopsticks. I grew up loving poutine, drinking Tims Iced Cappuccino, and cheering for the Montreal Canadians hockey team. Growing up, I spoke in Mandarin with Mom and Dad, spoke in "Frenglish" with my friends, and dreamed in all three languages. My Chinese roots taught me about family, courage, and the little happinesses in life. My Canadian upbringing taught me about friendships, adaptation, and trust.

For nineteen years, she has been standing on an unsteady bridge suspended between two worlds. Sometimes, the wind pushes her to one end; sometimes, it pushes her to the other. But slowly, she finds the strength to resist the wind, the will to stand on her own, and the courage to look at the world from the middle.

www.ingramcontent.com/pod-product-compliance
Lightning Source LLC
LaVergne TN
LVHW010732020926
846742LV00029B/63